Coastal Ghosts
of Southern California

Anita Yasuda

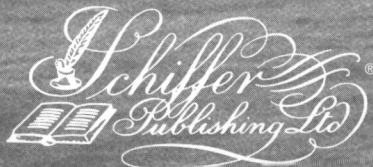
Schiffer Publishing Ltd®

4880 Lower Valley Road, Atglen, Pennsylvania 19310

Other Schiffer Books by Anita Yasuda

Japanese Children's Fabrics	0-7643-1967-1 $34.95
Japanese Anime Linens 1970s to Present	0-7643-2155-2 $34.95
Hello Kitty Cute, Creative & Collectible	0-7643-2352-0 $19.95
Traditional Kimono Silks	9-780-7643-2691-2 $34.95
Snapshots of San Diego	9-780-7643-2804-6 $24.95
Greetings from Buffalo, New York	9-780-7643-2888-6 $19.95

Schiffer Books are available at special discounts for bulk purchases for sales promotions or premiums. Special editions, including personalized covers, corporate imprints, and excerpts can be created in large quantities for special needs. For more information contact the publisher:

Schiffer Publishing Ltd.
4880 Lower Valley Road
Atglen, PA 19310
Phone: (610) 593-1777; Fax: (610) 593-2002
E-mail: Info@schifferbooks.com

For the largest selection of fine reference books on this and related subjects, please visit our web site at **www.schifferbooks.com**. We are always looking for people to write books on new and related subjects. If you have an idea for a book please contact us at the above address.

This book may be purchased from the publisher. Include $5.00 for shipping. Please try your bookstore first. You may write for a free catalog.

In Europe, Schiffer books are distributed by
Bushwood Books
6 Marksbury Ave.
Kew Gardens
Surrey TW9 4JF England
Phone: 44 (0) 20 8392-8585; Fax: 44 (0) 20 8392-9876
E-mail: info@bushwoodbooks.co.uk
Website: www.bushwoodbooks.co.uk
Free postage in the U.K., Europe; air mail at cost.

Copyright © 2009 by Anita Yasuda
Library of Congress Control Number: 2008937812

Designed by Stephanie Daugherty
Type set in Smudger LET/New Baskerville BT

ISBN: 978-0-7643-3150-3
Printed in the United States of America

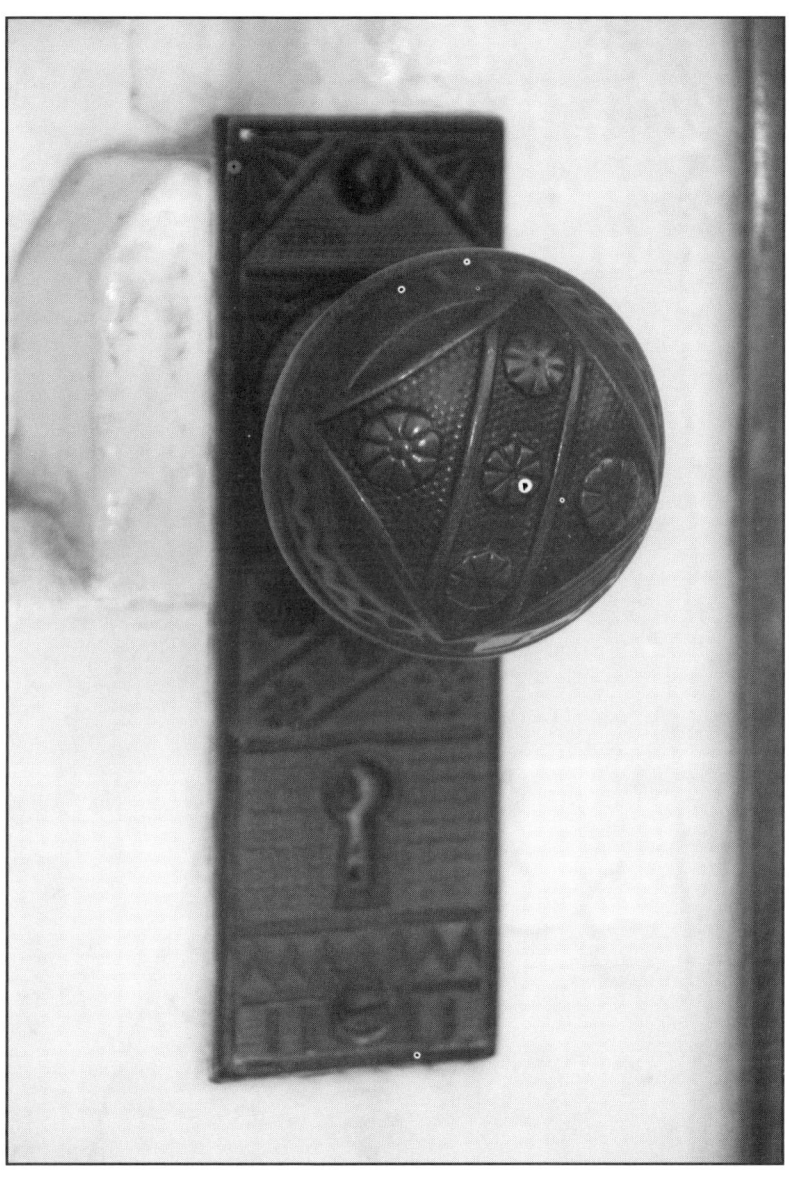

The doorknob of the Whaley House in Old Town, San Diego. Go inside if you dare; the family is waiting for you.

"...the conversation happened to turn upon supernatural agency. The stranger remained reserved and mysterious during the discussion, but when the baron in a jocular manner denied the existence of spirits, and satirically mocked their appearance, his eyes glowed with unearthly luster, and his form seemed to dilate to more than its natural dimensions."
—The Spectre Bride William Harrison Ainsworth

Dedication

To Kaylee Emi

Acknowledgements

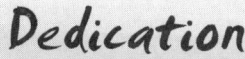hank you to everyone who kindly shared their ghost stories with me.

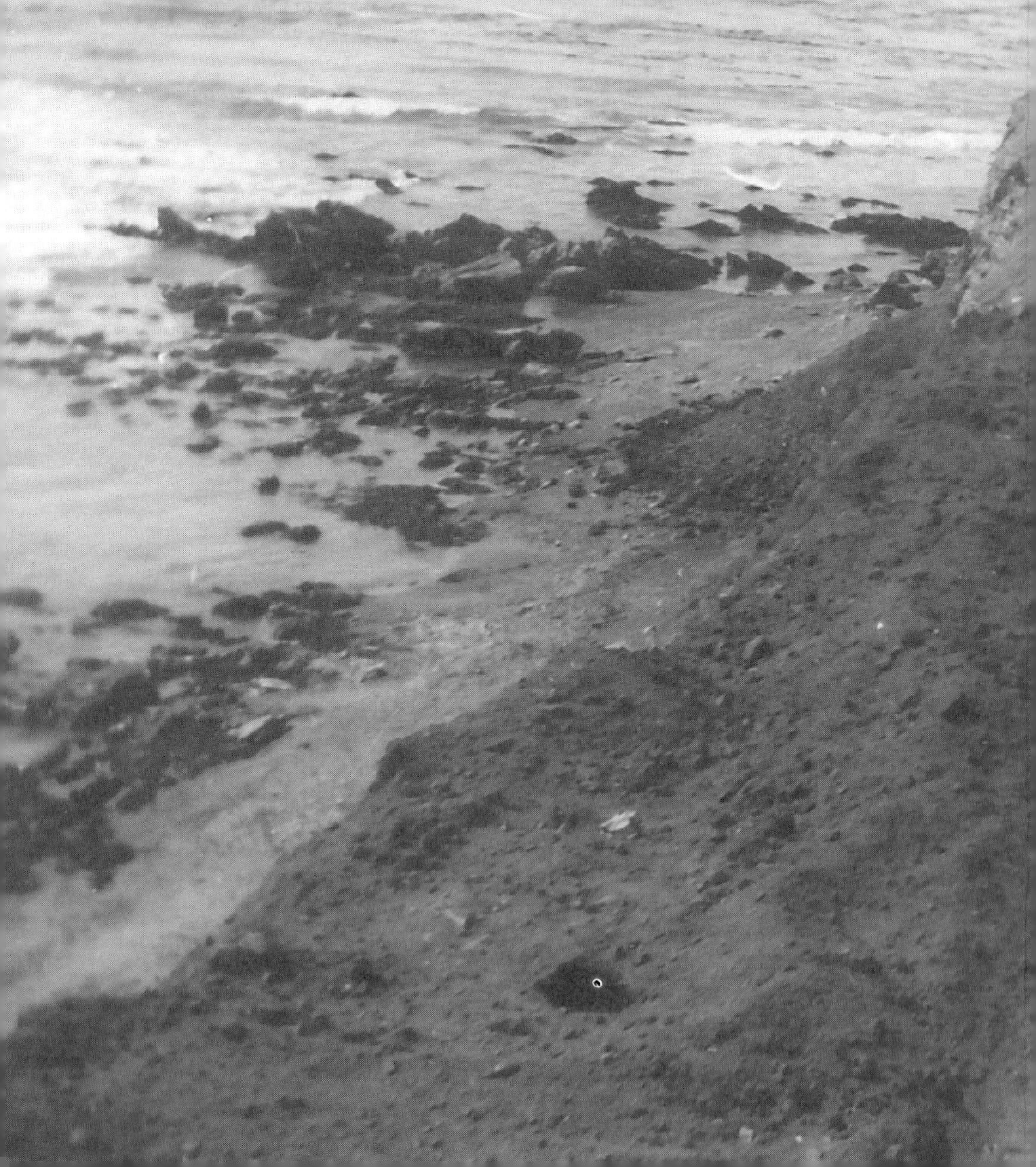

Contents

Author's Note   8

Introduction   9

Abbott Kinney~ Venice Beach   10
Albert Pryor~ San Juan Capistrano   12
Alice Halloran's Headless Spirit~ Nacimiento River   15
Andres Pico Adobe~ Los Angeles   16

Balboa Theatre~ San Diego   18
Big Yellow House~ Summerland   19
Billiwhack Monster~ Aliso Canyon   21
Black Lady Rising~ San Luis Obispo   22
Bless This Home~ Van Nuys   23
Bubbles Lives On~ Irvine   24

Cabrillo's Ghost~ Catalina Island   27
Captain Cass~ Cayucos   29
Casa de Rancho Los Cerritos~ Long Beach   30
Charman~ Ventura   32
Cheesecloth Ghost~ Long Beach   33
Conception Arguello's Curse   34
Curse of Griffith Park~ Los Angeles   36

El Adobe Restaurant~ San Juan Capistrano   38

First Christian Church~ Rialto   40
Fox Fullerton Theatre~ Fullerton   41

Georgian Hotel~ Santa Monica   43
Ghost of Foster Park~ Ventura   44
Glen Tavern Inn~ Santa Paula   46
Grand Colonial Hotel~ La Jolla   48
Guadalupe Adobe~ Santa Barbara   49

Haunted Gaviota Coast~ Gaviota   51
Haunted Rental~ Laguna   52
Hippolyte de Bouchard~ Long Beach   53
Horton Grand Hotel~ San Diego   54

Joyita~ Santa Catalina Island   57

La Casa de Estudillo~ San Diego   59
La Purisma Mission~ Lompoc   61

Lady in Pink~ Yorba Linda   62
Lamar Street~ Los Angeles   64
Le Milagro~ Santa Paula   66
Legend of The Swallows~ San Juan Capistrano   68
Leonis Adobe~ Calabasas   70
Lord Harry~ Santa Barbara   73

Mission San Fernando Rey De Espana~ San Fernando   76
Mission San Juan Capistrano~ San Juan Capistrano   78
Mission San Miguel Wishing Chairs~ San Miguel   82
Mission San Miguel Archangel~ San Miguel   83
Mission Santa Barbara~ Santa Barbara   85
Mission Santa Ines Ghosts~ Solvang   87
Mission Santa Ines Legend~ Solvang   89
Modjeska House~ Ventura   90
Montanez Adobe~ San Juan Capistrano   91
Morey Mansion~ Redlands   92

Old Cemetery~ San Juan Capistrano   94
Old Fort Tejon~ Grapevine Canyon   96
Old Point Loma Lighthouse~ San Diego   97
Olivas Adobe~ San Luis Obispo   102

Paso Robles Inn~ Paso Robles   105
Pepper Tree Legend~ San Juan Capistrano   107
Pierpont Inn~ Ventura   108
Pirate Lights~ Smugglers Beach   110
Pisgah Grande~ Santa Susana Mountain Park   112
Plummer Auditorium~ Fullerton   113
Point Vicente Lighthouse~ Palos Verdes   114
Possessed Bridge~ Pasadena   116
Possessed Rail Car~ Long Beach   118

Queen Mary~ Long Beach   120

Red Lady of Pendleton Road~ San Bernardino County   124

San Bernardino High~ San Bernardino   126
San Diego State University~ San Diego   127
San Pasqual Battlefield~ San Diego   128
Sea Serpent~ Long Beach   130
Sea Serpent~ Ocean Park   131
Sea Serpent False Alarm~ Malibu   132
Spirit of the Rios-Caledonia Adobe~ San Miguel   133
Stage Coach Inn~ Ventura   134
Stanley Ranch Museum~ Garden Grove   136
Star of India~ San Diego   137

The Bluebird Motel~ Cambria   141
The Clubhouse at This Old House~ Cayucos   142
The Cursed Ship~ San Clemente Island   143
The Del Coronado~ San Diego   145
The Drum Barracks~ Wilmington   147
The Sirens~ Channel Islands   148
Theodore Spurkuhl~ Santa Monica   150
Trained Serpents~ Southern California Coast   152

Valentino~ Hollywood   154
Villa Montezuma~ San Diego   155

Whaley House~ San Diego   160
Wild Goose~ Catalina Island   164
William Desmond Taylor~ Los Angeles   166
William S. Hart Park~ Santa Clarita   166

Conclusion   **169**

Top Ten Places To Find A Ghost   **170**

Glossary of Common Ghost Hunting Terms   **173**

Your Own Ghost Stories   **185**

End Notes and Selected Bibliography   **186**

Index   **190**

Author's Note

This book takes the form of a guidebook to places along the Southern California coast that are associated with ghost stories or supernatural events. The communities are arranged alphabetically and, wherever appropriate, specific directions are given to locate the "haunting." Sources are listed for all entries. Each entry in the bibliography is keyed to its entry in the body of the book.

* The author took all photography in the book unless noted. The collectible postcards range in value from $4 to $9 U.S.

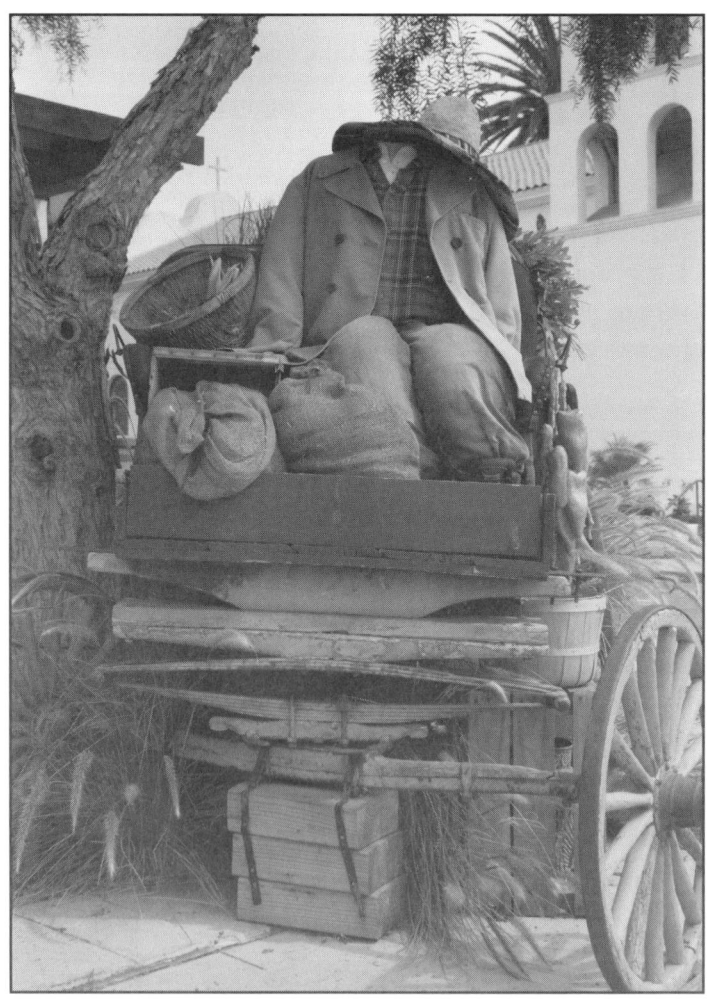

Begin your ghost tour with the headless wagon rider.

Introduction

Historical murders, executions, mysterious ghost sightings and hauntings—come and take a walk through the darkness. As the skies begin to darken over the city, your ghost tour begins. Select a spot, or two. You can go by foot, car, or even public transportation.

Imagine you are the guide striking a match and lighting the lantern. Each step brings you closer to a haunting. Go by yourself or with your family. You can learn how a murdered family at one Mission may explain the hauntings. The ghost of a construction worker beckons to the distraught on a bridge in Pasadena and learn how pirates walk the sandy bottom of the beach looking for their treasure.

Stories

All stories were researched using historic newspapers, eyewitness accounts, local libraries and, of course, firsthand experience. You don't have to make a reservation for this tour. Just bring a good pair of shoes, camera, a sense of humor, and an interest in history, and last but not least—an open mind.

Rules for Meeting Ghosts

• Remember to respect all private property.

• Obey all entrance rules and time restrictions.

• Just because you are forearmed with information on the type of haunting doesn't always mean you'll meet a ghost. But who knows? Stranger things have happened.

• Don't be in a rush to finish the tour and miss the very nuance of a place.

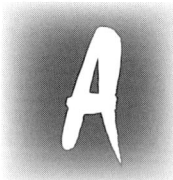

Abbott Kinney
Venice Beach

"I look for ghosts—but none will force their way to me..."
—Wordsworth

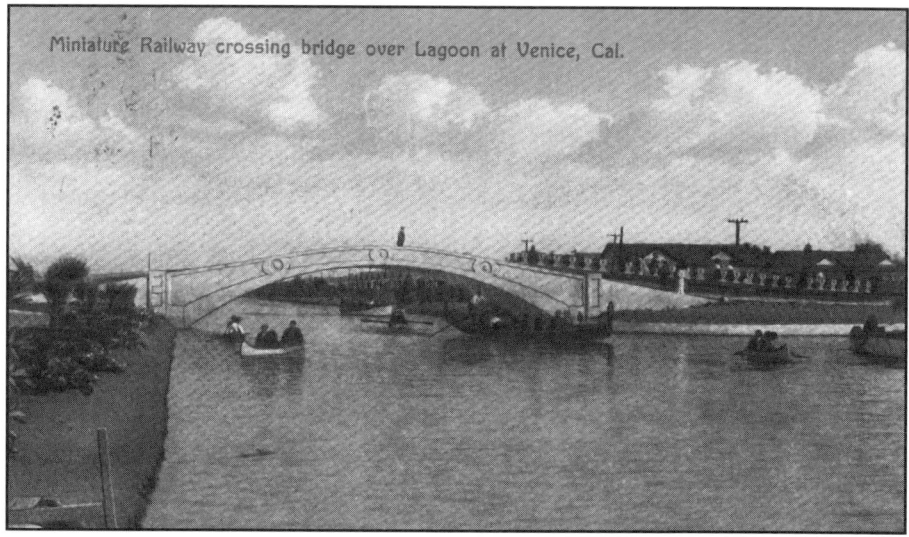

Miniature Railway crossing bridge over Lagoon at Venice, Cal.

**Miniature Railway crossing bridge over Venice, California, lagoon.
Collectible postcard. c. 1910 by Newman Postcard Company, Los Angeles.**

A new resident to Venice, Mrs. Y loved the location. The canals reminded her of a recent trip to Venice, Italy, and the proximity to the ocean was all she needed to call her new neighborhood home. Over the course of a few months, she established a routine of taking an after-dinner walk along the banks of the canal. One evening, while admiring the sunset, she noticed pair of shiny black shoes beside her. Surprised as she hadn't heard anyone approach, she looked up to see a man dressed in a black formal suit complete with hat. He smiled at her and passed by. She turned around quickly to see where he was headed, but no one else was on the bridge. The man wasn't on the path nor had he walked down the bank.

Feeling slightly disconcerted, she returned home. One of her neighbors was sitting out and she asked him if he knew of a special event going on in the area. After being told no, Mrs. Y described the oddly dressed man. How surprised she was to learn that she had just met the phantom of Venice Beach—Abbott Kinney.

In 1904 Abbott Kinney had a dream to create Venice in America, complete with canals and gondoliers. He wanted to "(sic)…make such a unique city a place where people would want to go." The canals connected to the Pacific Ocean at Playa del Rey and wound for three miles through residential districts under causeways fashioned after those in Venice between palm-bordered parks into a large lagoon. A miniature railroad at one time surrounded the canals. It was constructed simultaneously with the waterways. The news media was not kind, calling it "Kinney's Folly" and the public at large ridiculed such an outrageous idea. But with the opening of Venice, July 4, 1905, Abbott Kinney accomplished what he had set out to do. It was rumored that he and his associates invested $1, 500,000 in constructing Venice.

A year later, reports would surface of his plans to sell "the whole concern," but he never did. Originally marketed as "Venice by the sea," the combination of Chautauqua and pleasure resort, it was soon seen that more money could be made catering "(sic)…to those who dance and drink beer than to those addicted to plain living and high thinking."

"Venice of America" screamed with ads Kinney placed in papers across the country. Do not fail to visit this suburb resort with the best beaches in the world, prospective visitors were told. Besides fishing and boating, afternoon concerts and evening dancing, there was the longest miniature railroad in the world. What more could the vacationer ask for? For a mere $17 to $35 dollars, a family could rent a bungalow in Villa City or at the nearby Winward Hotel; a dollar could buy you a room with a bath!

A mere twenty years after transforming swamp into a mini-Italy, city trustees would order most of the waterways filled. Trustees claimed this was necessary due to an increasing need for development of automobile spaces. Also, many of the canals contained stagnant water and were mosquito breeding grounds. These changes coincided with the annexation of Venice by Los Angeles city proper in 1925. The new streets conveniently connected to boulevards leading to Los Angeles.

With the death of Abbott Kinney in 1920 at the age of seventy, the subsequent filling of the canals, and with the discovery of oil in Venice, rumors of Abbott Kinney's ghost became legendary in the city. In 1939 one reporter wrote, "Surely the discovery of oil beneath the acreage over which he worked so hard to develop into an unusual watering place for the rich, the new and the near rich would make his ghost come back to haunt those who will make vast sums from the black gold coming forth from the earth."

11

While Abbott Kinney saw value in investing in Venice, there were those who said, "…investing in Venice was a coin thrown in the wind." The discovery of oil was seen as further proof the skeptics were wrong.

In articles from the 1970s, the ghost of Abbott Kinney returns distraught over his "souring dream." In recent years in which this pedestrian-friendly city and current gentrification is praised, the ghost of Abbott Kinney returns pleased with the rebirth of an area he loved. {1, 2}

Location

See The Venice Forum Web site for community details at www.veniceforum.org. Visit the Chamber of Commerce site at www.venicechamber.net to download a free walking tour.

Albert Prior
San Juan Capistrano

"Why do spirits not speak of their spirit world? He is not yet prepared to give much concerning his present state, because of his difficulties in becoming attuned with the sphere of mortals from which he has so recently gone."
—Dr. James H. Hyslop 1909

Across the green expanse of lawn is a small grey and white clapboard cottage. You will notice the crisp white porch that wraps around the home. Sitting on the porch this sunny spring day, is an elderly man. He slowly rocks back and forth taking long puffs on his pipe. Smiling at him, you approach the home, feeling that you are trespassing on private property.

The Garcia/Pryor residence was turned into the O'Neil Museum years ago. The smell of pipe smoke fills your nose as you walk up the steps. Looking to your right, the elderly man is no longer on the porch. Shrugging your shoulders, you give him no more thought, until perusing the museum's handout— when you read about the ghost of Albert Pryor.

Mr. Pryor purchased the home in 1903 and his family lived there until 1955. The home would then be tenanted periodically. It was very hard to keep renters as Mr. Pryor kept returning to the little cottage. Mr. Pryor wasn't returning from a nursing home, but from the beyond, preferring his porch to whatever lies after death.

Today, this bungalow is filled with priceless antiques, including 1800s furniture, clothing, and glassware. The staff will be able to tell you about Jose Dolores Garcia, a saloon owner, who built this home for his wife, Refugio Yorba. He was murdered a few years later in 1896, and his wife later sold the home.

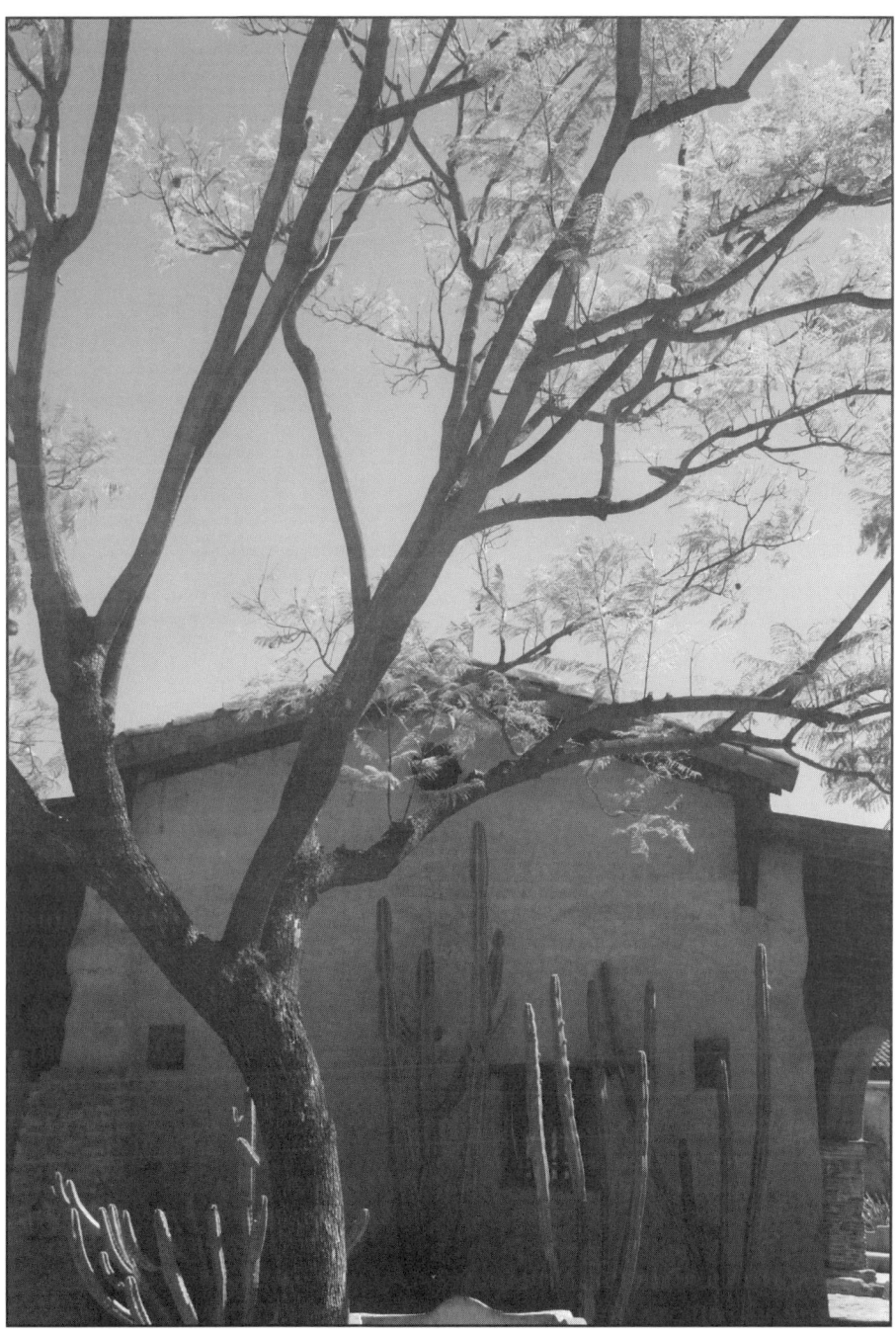

The Los Rios Historic District is the oldest neighborhood in Orange County. This photo was taken at the Mission San Juan Capistrano.

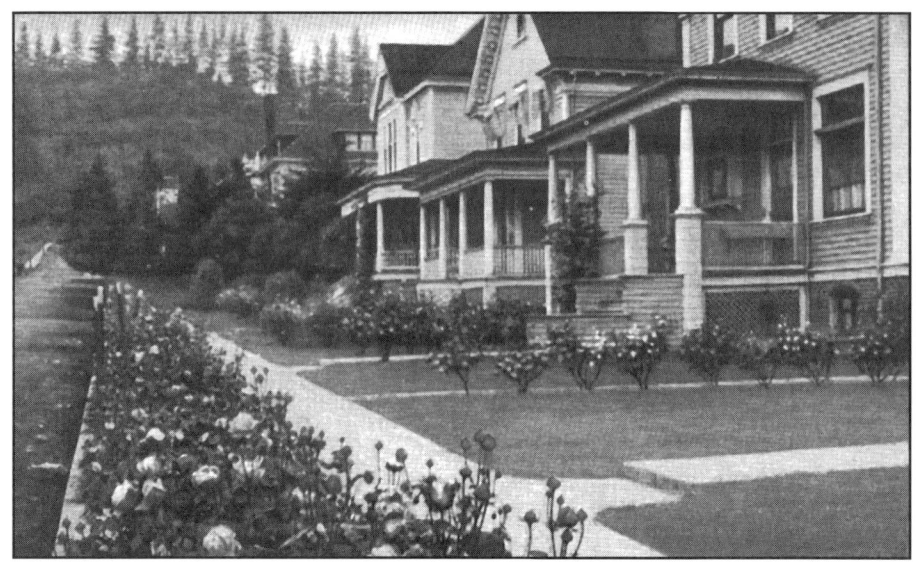

Who haunts the porches of these homes in this vintage California Rose Walk postcard? Produced by Pacific Novelty Co., San Francisco & Los Angeles.

The Los Rios Historic District, has the greatest concentration of old structures and lies just across the railroad tracks from the town's restored depot, a short block from the Mission, and just steps from bustling downtown. Crossing to the other side of the tracks and walking the dusty, unpaved streets is like taking a step far back into history. With some buildings dating from 1794, historians credit it with being the oldest continually occupied neighborhood in California. Today, it's a mix of shops and private homes.

Location

The Los Rios Historic District, has the greatest concentration of old structures and lies just across the railroad tracks from the town's restored depot, a short block from the Mission, and just steps from bustling downtown. Crossing to the other side of the tracks and walking the dusty, unpaved streets is like taking a step far back into history. With some buildings dating from 1794, historians credit it with being the oldest continually occupied neighborhood in California. Today, it's a mix of shops and private homes.

> 31831 Los Rios Street
> The San Juan Capistrano Historical Society leads hour-long tours of the town's adobes.
> Hours: Sundays at 1pm
> (714) 493-8444

14

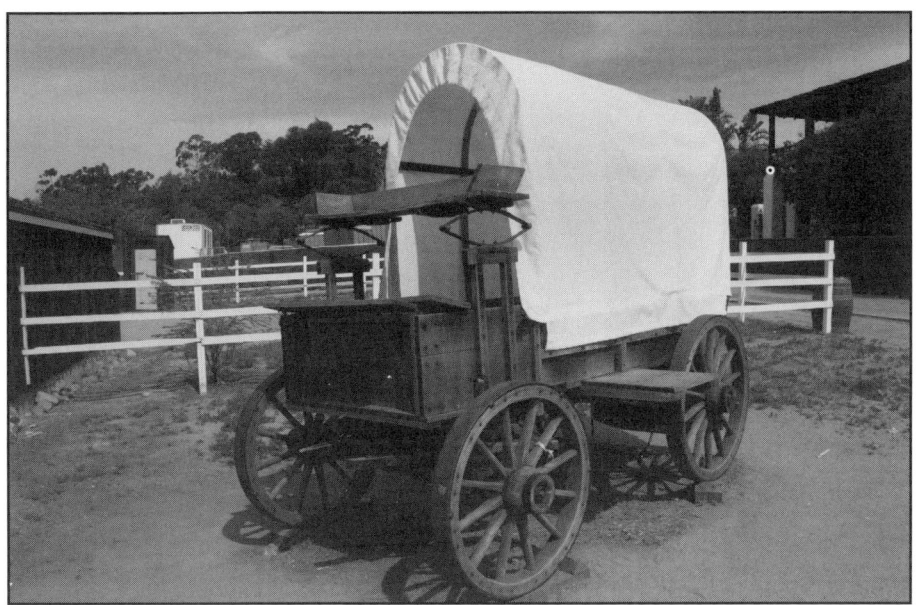

Does the headless spirit of Alice Halloran wander near the Nacimiento River?

Alice Halloran's Headless Spirit
Nacimiento River

"When people talk of ghosts I don't mention the Apparition by which I am haunted, the Phantom that shadows me about the streets, the image or spectre, so familiar, so like myself, which lurks in the plate glass of shop-windows, or leaps out of mirrors."

—Logan Pearsall Smith

If only Alice Halloran's husband had listened to the local Indians when he stopped in the town of Jolon. They tried to tell him that the Nacimiento River was running fast and not to cross, but Michael Halloran didn't listen. He believed they were trying to cheat him out of his land. No river was going to stand between Michael Halloran and his land. Michael, his wife, Alice, and their baby, Clara, headed for the river that spring day. Michael could see that the current was swift but he drove his team of horses and the heavily laden wagon into the Nacimiento. The wagon was no match for the river; the wagon flipped, spilling its human cargo and other contents into the water. Alice became entangled in the reins, severing her head. Baby Clara's body was never found.

Since that day, the headless spirit of Alice Halloran is said to wander near her grave or along the banks of the Nacimiento River. One night, in the 1950s, two soldiers stationed at Fort Hunter Liggett, near Alice's gravesite, encountered her spirit. The men were on a routine night watch, not expecting any company but what happened next would become one of the most frightening Halloran twists in this story.

The men a had no idea Alica Halloran was one of the most famous spirits wandering the Santa Lucias. She certainly wasn't included in any army briefing. Without warning, Alice Halloran materialized in front of the men, her glowing misshapen form hovering a few feet above the ground, causing one man to suffer a massive heart attack. He died on the spot. The other man was found rambling incoherently in the woods. He was unable to give any insight into that fateful night until months later. It was never noted if he fully regained his mental capacities.

There haven't been any recent sightings of Alice but the grave is still off limits. See the directions below to a nearby bridge where, if you are brave enough, you might see Alice floating along the banks looking for her head and baby Clara.

Location

The Jolon grave is on federal property and off limits. A great view of the Nacimiento and therefore Alice is to be had from the Nacimiento-Ferguson Bridge. Or try camping at the Nacimiento Campground. Web site: www.campone.com for more information.

Andres Pico Adobe
Los Angeles

"The illimitable, silent, never-resting thing called Time, rolling, rushing on, swift, silent, like an all-embracing ocean-tide, on which we and all the universe swim like exhalations, like apparitions which are, and then are not...."

—Thomas Caryle

In 1834, Indians from the San Fernando Mission constructed a small building (which today is the living room of the Andres Pico Adobe). Forty years later, Catarina and Romulo Pico would make renovations to this structure making it their home. The couple lived at the adobe until the late 1800s.

According to caretakers and mediums visiting the dwelling, Catarina is still tending to her daily chores and taking time to knit by the stairwell. She is the unofficial guardian of the second oldest adobe home in Los Angeles. Why her spirit still lingers over the adobe is unknown, but all who have lived here since the restoration in the late 1920s have felt her presence.

Since the Picos occupied the adobe it has been sold many times, until it finally stood vacant and deteriorated. Its historic value wasn't understood until 1930 when Dr. M. Harrington, curator of the Southwest Indian Museum, bought the home and the surrounding twenty acres. During this period, Dr. Harrington "sensed" the presence of a spirit in the home. It is not clear who asked for a medium to come to the adobe. This medium identified the spirit as Andres Pico's daughter–in-law, Catarina, who was "pleased with the restoration work on the adobe."

In the early 1960s, the adobe was owned by the North Valley YMCA and used as its district headquarters. Once again facing demolition, The San Fernando Valley Historical Society raised funds to buy the historic home. In 1968, the city of Los Angeles purchased the adobe through the efforts of the San Fernando Valley Historical Society.

Reports of a haunting once again surfaced at the adobe with the installation of a new caretaker. A reporter from the Van Nuys newspaper conducted interviews with Mrs. Pat Knipschild, wife of the caretaker, who also acted as tour guide. Mrs. Knipschild was certain a ghost resided at the building. The spirit she described as quiet, but ever present.

Reporter J. Hanrahan conducted an interview in 1997 with Elva Meline, resident curator of the home. She spoke about asking Catarina to take care of her on her first night at the adobe. "I never felt scared," she (Elva Meline) said. "I believe ghosts can't hurt you. Usually they're there to help."

Once Elva saw Catarina looking out of an upstairs window. This room was formally Catarina's bedroom where she is said to have died. The spirit of Catarina not only haunts the rooms of the adobe, but the very mortar itself. There are reports of her image appearing in the cracks of the exterior. {3, 4}

Location

10940 Sepulveda Boulevard
Mission Hills, CA
(818) 365- 7810
 Driving directions are available on the LA Parks Web site: www. laparks.org.
Hours: Monday 10 am to 3 pm and every third Sunday. Admission is free.
San Fernando Historical Society Web site: www.sfvhs.com.

B

Balboa Theatre
San Diego

*"These fields may also induce more elaborate forms of sensory hallucinations
ranging from the feeling of a 'sensed presence' to seeing a fully formed apparition."*
—Peter Frost

Locals say that a man was murdered at the Balboa Theatre when it was used as a speakeasy. But are the rumors true? Construction workers renovating the building experienced some very mysterious happenings.

The theatre is named for Vasco Nunez de Balboa, the first European to discover, in 1513, the Pacific Ocean. The theatre was an important cultural institution in San Diego from 1924 until 1930 with nationally recognized vaudeville acts. Famous stars appeared at the theatre making it a popular place. From 1930 until 1940 it was renamed the El Teatro Balboa and showed Spanish language cinema and stage shows. The Navy would later use it for office space and housing for sailors.

Unbelievably, the building faced demolition in 1959, as developers wanted the space for a parking lot. The city took ownership of the building, but gradually the once-grand theatre fell into disrepair. In 2005, renovations began on the building and it opened to the public in 2007. The building, in 1972, was placed on the local Register of Historical Places and, in 1992, on the National Register of Historic Places.

Over the past few years, during theatre renovations, reports of ghosts surfaced amongst the construction workers. One man looked up from his work to see a small child watching him. He was even more surprised when she simply vanished. Is this the restless spirit of a performer's child from the 1930s?

Other workers complained of tools going astray. When workers arrived on the job in the morning they could never be certain their equipment was going to be in the same place. More unnerving was when they turned their backs, tools would go missing. Is this

18

prankster ghost the little girl or are there several entities in the building?

In a 2007, an article from the *San Diego Union Tribune* by J. Herbet, the senior project manager, Gary Bosse, told him, "One carpenter required that someone else work with him at all times, after incidents in which tools allegedly were moved while his back was turned. Some ironworkers, Bosse says, "asked not to come back" after hearing the sound of children running and laughing above the plaster ceiling in the audience chamber. Mr. Bosse had a paranormal experience when he heard the sound of a piano but no one was about.

With the reopening of the Balboa Theatre, you too may experience something not included in the performance. You never know who may be sitting in the seat next to you.

Location

868 4th Avenue
San Diego, CA
Web site: www.sdbaloa.org

Big Yellow House
Summerland

"I like the ephemeral thing about theatre, every performance is like a ghost—it's there and then it's gone."

—Maggie Smith

New to the kitchen Mike (pseudonym) was happy to be working for the summer at the restaurant. He had heard rumors of ghostly happenings at there but thought them to be bogus. *Sure there were ghosts,* he thought. Busy at his station, at first, he didn't notice anything strange that July evening. Close to his workstation was a large steel vat that the restaurant used for whipping honey-butter. He had probably consumed oodles with the house bread in his first week alone at the restaurant. What happened next was something no cooking school could prepare one for.

As he chopped, he noticed a slight movement to his left where the vat stood. Calling out to the spooks in the kitchen, he said out loud, "You got to do better than that." The heavy pot suddenly came directly towards him as if shoved by unseen hands. Another staff member in the kitchen said to an obviously shaken Mike, "Well I guess you won't say

19

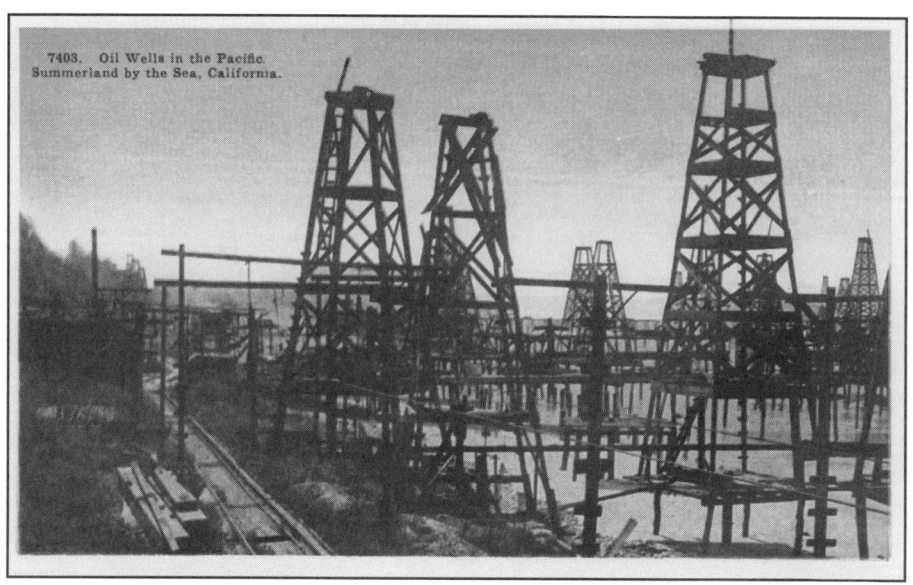

Vintage Postcard c.1940 Summerland by the Sea. Produced by Pacific Novelty Co. San Francisco. The Summerland Oil Field has the distinction of being the first off-shore oil field developed in America.

that again." And he didn't. Mike learned to accept the kitchen spirits and didn't taunt them again.

Besides kitchen staff witnessing unusual happenings, others sensitive to the paranormal requested to be moved from a certain room because of its atmosphere and cold spots.

H.L. Williams, the founder of Summerland, built the home in 1889. Now if you glanced at his biography and read "former Treasury Agent," this would certainly not seem odd, but rather mundane. But Williams and his wife shared another interest. They were spiritualists and they wanted their new town to be a Spiritualist haven. Summerland is the term Spiritualists use for "heaven."

People around the area had another name for the town—Spookville. From the early twentieth century rumors have spread throughout the area of the "unusual" activities going on in Summerland. Is it any wonder that the home built by Williams himself is also a center for spirit activity?

The house was a focal point for Spiritualist séances. There have been many reports that during séances, a man of huge, almost giant, proportions was summoned and it is this man who continues to reside at the home.

For more information on this, consult Rod Lathim's book, *"The Spirit of the Big Yellow House."*

Location

The Big Yellow House on Pierpont Road no longer operates as a restaurant. At the time this book was printed, new owners were renovating the home.

Billiwhack Monster
Aliso Canyon

"…Ghosts are not so different from ordinary people—that is, when they have become materialized."
—The Ghost of Guir House Charles Willing Beale

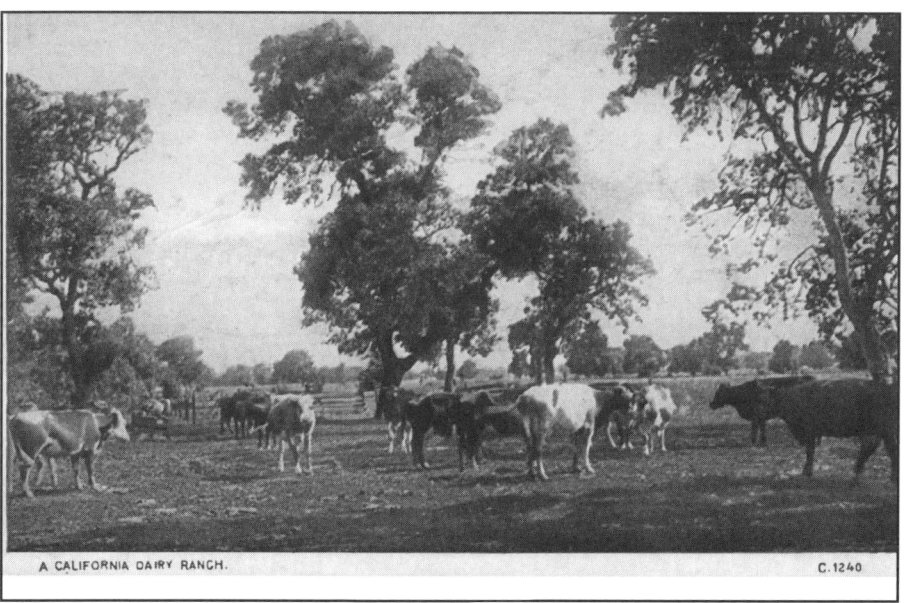

A CALIFORNIA DAIRY RANCH.   C.1240

Vintage postcard of California Dairy Ranch similar to what August A. Rubel envisioned for his land. His herd of Holstein cows was considered the finest in the country. Produced by Pacific Novelty Co. San Francisco & LA.

In 1960,, an article appeared in the *Los Angeles Times*. It spoke of a terrifying creature lurking in the ruins of the old Billiwhack dairy. Local kids had come across the creature several times and described it as a snarling beast unlike any other they had ever seen. Is the Billiwack monster an urban legend or a military experiment gone wrong?

21

August A. Rubel purchased Rancho Camulos, situated between Piru and Castaic, in 1924, from the De Valle family who established the ranch back in 1853. This former New Yorker of Swiss parentage was going to try his hand at Dairy Farming. August Rubel was enticed to buy the land for the deal which also involved the most valuable water rights in Ventura County. "…300 inches of water estimated at $1,000 an inch."

He raised Holstein cows and according to historical documents, it was considered one of the finest herds in the country. Nothing so far would make you believe a monster was also at the ranch, or is there? The story takes a twist with Mr. Rubels untimely death in World War II while driving an ambulance in North Africa. The vehicle hit a mine.

Some believe Mr. Rubel was much more than an ambulance driver but involved in top-secret experiments. What kind of experiments? They were like something from an episode of the *X-Files*, developing a new species of animal. None of this can be proven of course; it isn't as if the Pentagon is going to answer queries regarding Dairy Farm slash Bigfoot breeders now is it?

Sightings of the Billiwhack monster peaked in the fifties and sixties, which correspond to a time when the ranch was a ruin. Current sightings of the beast are few and far between. Some have claimed they saw a hairy Sasquatch like creature around dusk near the canyon road. {5}

Location

Rancho Camulos Museum—a forty acre National Park. Web site- www.ranchocamulos.org.

To find out about tours and hours of operation phone (805) 521-1501.

The ranch was used as one of the settings for Helen Hunt Jackson's novel, *Ramona*. One of the stipulations of the 1924 sale was that Mr. Rube preserve the original adobe and chapel.

———————————————

Black Lady Rising
San Luis Obispo

How to catch a monster. Advice from August 26, 1906 Los Angeles Herald Anon. "..to capture the monster…they are constructing a net made of a section of Page wire fence. The ferrymen say their net is horse-high, hog-tight and bull-strong. They believe it will hold the winged horror."

The Black Lady is said to rise from the depths of Black Lake near Nipomo. A punctual ghost, she makes her nightly appearance around 12:30 pm.

There are many local legends regarding the ghost. The next account is one supposed encounter with the lady. Did it really happen or is it yet another urban myth?

A couple driving along the road, near Black Lake saw something move in the shadows by the side of the road. They slowed down, thinking it could be a stray dog. They saw instead a woman in a long black dress. Not a new one, mind you, but a dress you might have seen in the 1800s! She had her back turned to them. Thinking she was in distress, the lady rolled down her car window and called out to her. The figure slowly turned to reveal a faceless phantom. Terrified, the couple sped off and did not look back. Cue the scary music...

Local legend says she was a drowning victim; others say she was murdered and dumped in the lake. What ever you believe, it is a creepy drive at night with the wind rustling through the branches.

Location

The lake is on private property so the closest you can get to it is along a roadside. You probably have a better chance of seeing the ghost along Highway 1, which she is also said to haunt.

For more information on Nipomo or to read a few more local stories, check out the Web site at www.nipomochamber.com.

Bless This Home
Van Nuys

"...when a spirit returns to earth in visible form, it is the result of some disquieting influence immediately before the death of the body, or, as I might say, previous to the new life."
—The Ghost of Guir House Charles Willing Beale

Writer Mrs. Young, in the spring of 1970, wrote of her haunted home in Van Nuys. She knew for sometime, though her husband was not certain, of the haunting. She had resisted speaking to him until odd occurrences escalated.

In the first few years, she was awakened by the sound of footsteps moving about the upper floor. Knowing the doors to be locked and her husband to be asleep, there was no logical explanation for them. Concerned that someone had broken into the home, she got up to investigate but no one was out in the hallway. Night after night, Mrs. Young was disturbed by this sound, but when she looked for the source found nothing. Her husband, who had no time for ghosts, told her the ceilings and walls of the old house cracked as they cooled or settled.

Mrs. Young was not impressed with her husband's answer as the sounds she heard were definitely footsteps. She could tell the difference between a home settling and a footstep. As years passed, the author got accustomed to her phantom walker.

Nothing more was ever written about Mrs. Young's haunted home in Van Nuys. We are simply left to wonder if the haunting ceased. {6}

Location

Van Nuys is in the heart of the San Fernando valley.
Convention & Visitors Bureau
15205 Burbank Blvd. 2nd Fl.
Van Nuys, CA 91411
(818) 782 7282

Bubbles Lives On
Irvine

"…(sic) again that creep of horror came over me; but this time it was more cold and stubborn. I felt as if some strange and ghastly exhalation were rising up from the chinks of that rugged floor, and filling the atmosphere with a venomous influence hostile to human life."
—The Haunted & the Haunters Sir Edward Bulwer-Lytton

Irvine's Lion Country Safari had a repeat escapee by the name of Bubbles. Bubbles was a female hippo that preferred life out of zoo confines. Once she had to be brought back to the zoo in front of an end-loader!

February and March 1978, Bubbles fascinated the public with her latest and most brazen escape. Hundreds of volunteers looked for Bubbles in the Laguna Hills. Finally she was spotted in a rain-filled pond along the Laguna Canyon Road. It was here, media crews caught her daily swims. While she swam, lawyers were busy at work on her behalf. A Superior Judge forbade anyone from harming Bubbles unless she became a danger, but sadly this would not be enough.

Nineteen days after she first broke out, Bubbles lay dead. During yet another attempt by zoo employees to capture her, tranquillizer darts were fired. Bubbles fell in such an awkward way her windpipe was closed off causing suffocation.

Bubbles escape was only one of many incidents. Over the years at Lion Country Safari, a visitor was mauled, and a worker died during the capture of a wayward elephant. The Lion Country Safari entertained visitors from 1970 until it closed its gates in 1984. When the signs appeared "No Trespassing. Violators Will Be Eaten!" screams in the car would erupt: "We're Here, We're Here." For less than $5 dollars, families would drive through the preserve as lions, elephants, giraffes, and zebras passed within feet of their cars. Needless to say, convertibles were discouraged. The zoo officially closed in 1984, but the image of Bubbles swimming by the freeway remains with residents of Orange County.

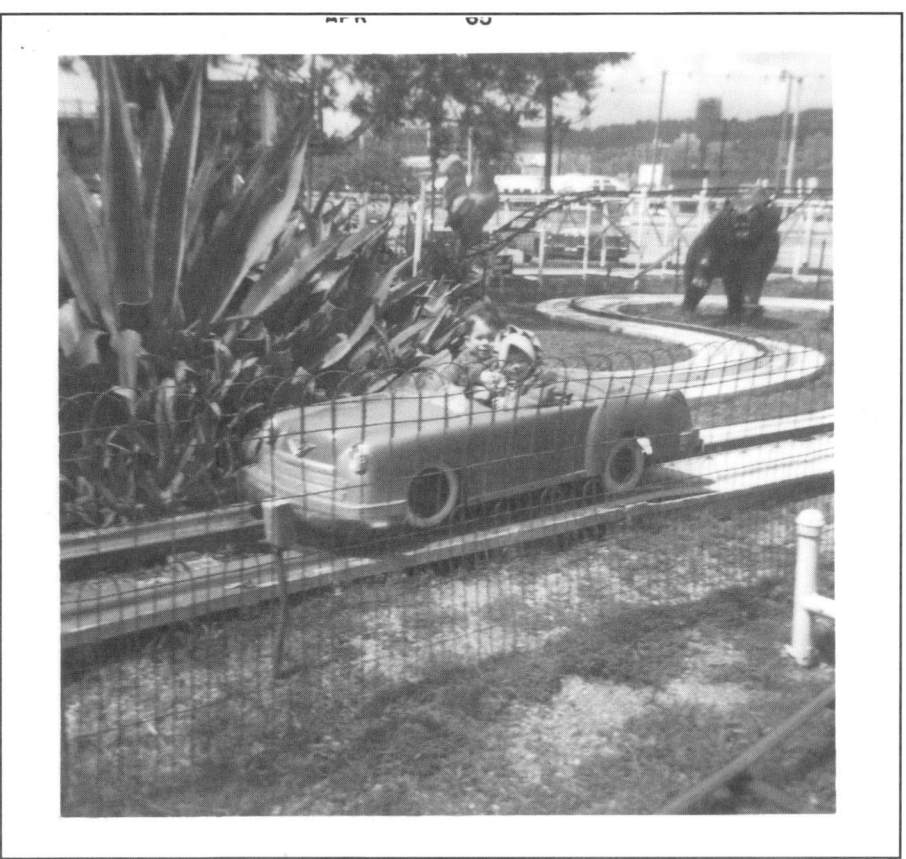

Vintage photo of an unknown Californian amusement park. Ghost hunting is definitely more interesting when you venture off the "rails."

Local lore states Bubbles is still enjoying her freedom. Don't be surprised if driving down Laguna Canyon Road your children start yelling, "There's a hippo over there!" It might be the apparition of Bubbles enjoying herself in her pond. If you don't spot her, you could keep driving south to the San Diego Zoo. Laguna Canyon Road also gained notoriety in 1996 when crop circle formations were spotted. Maybe there is more to this stretch of highway than meets the eye? {7,8}

Location

Laguna Canyon Rd or Route 133 is fifty miles South of Los Angeles. Wild Rivers Amusement Park occupied the site until 2007; its lease was not renewed to make space for a housing development.

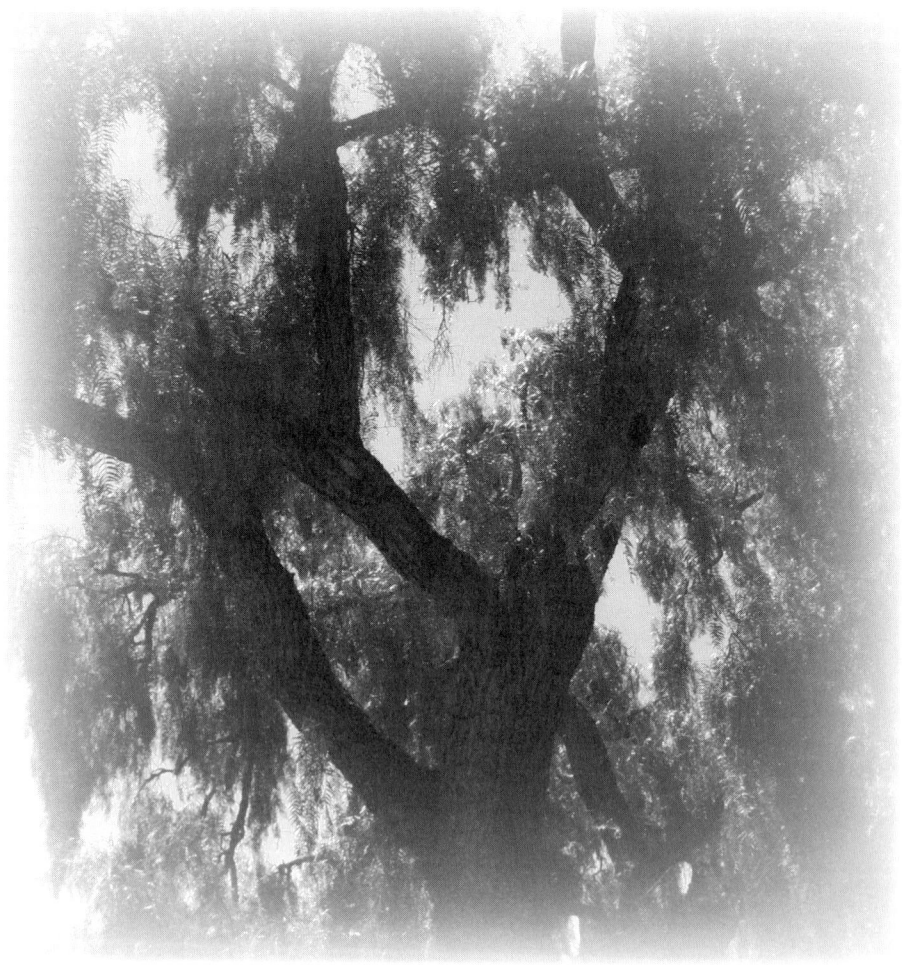

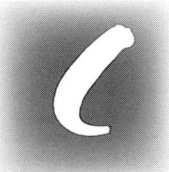

Cabrillo's Ghost
Catalina Island

"I never daunder by its shores, and see the waters hurrying like messengers from the greet deep, without solemn thoughts..."
—The Outgoing Tide John Buchan

In 1966, the *Press Courier* wanted to know if San Miguel Island was a place of death where "ghosts and death abound?" The island's reputation began in 1542 when Juan Rodriguez Cabrillo wintered his fleet off one of the Channel Islands. A small party of men sent ashore came under Indian attack. Cabrillo organized a second party to go ashore but he was injured during this rescue attempt. He contracted an infection, died, and may be buried on San Miguel. The location of the grave has never been discovered and is still debated. Those who believe in Cabrillo's ghost say he is wandering San Miguel Island and curses anyone who tries to live there. "In the centuries following Cabrillo, San Miguel Island has always fought with Point Conception for title graveyard of ships."

The Tale of the King of San Miguel Island

The last man to live on the island was Herbert Lester, a self-styled king, who settled on the Island in 1930 with his wife, Elizabeth. The couple spent twelve years on San Miguel attracting celebrities, due in no small part to their hospitality and charm. You can read more about their lives in Mrs. Lester's book, *The Legendary King of San Miguel*. When the Navy ordered the family to leave the island in 1942, Herbert Lester swore he would never leave, and killed himself. His family abandoned the island leaving behind their belongings and, in one report, the "king's last meal." The King's ghost is said to wander the sand of San Miguel, perhaps keeping company with a famous Spanish explorer. {9}

The island is still uninhabited, as it has belonged to the U.S. military since W.W.II. Is this proof of the curse?

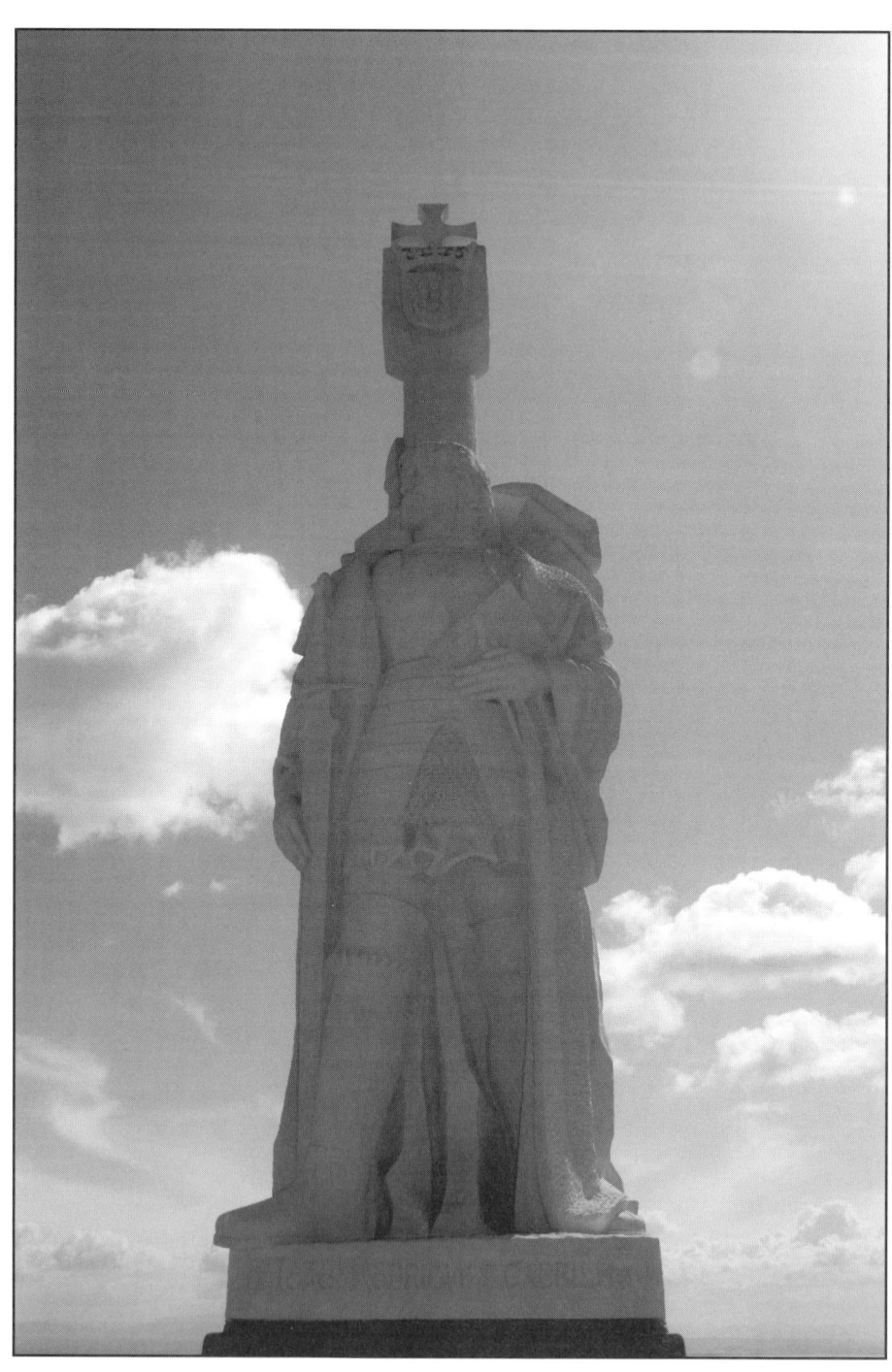

Cabrillo National Monument, San Diego, California.

Location

Channel Islands National Park
Visitor Information: (805) 658-5730
The park is open year round but visitor centers do close on certain holidays.
Transportation: www.nps.gov/chis/planyourvisit/publictransportation.

Captain Cass
Cayucos

"The ethereal world interpenetrates all the physical world. The horizon line of the unseen, the incalculable, is constantly receding, and we are increasing utilizing the ethereal forces. All these are a part of the conditions of which communication with 'the dead' is one of the possibilities."
—Lilian Whiting, 1909

Music drifts through the old home of Captain James Cass but no one is at home. One lady walking her dog in the early evening hours couldn't understand why her dog would not pass the home. "We walked by it daily for years." But on this occasion the dog wouldn't budge. Exasperated, the woman picked up her dog. As she did so, she glanced towards the house. "There was the shape of a man by the side of the home, then there wasn't." The lady hurried home. She has never had another encounter and wonders to this day if it was Captain Cass himself. It certainly wasn't a contractor.

Captain Cass built the home in 1887. The home was completely renovated by its new owners from the early 1990s up until 2007. In various news articles, the owners have spoken about workers' tools missing and unusual noises in the home which couldn't be explained. There is even a report by a previous owner of an old record player suddenly playing.

Who ever is haunting the home, they obviously enjoyed music. The home is now open as a luxury bed and breakfast, of which the Captain would approve. {10}

Location

The Cass House Restaurant
222 North Ocean Avenue
Cayucos, CA 93439
Web site: www.casshouseinn.com
* Cayucos is the Native Indian word for *canoes*

Casa de Rancho Los Cerritos
Long Beach

What is a ghost? The following answer comes from Dr. Alexander J. McIvor-Tyndall who "…(sic) defined the word from the theosophical viewpoint as "an empty shell, something non-vital and having no real power itself."
—Los Angeles Herald March 13, 1905

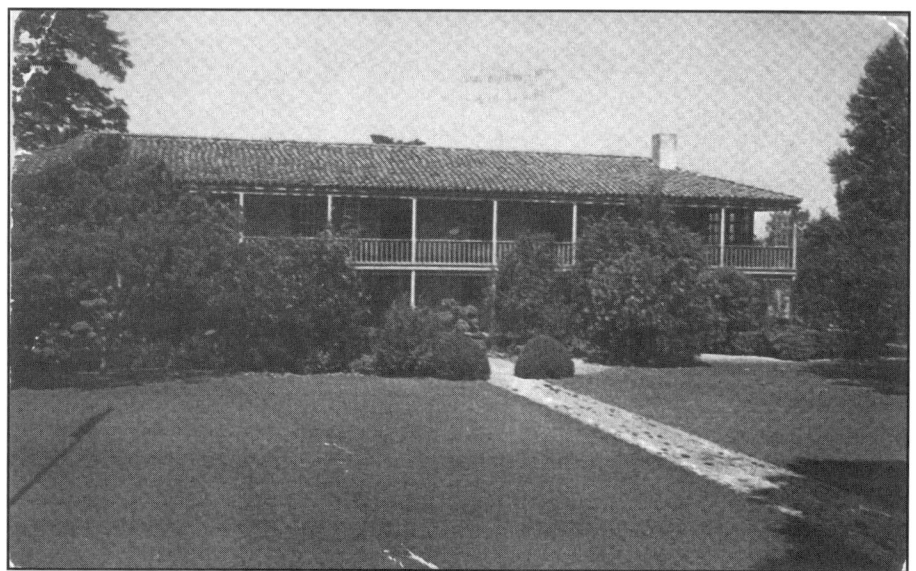

Collectible postcard c. 1960 of the Casa de Rancho Los Cerritos, Long Beach.

Don Juan Temple built Rancho Los Cerritos (meaning *Little Hills*) in 1844. The ranch is a National, State and Long Beach landmark. Los Cerritos along with another ranch Los Alamitos (Little Cottonwoods) totaled 55,000 acres.

In 1974, the caretakers of the adobe spoke with *Long Beach Independent*, reporter T. Thomey of their paranormal encounters while living in the home. The unnerving thing was the Schrubbe's experienced the ghosts of Los Cerritos at all times of the day. Living in such a haunted place you might wonder why they didn't leave, but the Schrubbes explained that the ghost was a benevolent presence.

On several occasions, Mrs. Schrubbe was awakened by a rustling sound. She never determined the source of this noise, but it was certainly loud enough to rouse her from sleep. At first, it was an annoyance but as it kept happening, she realized there was a pattern.

Within moments of being awake, inevitably a police car, fire truck, or other emergency vehicle would pass by the home. This led her to believe that the ghost was warning her of oncoming danger.

Mr. Schrubbe thought a murder may have been committed on the premises and it was this spirit that wandered the home. "...(sic) that the victim—still unhappy about his fate—has remained on the premises in a ghostly state, awaiting satisfaction." This was never historically proven.

Frequently, footsteps were heard in the hallway. When the children heard the sounds and investigated, there was no one there. One of the children turned a light on to investigate the sound. He managed to take a few footsteps in the direction of the sound before the light turned off. That put a quick end to ghost hunting.

The spirit also exhibited poltergeist activity. Keys and other little objects were forever being moved about the dwelling. They would turn up in an obvious spot in plain view.

The caretakers consulted with a psychic medium who was convinced "...(sic) the ghostly activities are in some way connected with a man known to have abnormally short arms." An interesting piece of information but as the spirit never revealed its name, it was a dead lead, and no more information was obtained.

Disbelievers of the ghost theory point to docent Mike Morillos who knew some of the original characters associated with the home. He thrilled children with stories of haunted staircases, murder, and even silver bars, which he said he threw down the well at the ranch. Mike Morillos died in 1931, but his recollections of the ranch are preserved forever at the Long Beach Library's oral history collection. While treasure was never found at the ranch, Indian artifacts have been found as Don Juan Temple built his home in 1844 over an old Indian village.

Los Cerritos originally belonged to the vast Los Nietos Rancho, granted in 1784 by the Spanish to soldier Manuel Nieto. Upon his death in 1804, his daughter Manuela inherited Los Cerritos and occupied it with her twelve children. A daughter, Rafaela, married a merchant named John Temple who would eventually buy out the other heirs' interests in Los Cerritos. In 1844, he built his new home in Los Cerritos, which served as headquarters for his ranching operations.

The hacienda soon became famous for its hospitality and good food. Spectators watched bullfights from seats outside of the ring and an annual rodeo brought many visitors to Los Cerritos.

If you pass by Los Cerritos in the evening hours and see a soft glow on the grounds, it might be the spirit of Mike pointing the way to the buried treasure. Or you can visit during daylight hours and may feel the presence of Don Juan Temple, Rafael, or one of their children. {11, 12}

Location

Rancho Los Cerritos
4600 Virginia Road
Long Beach, CA 90807
(562) 570-1755
Hours: Wednesday to Sunday from 1 pm to 5 pm; not open on major holidays. For tour information, see the web site www.rancholoscerritos.org.

Charman
Ventura

What do ghosts feel about the world? Here is one view: "Here's a year of my life written in pen or pencil but already it's blunted. The feeling has gone out of it. This must be the way ghosts feel about the world they've left behind. No passion. Only poignancy."
—Rob Wells, *The Independent.* January 1, 1964

The Charman is coming! The Charman is coming! Charred flesh hangs from his bones, eyes loose in their sockets, and scraps of clothing clinging to his frame. You'll probably smell Charman before you see him. No, you are not waiting in line for a double showing of a B-movie classic; this is Ventura County and you are (flashlight in hand) waiting for the creature to appear. Yes, it might have been safer to buy some popcorn and rent a DVD but *nooooooooo*, you wanted excitement.

This monstrous figure from Ojai has been a classic campground tale for years. The variations of the story increase with its age. Sometimes he is an old man burned by teenagers in an arson attack, or a firefighter killed fighting a blaze, which according to history records didn't happen. Or is he the spirit of a car accident victim? No one knows for sure, but this doesn't stop the curious and paranormal groups from staking the area around Camp Comfort in order to see for themselves. There is also a bridge, which he is said to be haunted. The area has two bridges; look for the one with an *x*. Some helpful person put an *x* on one, but it is sometimes removed.

This spot should never be visited alone, as it does attract certain elements best not met with at night. It is easy to see why so many believe that something lurks in the woods.

You can really try testing your metal and stay overnight at Camp Comfort. You never know who may show up.

11969 Creek Rd.
Ojai, Ca 93023
Camp Comfort—a number of ghoulish inhabitants, including a Vampire from Spain, according to Dennis Hauck author of *Haunted Places: The National Directory*, though none showed up on our picnic day.

Cheesecloth Ghost Long Beach

Not all phantoms appear as benign glowing orbs. "…(sic) a brilliant light illuminated the drive and to her horror the figure of a young woman, all in flames, bearing a child in her arms, appeared, tearing down the avenue."
—Anon. *San Francisco Call*, September 25, 1904

What could a dollar buy you in 1928 Long Beach? A dollar went a long way back in 1928, but some foolish residents of Long Beach soon found out it couldn't buy them a spirit. One evening, an off-duty policeman noticed a steady stream of people entering a small apartment building. It seemed more than a bit odd, as no business was located on the premises, at least no legal business. Thinking he had uncovered yet another speakeasy, he went to investigate.

The policeman watched from the stairwell as a couple handed a dollar to a man standing outside one of the units. He stashed the money in a coat pocket and allowed them inside. Determined to get to the bottom of the mystery, the policeman also paid the doorman. The policeman slipped quietly to the back of the dimly lit room and waited.

Suddenly, a long curtain parted dramatically and out stepped a man wearing a long piece of jeweled cloth wrapped around his head. The crowd held their breath in anticipation as he sat down at the small table. He demanded in a loud voice for the spirit to show itself. The crowd edged a little closer to the table but no spirit appeared. More money was collected and it was explained the spirit was feeling a little shy.

The man once again implored the spirit to materialize; from behind the curtains where the man had entered the room, a slight motion was detected. People were now on the edge of their seats as curtains parted to reveal a white form. Some in the audience gasped and others fainted, as in front of their eyes was a ghost!

The policeman quickly put a stop to the spiritualist's séance and charged them with illegally collecting money.

A dollar bought you many things in 1928, but not a ghost. A Long Beach dollar did buy you a woman dressed in black tights and veil made of several yards of cheesecloth.

Spiritualist Licenses

In 1905, ordained ministers of spiritualism and mediums tried to petition the city of Los Angeles for tax exemption in regard to licenses. "We do not think that our ordained ministers should be licensed," they said through a representative from the spirit world. The representative pointed out that people go to spiritualists for "comfort for their souls." The council was not swayed. Instead it decided to double the licensing fees for spiritualists! {13}

Location

If you are planning a visit to Long Beach see www.longbeach.gov/visitors or www.visitlongbeach.com.

Conception Arguello's Curse

"Dr. Forbes Winslow says that insanity from spiritualism increases daily in England, and that 10,000 lunatics are now under treatment in America from this cause."
—Thoughts on spiritualism from December 9, 1876,
Oakland Evening Tribune

Conception Arguello was interested in the Russian Chamberlain of Tsar Alexander I, Nikolai Petrovich Rezanov. He had come from Russia to establish trade between the two countries but had no success. He then began his pursuit of Conception Arguello. Here the romantics insist he was truly in love with the girl and the pessimists insist he was using her as a ploy to gain access to trade. In Nikolai Rezanov's own journals he noted, "A close bond would be formed…" between the two countries if they were married. Before the "star crossed lovers" could be married, Rezanov sailed back to Russia to ask the Csar's permission.

Rezanov died of pneumonia on his way to St. Petersburg. No word was sent to California, leaving Conception to wonder for five years of his fate. When word came of his death, Conception entered a convent where she devoted her life to the infirm, elderly,

34

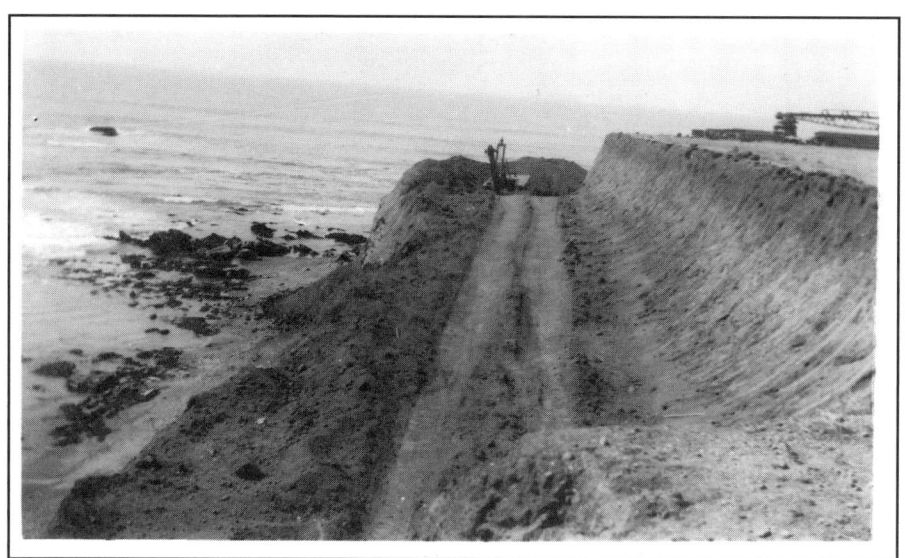

Vintage photo of Point Arguello, Coast Guard Station.

and poor. She became the first Californian to take the vows of a Dominican nun.

The Curse

By all accounts, Conception was contented at the convent, but curse theorists would have you believe otherwise. Many have wondered whether the misfortune that was attached to Conception hangs over this coastline, as after her fiancé died, the list of seafaring accidents grew. Over fifty ships and countless lives have been lost on this three-mile stretch of ocean, known as the "Graveyard of the Pacific." Here is an account of one horrific accident and it's ghostly legacy.

In 1854, the captain of the *Yankee Blade* was engaged in a race with the steamer *Sonora,* but the ill-fated race ended when the *Yankee Blade* crashed onto the rocks. The captain abandoned ship, and his ten-year old son. The ship's crew even robbed many of the survivors on shore! "…(sic) the actual sufferers never received the provisions sent them, for a party composed of the ship's firemen, insensible to humanity took for themselves almost everything that went on shore and money was seen in their possession which they could not have obtained only by dishonesty."

Fifty-two passengers died and echoes of this tragedy are heard. Some say they have actually seen the *Yankee Blade* and heard her passengers' cries of distress. The ship, *Dancing Feather,* sent out to retrieve the *Yankee Blade's* treasure of gold returned to port after twenty-five days empty handed. In an interesting twist, the Captain was later charged with stealing the *Yankee Blade's* treasure—no wonder there was no room for passengers aboard his lifeboat! Further research will reveal a lengthy list of lost steamships and Navy destroyers. These incidents further cement the area's cursed reputation.

Point Conception Lighthouse is located on the west entrance to the Santa Barbara Channel. The lighthouse was established in 1856. The original one-story Cape Cod lighthouse was constructed in 1856. It had to be partially taken down to accommodate a Fresnel lens imported from France. The original tower had sustained damage from the constant wind. The light was activated on February 1, 1856, and automated in 1973. {14,15,16}

Location

The lighthouse is not accessible or open to the public, as a large private ranch surrounds it. Whether or not one believes in haunting legends, the fact remains that this jagged area of coastline northwest of Santa Barbara has seen enough tragedy to justify every kind of supernatural claim.

Curse of Griffith Park
Los Angeles

"Ghosts aren't trained seals that perform on command. What we parapsychologists call 'spontaneous phenomena' do not occur except when the actual emotional situation exists."
—Hans Holzer, *Eureka Humbolt Standard*, February 15, 1964

Griffith Park, Los Angeles, was originally part of an 8,000-acre ranch owned by Antonio Feliz. The odd series of supernatural events leading up to this event linger over the park today.

In 1863, Feliz died of smallpox. His niece, Dona Petranilla, who usually resided with her uncle, was not at the home. When she did return, Dona Petranilla was both saddened by her uncle's passing and horrified to find that an unscrupulous man named Antonio Coronel had disinherited her.

Petronilla was not one to take this lying down and she cursed Coronel and his family. She swore anyone who owned the ranch would never enjoy or profit from it. Soon after uttering the curse she collapsed and died.

36

In short order, members of the Coronel family died untimely deaths. The property was bought by Leon Baldwin, who restocked the ranch. His dreams of ranching ended when he was killed in Mexico.

A Colonel Griffith, the next owner, also met with misfortune. In 1884, the Los Angeles River flooded bringing ruin to Rancho Feliz. Native Indians said, "Old Don Antonio rode the crest of the flood that carried much of the rich bottomlands out to the sea. Legend has it that the Don was seen dancing El Jarabe (a tap dance) over the ruins." (El Jarabe means Mexican Hat Dance.)

Colonel Griffith's woes continued after the flood with workers refusing to step foot on the property. They swore they had seen the Ghost of Don Antonio. Even a portion of the land leased for a time to an ostrich farm was not immune. The ostrich keepers swore the place was haunted as every night the ostriches would stampede.

By 1896, Colonel Griffith had had enough and gave the land, 3,000 acres, to the City of Los Angeles. The dedication banquet, attended by city officials and other dignitaries included one surprise guest from the past. At some point during the evenings festivities, invitees looked with amazement at the table. Who was there? Why it was Antonio Feliz himself, back from the dead who came to join in the celebration. The ghost's appearance put an abrupt end to the evening.

As for Colonel Griffith, he didn't escape the curse either. Seven years later, he was sentenced to twenty months in San Quentin for seriously wounding his wife in the Hotel Arcadia, Santa Monica. He swore he accidentally shot her after a heated argument, but his wife, her family, and ultimately a jury, didn't believe him. He was a social outcast for the rest of his life. {17}

Location

4730 Crystal Springs Dr.,
Los Angeles, CA 90027
(323) 913-4688
Web site: www.laparks.org for more information.
The park is open from 6 am until 10 pm.

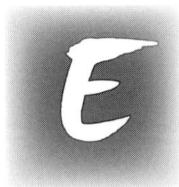

El Adobe Restaurant
San Juan Capistrano

"I want to have goblins about me, for I am courageous."
—Friedrich Nietsche

Smoke fills the air, my daughter nervously awaits the ghost of perhaps a prisoner from the time the El Adobe was two buildings—a private residence and a jail. But no, the smoke is from neighboring tables'deep-fried chimichangas.

The jail portion has been converted into a wine cellar for the restaurant and it is here that the waiters report a feeling of being watched. Wait staff are said to be reluctant to enter the wine cellar, though mine certainly said he had no problem! In addition, the ghost of a headless monk has been seen wandering the street outside of the restaurant.

Alfred Cornwell of Long Beach owned the El Adobe Restaurant; it was one of Southern California's most historic dining places. A portion of it was built in 1778. Another portion of the restaurant was built in 1810. In former decades, it was used as a stage depot, trading post, and justice court.

Though Nixon is said to have loved this restaurant, he isn't one of the specters coming back to El Adobe. When the smoke clears, look out for a monk outside and ask the hosts about the "dungeon" below the restaurant.

Location

31891 Camino Capistrano
(949) 493-1163
Web site: www.eladobe.net

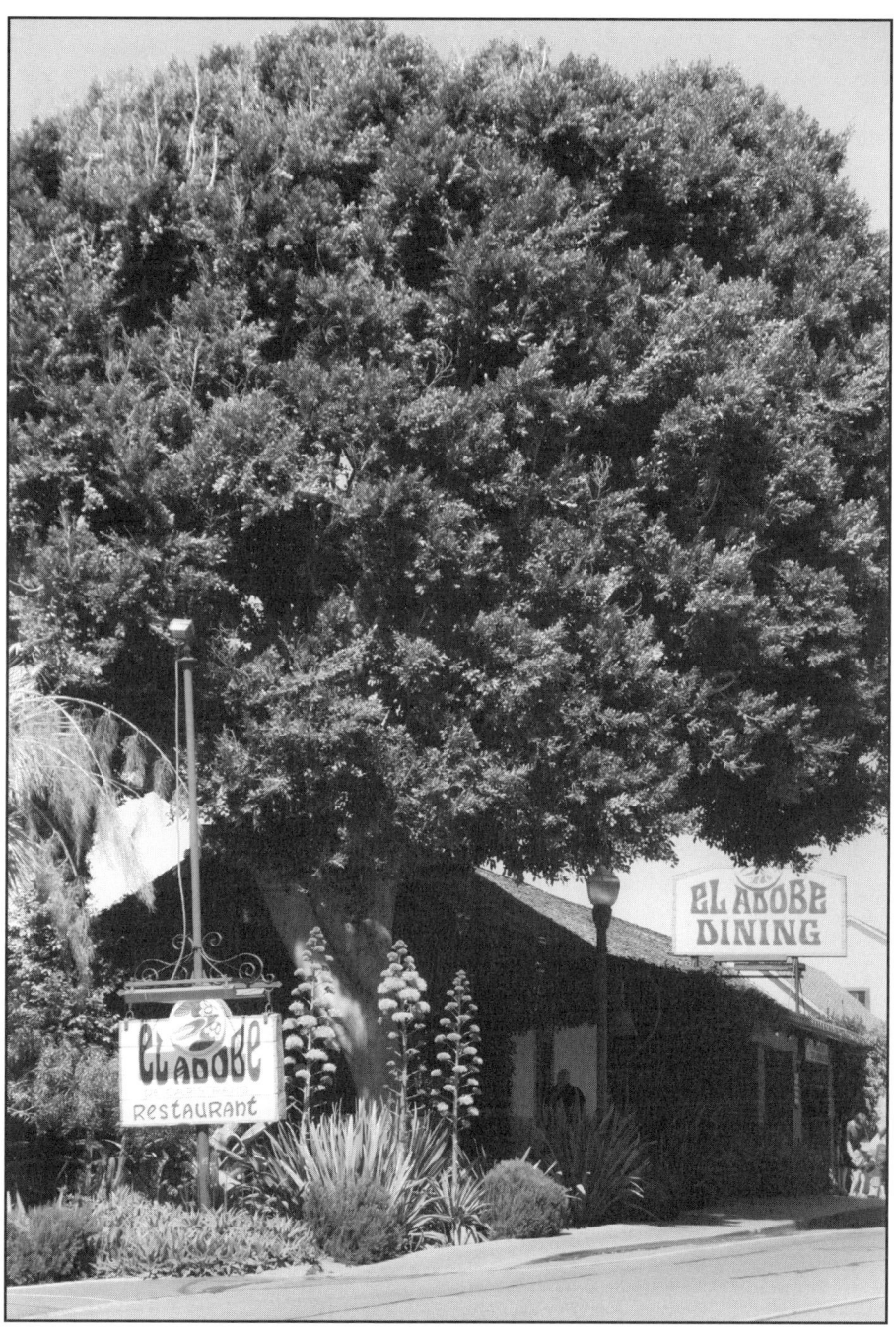

The El Adobe restaurant on Los Rios Street is a short walk down from the Mission.

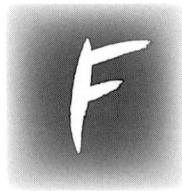

First Christian Church
Rialto

With a surge of public interest in spiritualism in the 1900s, fake mediums flourished, preying on the unsuspecting. Police were kept busy raiding séances. "Spookdom received a terrible jolt last night. Two mediums were captured and the regalia of a ghost with three trumpets will rest peacefully at police headquarters."

—Los Angeles Herald, Anon. November 3, 1907

The white clapboard former church on Riverside Avenue is not holding service any longer. Ever since it came under the wing of the Rialto Historical Society, reports of ghosts have been appearing in local papers. One ghost is thought to be of a young girl named Kristina. She was the daughter of a Rialto physician, Dr. Merlin A. Hendrickson. He bought the building in 1963 and donated it for use as a museum a few years later. It is listed on the National Register of Historic Places.

Kristina died of leukemia in 1967. The old building was renamed in her honor, Kristina Dana Hendrickson Cultural Center. After the Hendricksons placed her ashes in the church basement, people started claiming they had seen Kristina in the church. Busy at work, one volunteer suddenly stopped her work when the form of a child appeared before her. In the blink of an eye, the image disappeared leaving the worker terrified. Though Kristina was never considered a malicious spirit, her appearance caused many to feel unsettled. According to an article published in the *Inland Valley Daily Bulletin* in 2006, "Kristina's ghost was seen, heard, or felt by at least ten different people. After three very emotional séances designed to release her, Kristina disappeared from the church."

In 1997, volunteers at the museum arranged for Tom Hagman, president of the Parapsychology Association of Riverside, to investigate the building. The volunteers did not tell Mr. Hagman of Kristina, but he was able to see her looking out of an upper-story building. His description of Kristina matched a picture of her in the museum's possession.

Though Kristina is now believed to be gone, two area policeman responding to a burglar alarm encountered a woman dressed in Victorian-era clothing at the base of a stairway. They could see every detail of her features. She had normal color, but was transparent and had no feet! Though she had no feet, another pair of officers who responded to a call earlier, heard footsteps on the same staircase. In addition to these ghosts, other investigators are certain many more spirits exist here. {18}

Location

The old Christian Church is now the location of the Rialto Historical Society. It is located at 201-205 N. Riverside Avenue.

The museum is open to tours Wednesdays from 2 pm until 4 pm and Saturdays from 10 am to 2 pm.

Telephone: (909) 875-3776

Web site: Rialto Historical Society- www.ci.rialto.ca.us

Fox Fullerton Theatre
Fullerton

"Not every haunting is real. A true ghost hunter must ask questions. The next 'paranormal experience' occurred in an unidentified town with many observers gathered around. "There was a raised place in the center of the bed and it was moving as if something uneasy was under the sheet." Was it a ghost? Drawing back the bed sheet a full-grown hen was revealed!
—*The Paris News* January 1, 1975

The Fox Fullerton Theatre is reputed to be haunted by the ghost of a former theater manager. It is said his ghost still walks the aisles from time to time. No one knows why the spirit keeps returning. Also, reported accounts of a strong floral scent that suddenly wafts past you inside the building, and then quickly dissipates have been mentioned.

History

C. Stanley Chapman who was the son of Fullerton's first mayor, Charles C. Chapman, built the theatre. It was known as the Alician Court Theatre, named for C.S. Chapman's wife, Alice. Theater architects, Meyer and Holler, Inc., who also designed Grumman Chinese Theatre in Hollywood, designed the building.

41

Location

510 N. Harbor Boulevard
Fullerton, CA
Corner of Harbor Boulevard and Chapman Avenue
Fullerton Historic Theatre Foundation: (714) 870-0069.
Web site: www.foxfullerton.com.

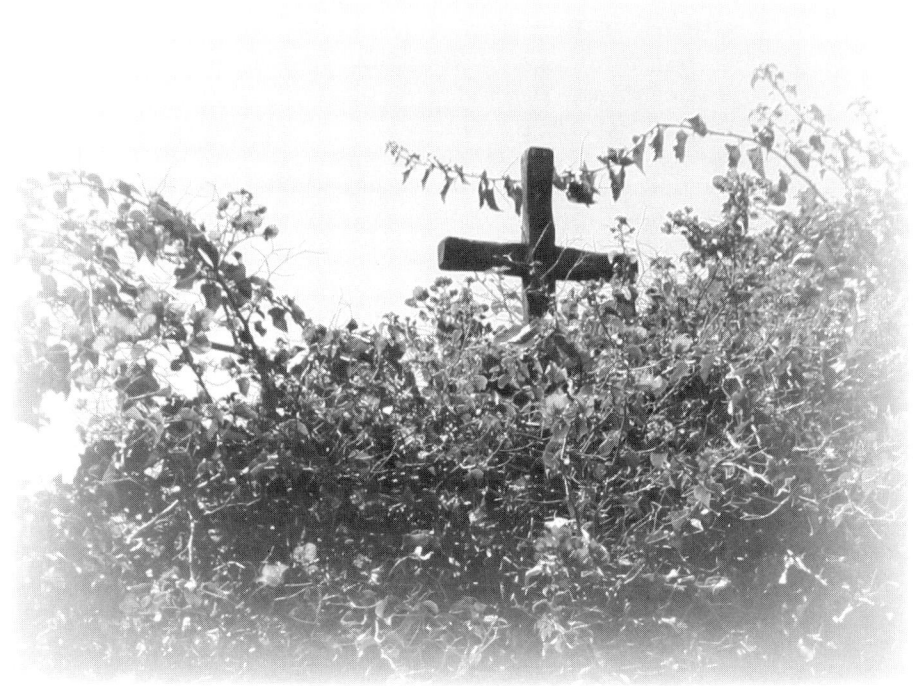

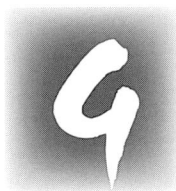

Georgian Hotel Santa Monica

"The figure did not appear to be thoroughly solid, but to be of the consistency of curd..."

—*A Dead Finger,* Sabine Baring-Gould

The bartender made sure everything was in place for the evening. Glasses were wiped and put away, ice, checked. Out of the corner of his eye, a slight movement caught his attention. He looked up to see a man dressed in an old-fashioned suit complete with hat sitting at the bar. He could also see the rest of the speakeasy through this diaphanous figure. Before he could blink, the figure disappeared as quietly as it came.

In an area of the hotel known as the speakeasy, liquor was served during prohibition. When you go for a drink at the Georgian, you never know who might be rubbing elbows with you, but of course some of them will be hard to see. Tales of ghosts have swirled around this Art Deco gem for years. Clark Gable, Carole Lombard, and Bugsy Siegel were known to frequent the bar.

This hotel was *the* place to stay. Martinis flowed freely for this was not the Georgian of today, whose gorgeous blue façade beckons to all who pass. This little gem was

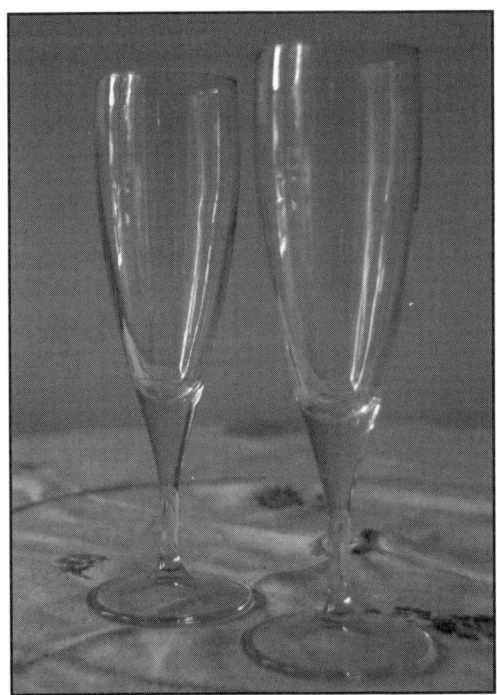

Georgian Hotel Santa Monica.

tucked discreetly away from prying eyes during prohibition. The authorities did not look kindly on alcohol being served.

The ghosts at the Georgian Hotel are not shy about their presence being felt. There are mysterious pockets of cold, voices and laughter echoing in the Speakeasy when it is empty—well, empty of the living. The sounds of music drift through the air when no auditory device is turned on.

One hotel employee came across a very polite ghost who wished him a good morning. Another man heard the distinct sound of a person sighing but no one was beside him. There are tales of guests encountering guests from the past in the halls. Some of these well-dressed guests, in outfits from the 1930s, roam the halls only to vanish after wishing present guests a good evening. None are malicious, and in fact, simply add to the spirit of the hotel.

The Georgian Hotel opened in 1933 to raves. It was a grand hotel owned by Mrs. Rosamond Borde who hired architect, Eugene Durfee, to design in Art Deco style. The hotel was renovated in 2000 to enthusiastic reviews. A few hours spent at the Georgian will whisk you back in time, and who knows who may appear to have a drink with you.

Location

1415 Ocean Avenue
Santa Monica, CA 90401
(310) 395-9945
Web site: www.georgianhotel.com

Ghost of Foster Park
Ventura

"No work begun shall ever pause for death."
—Robert Browning

In the late 1800s, a group of ladies traveled to the banks of the Ventura River for a picnic. Their picnic was cut short when dark storm clouds came rolling in. Frantically, the ladies packed everything into their carriage. They couldn't move fast enough as it started to pour. As they whipped the horses to get going, they saw a hooded figure coming out of the willow trees. It swayed back and forth beckoning to them. The ladies wasted no time in racing to Ventura.

They told their husbands of this phantom down by the river, demanding that they do something. Many weeks went by and the incident was forgotten, until the next stormy night, when a man walking near the willow trees also saw the phantom moaning near the willow trees. The terrified man galloped back into town. By the next morning, everyone knew the ghost had returned.

The ladies' husbands decided that they would be brave and seek the ghost out. The next evening, they set out for the river wondering if the ghost would make a third appearance. They didn't wonder long. As the wind picked up and thrashed the boughs of the willows, the ghost made its appearance. It moaned and groaned as if in agony, frightening the men away.

It was decided by the men of the area and the Sheriff to get rid of this phantom. The next rainy evening the sheriff assembled a group of men to go down to the river. The Sheriff did not believe in ghosts and thought this was a great waste of time, but if he did not appease the town's people, he was never going to get any peace.

The rain subsided as the group neared the river. The Sheriff asked the men to remain as quiet as possible. All eyes were on the river when the ghostly figure stepped out from the trees. It swayed and moaned just as before, but the Sheriff ordered the men to keep their calm. The Sheriff ordered the phantom to surrender, but when the order was ignored, he pulled out his gun and fired. Instead of vanishing into thin air, the creature crumbled to the ground.

The men crept forward until one got up the nerve to pull the hood from the figure. To their shock, it wasn't a phantom but the local judge! The men placed the Judge's body on horseback and rode to the man's home. The maid gave them access to the home where the Sheriff searched the Judge's personal writings. He came across a written confession.

To what had the Judge confessed? He had confessed to killing a man who had been a rival for a local woman's affections. He had told the woman of his crime and she, overcome with fear, died. He was too much of a coward to take his own life so concocted this river phantom as a way to provoke someone into shooting him!

Days after the Judge's death, rumors of a hooded figure by the river spread through the county. Did the judge's ghost return to the spot where once he had been a fake phantom? Was he destined to spend eternity by the river as a penance for the crimes he had committed?

The Park dates back to 1906. Today, it is a popular location for those hiking the Ojai Valley Trail. The real ghost of the Judge is said to come back to this spot on rainy evenings. There haven't been any recent sightings, but as the park is closed to the public well before the evening hours, it is little wonder. {19}

438 Casitas Vista Road
Hwy 33, Exit Casitas Vista/ Santa Ana Road
(805) 654-3951
Map available on the County of Ventura Web site: www.
countyofventura.org.

Glen Tavern Inn
Santa Paula

For acts of disobedience, the anonymous author writes about popular strategies of the day. *"...(sic) they (children) are told strange stories of ghosts and threatened that if they do not behave they will be sold to the ragpicker..."*

—*Oakland Tribune March 28, 1906*

The Glen Tavern Inn is said to be the most haunted place in Ventura County, host to paranormal conferences and more than its share of séances. The Tudor-style hotel, built in 1911, has owners even talking about its resident ghosts on the hotel's We site. The Web site states, "A number of guests have reported odd manifestations in their rooms late at night, and at least seventy-five percent of the hotel staff has encountered one of several phantoms that wander the inn."

Additionally, newspaper accounts of hauntings at Santa Paula's Glen Tavern Inn have been reported for over twenty years. Why so much interest in this inn? Not because of the famous guests like Clark Gable, Carole Lombard, and Harry Houdini, but because of the ghostly guests who were already in residence.

The Inn was a popular stop for those working in the film industry. One of these guests is the ghost of Buffalo Bill Cody—or an actor resembling the famous man. It attracted a long list of colorful characters that apparently stayed on. Buffalo Bill's ghost is said to haunt Room 306. A group of Ventura College students taking a ghost-hunting course decided to investigate the room. One of them, Catherine Dickerson, took thirty-six photographs of the room. Later, they were developed revealing thirty-five blank shots and one with a strange green ectoplasm image of Buffalo Bill.

The Inn has seen its fair share of séances, too. Through the work of medium Debra Christenson Senate, Grace Coveney, and paranormal investigator Heather Woodward, some of the Inn's spirits have been identified. In 1986, Debra Christenson Senate was able to contact the spirit of Jennifer, a woman who died around the 1930s in Room 306.

Grace Coveney, after her time at the Inn, came to the conclusion there were at least three spirits there. There was the spirit of a child on the first floor, a woman in Room 218, and the previously mentioned Buffalo Bill.

In 2007, as reported in the *Ventura County Star* by Kim Lamb Gregory, Heather Woodward was able to contact the spirit of a French perfume saleswoman who died at the Inn in the 1930s. Heather Woodward used a technique called automatic writing, in which the medium is able to channel the spirit of a deceased person.

Though the reported ghosts certainly are colorful one deeply touching story comes from Glen Tavern night innkeeper, Susan Gallagher who spoke of her experience in the same article. At the inn's bar is a piano, which one-day started playing all by it self and it wasn't a player piano. The next day a woman whose father loved to play piano at the bar paid the inn a visit. Her father had just died. It seems there is something at the Glen Tavern Inn, which keeps old spirits about and draws in new ones.

For the staff at the Inn, most occurrences are ordinary, not as exciting as ectoplasm resembling past stars. One girl working as a waitress in the now closed restaurant heard the ghost stories, but didn't pay much attention to them. Even when the Inn hosted a paranormal conference, she wasn't convinced.

She changed her mind one day after cleaning up after the lunch crowd. She was straightening tables and pushing in chairs when she heard someone come in the room. She thought it was the other waitress so continued to push in chairs, chatting away. Then her colleague appeared apologizing for not coming to help sooner. The first girl more than a little nervous turned slowly around to the table where she thought the other girl had been working. She noted three of the four chairs were tucked in neatly, but one chair was pulled out, facing her as if someone had been sitting in it listening to her chatter. Which of the spirits of the Santa Paula Inn had come for a late lunch? {20}

Location

134 N. Mill Street
Santa Paula, CA 93060
(805) 933-5550
Web site: www.glentavern.com

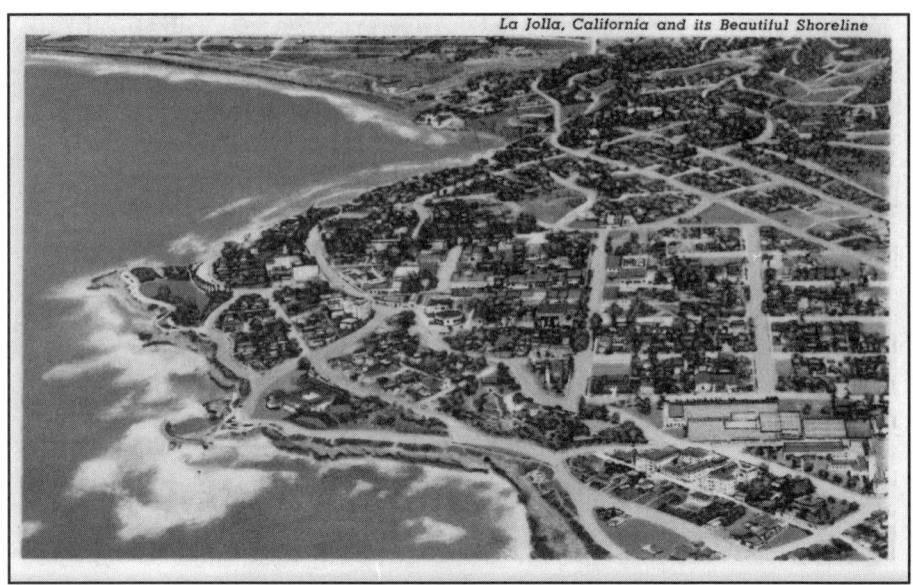

Vintage collectible postcard of La Jolla.

Grand Colonial Hotel La Jolla

"The spirits of the dead, who stood In life before thee, are again In death around thee.."

—*Spirits of the Dead,* Edgar Allan Poe

The Grand Colonial, La Jolla, began life in 1913 as The Colonial Apartments and Hotel. The original building was moved to the rear of the property in 1925, and a new modern hotel opened in 1928, offering rooms at $25 to $50 a month. Thanks to several multimillion-dollar makeovers, from 1976 to 2007 the Grande Colonial has retained its historic charms and remains a favorite hotel for visitors to La Jolla.

I have stayed at the hotel several times; there is one visit I will never forget. This incident took place over ten years ago when I had no idea that the Colonial was haunted.

Our usual room was not ready when we arrived but the effects of jetlag convinced us to check into another room. The room was in a part of the hotel where we had never stayed. After unpacking and enjoying an early meal, we retired.

Shortly after 2 am, I was awakened by loud crashing sounds. My husband woke up soon after, and he is a very heavy sleeper. "Did you hear that?" I asked. Before he could respond, the sound was back again, followed by voices. The more we listened, the more it sounded as if a raucous party was in progress below us.

Impatient with being disturbed I phoned down to the front desk. They informed me there were no rooms below mine, just a bakery that was closed. I told them that I wasn't crazy and obviously their employees were having a party at my expense and could they stop it.

A little while later the front phoned up to say they had checked the bakery and it was locked up. Perhaps it was a sound from the hall, they suggested. I said I was certain it was not and that I would call down if I heard it again. Within ten minutes, the noisy party continued. In the end, my husband put in a pair of earplugs and I tried to get back to sleep.

It wouldn't be until seven years later, while doing research, that I would come across an article about the haunted Colonial. The "raucous" partygoers are said to be the spirits of two men and two women who enjoyed throwing parties when the hotel first opened. These spirits also act up in the kitchen with chefs noticing pilot lights mysteriously turning themselves off and kitchen equipment moving on its own.

Other unusual occurrences in the hotel include two glamoursly-dressed apparitions, disembodied voices, doors slamming, and the sounds of footsteps in empty hallways. The Grande Colonial is a wonderful place to stay, but some rooms come with unseen occupants.

Location

910 Prospect Street
La Jolla, CA 923037
(858) 454-2181
Web site: www.thegrandecolonial.com

Guadalupe Adobe
Santa Barbara

"The supernatural is the natural not yet understood."
—Elbert Hubbard

Long Before Cecil B. DeMille used the sandy landscape of Guadalupe west of Santa Maria for his 1923 movie *The Ten Commandments*, the town was making headlines. The town of

Guadalupe takes its name from Rancho Guadalupe, established in 1840. The small town is just west of Santa Maria. The town was founded in 1873, and for a short period in the late 1800s, it was one of Santa Barbara County's boomtowns.

Readers of the *Santa Maria Times* in 1890 were particularly intrigued with the reoccurring story of the un-rentable adobe of Guadalupe. They all knew this adobe, as the land was linked to the very founding of Guadalupe itself.

In 1840, the Mexican government granted Teodoro Arellanes and Diego Olivera more than 32,000 acres of good ranch land near the Santa Maria River. A cattle operation was begun and a large adobe home built, later destroyed by John C. Freemont and his troops in 1846. In the following years, the ranch lands would be divided into parcels and pass through many hands.

John Ward built a large two-story adobe in 1868. It would become the center of activity for the town of Guadalupe serving as meeting place, a stagecoach stop, a newspaper office, and a justice court.

For a time, the building was having difficulty getting tenants. According to the article, this adobe in town could not be let. Unsuspecting tenants would agree to rent out the place only to desert the adobe days, sometimes weeks, later.

What was driving the people out? Loud knocking on the walls rudely awakened tenants. The sounds did not originate outside the dwelling, but from within the walls. Townsfolk didn't know what to make of the matter. There were those who insisted the tenants were easily spooked. The sounds they kept hearing were probably coyotes. Others claimed they were the spirits of previous owners.

What exactly was happening at the adobe will forever remain a mystery as it was torn down to 1960.

Location

Santa Maria is located in the foothills of Santa Barbara's wine country.

Web site: www.santamaria.com

For a trip to Guadalupe see www.ci.gudalupe.ca.us.

To visit the Guadalupe-Nipomo Dunes where the set used in *The Ten Commandments* was located, though now buried under the sand, see www.dunescenter.org.

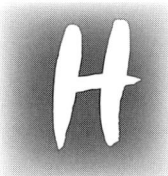

Haunted Gaviota Coast
Gaviota

"There are certain beliefs as old as the world, that have encountered more or less scepticism in all ages, and nevertheless endure today."
—*A Ghost Story,* Lafcadio Hearn

Somewhere along the Gaviota coast is a rock with the carved face of a Native Indian, hundreds of years old which is said to house a spirit. Sacrifices were made and large fires built until the face on the rock glowed. The Indians would then say the rock was alive. Those days are long gone, but on certain nights, the rock is said to awaken, emitting an unearthly glow.

As the fog rolls in, it is said ghostly riders appear causing unsuspecting drivers to lose control of their cars. If you walk on this road you may hear the rock moaning and groaning...beware.

History

Gaviota takes its name from the Spanish word for seagull. Members of the Portola Expedition named it after a soldier killed a seagull. This area is also famous for another story about a haunted trestle bridge, which crosses a creek.

Location

Gaviota State Park
10 Refugio Beach Road
Gaviota, California 93117
(805) 968 1033
Web site: www.parks.ca.gov

Haunted Rental
Laguna

"The mysteries of ages is not death, but is the unseen life of the spirit ordinarily hidden from dulled senses onearth."

—Dr. James H. Hyslop 1909

Astrologist K. Maurer was initially thrilled with her new rental on Laguna's famous Cliff Drive. At night she was lulled to sleep by the sounds of waves, and in the morning, the beach was a short walk away. It was like being on vacation, she thought.

All good things, even holidays, come to an end though. For Miss Maurer, this was when unusual things started to happen at her apartment. The apartment was located in an old home on the drive, which had been converted into rental units. Her journey into the paranormal began with odd creaks and groans. Being an older home, this wasn't unusual, until Miss Maurer realized there was a pattern to them. They weren't old-home squeaky floorboard kinds of sounds, but loud bangs, as if people were scuffling outside the door. When she checked, the hallway would be empty.

Soon after, at exactly midnight, the doorbell would ring. Living alone, Miss Maurer cautiously approached the door. Peering through the keyhole, no one would be standing there. Miss Maurer put it down to neighborhood pranksters and resolved to buy a pair of earplugs.

Just as Miss Maurer was beginning to settle in her home, she started hearing voices in her apartment. Once the ghost called her "girlie" leading Miss Maurer to believe one phantom was female. One evening, at exactly midnight, a female form materialized by the door for a few brief seconds.

Alarmed, Miss Maurer decided to research her apartment. Tracing the history of the house, she discovered a murder occurred there fifteen years ago. In what was now her apartment, a husband bludgeoned his wife to death. It is this woman's ghost that Miss Maurer believed was returning to her apartment every night at exactly the same time she was murdered.

At the time this story appeared, Miss Maurer hadn't decided if she could tolerate the spirit much longer, though she knew she meant her no harm.

Location

Laguna is 50 miles south of Los Angeles.
The Laguna Beach Visitors Bureau
252 Broadway Street, Laguna Beach
(949) 497-9229

Hippolyte de Bouchard
Long Beach

"If buccaneers have ghosts, then the spirit of a very angry pirate lingers over the Long Beach strand—standing guard with drawn cutlass over the stolen Spanish treasure he is alleged to have buried here more than a century ago."

—Spencer Crump, Journalist (1952)

Hippolyte de Bouchard (1783-1843) born in France, later became a citizen of modern day Argentina. A career sailor by 1817, he commanded his own vessel. Most importantly for our story, he was granted a "corsair license" by the Navy, which meant he could raid and harass any ships and territories of the Spanish Empire. In 1818, this Mission brought him to the coast of California where, after attacking first the Presidio of Monterey, he made his way to Santa Barbara.

The crew could see the deserted Ortega Ranch in Refugio Canyon, and decided to come ashore and plunder it. After setting fire to the structure, the pirates were cornered in the canyon but managed to elude the Spanish. Men on both sides were taken prisoner, but later, in the harbor, prisoners were exchanged and the Mission Santa Barbara was spared.

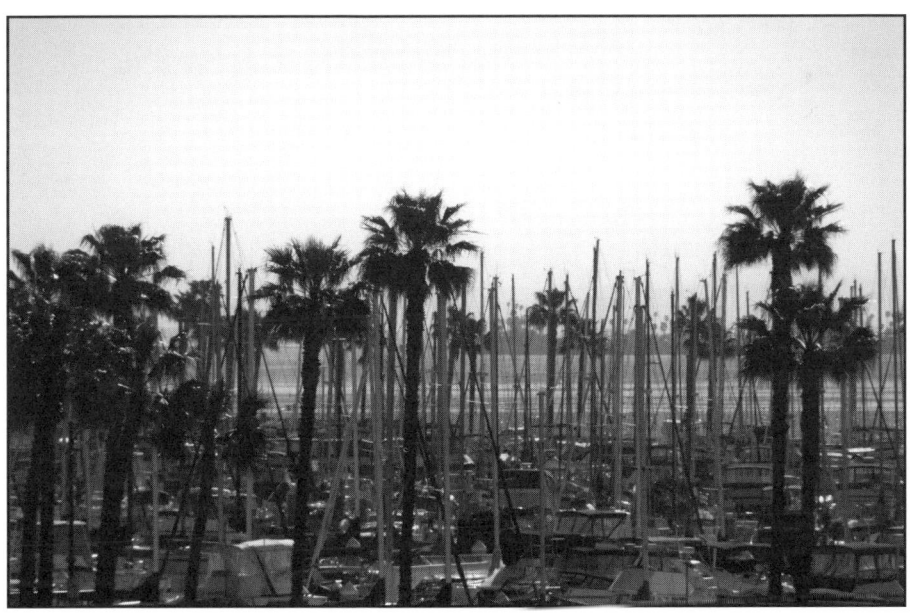

Present day harbor view in Long Beach, California.

In this legend, Hippolyte instructed his crew to lighten the ships before heading to Mission San Juan Capistrano. The pirates quickly chose to bury their treasure off the unpopulated El Camino Real at San Pedro Bay. Gold, silver, and priceless objects stolen from homes in Monterey and the Missions were hidden. In fact, no one has ever found the treasure.

After leaving Capistrano where they successfully plundered the Governor's house, the King's stores, and the barracks, Hippolyte sailed to San Diego where his plot to take California failed. Bouchard returned to South America and a few years later died in poverty—undoubtedly thinking of the treasure he left on the Long Beach strand.

From the eighteenth century, there have been many legends of buried treasure and ghost pirates walking the beaches of the Californian coast. In one story, an elderly couple strolling the beach came across a man digging a deep trench. Before they could inquire what he was up to, the man disappeared. Depending on which version you hear, sometimes a piece of gold bullion is left behind. {21}

Location

To learn more about San Pedro Bay, visit the archives.
638 S. Beacon Street, Room 626
San Pedro, CA 9073
(310) 548-3208
The archives are open Mondays to Wednesday from 1 pm to 4 pm.
There is a self-guided walking/driving tour of San Pedro map available from the San Pedro Chamber of Commerce.
Web site: www.sanpedrochamber.com

Horton Grand Hotel
San Diego

"The murdered do haunt their murders, I believe. I know that ghost have wandered on earth."

—Wuthering Heights Emily Bronte

The Horton Grand Hotel is in fact two hotels. In 1886, two hotels opened in San Diego, The Grand Horton Hotel and the Brooklyn Kahle Saddlery Hotel. Visitors to San Diego flocked to stay at the Grand, built by German immigrants as a replica of the Innsbruck Inn in Vienna, Austria. San Diego's Grand Hotel welcomed visitors who could now access the town via the newly opened railroad. The second hotel, the Brooklyn-Kahle Saddlery Hotel, was a less formal hotel. The Saddlery occupied the first floor. Wyatt Earp occupied the hotel during the seven years he resided in San Diego.

In the 1970s, both hotels faced demolition but they were purchased by the City of San Diego for $1. They were taken apart brick by brick and rebuilt in a new location. The ghosts moved with the hotel, so the psychics say.

In the late 1980s, the Horton Grand Hotel had an official psychic by the name of Shelley Deegan. It was during this time the Horton garnered a reputation for housing a few permanent visitors—all of them deceased. The most famous of these was Roger Whitaker who liked Room 309. Not a malicious ghost, but he did make his presence known. Before you start thinking you are going to be serenaded in the wee hours with ghostly versions of "Durham Town" or "New Word in the Morning," the ghost is not related to the musician with the same name.

In 1988, Shelley Deegan, the hotel's psychic, did a number of interviews. In an interview with D. White for *The Boston Globe,* she had this to say, "The ghost stayed with the hotel in the warehouse. He was a gambler who was shot to death in the 1850s by one of his associates."

In Room 309, there are reports of lights flashing, though no electrical problem can be found. No matter how many times maids straighten the pictures, they end up on the floor with frames intact. At the height of the haunting, in the eighties, visitors reported being shaken awake. Calls to the front desk included many complaints of rapping, thumping, and stomping. When the front desk came to investigate, there was no one on the floors above or below. At one point, the chambermaids at the hotel refused to clean the room.

After the hotel employed a psychic, events calmed down in Room 309. Guests were even disappointed that they neither met Roger nor were treated to a few flickering lights. But he does put in an appearance now and then. There have been reports of strange noises and mysterious footsteps. A woman guest said she was "touched" by an unseen presence.

A family friend will never forget her visit to the hotel. She was meeting friends from out of town at the hotel and had arrived early. She decided to explore as she had never been inside this hotel. Down a corridor just off the lobby, she peered into a room and saw a group of people dressed in period clothing—"straight out of an old western movie" was how she put it, "with women in long dresses and men wearing cowboy hats." Thinking they were for a special event, she gave it little thought, until they simply vanished.

Though now there is no official psychic, you can still go back in time at the Horton Grand Hotel. You might meet Roger wandering the halls. {22}

Location

311 Island Avenue
San Diego CA 92101
(619) 544 1886
Web site: www.hortongrand.com

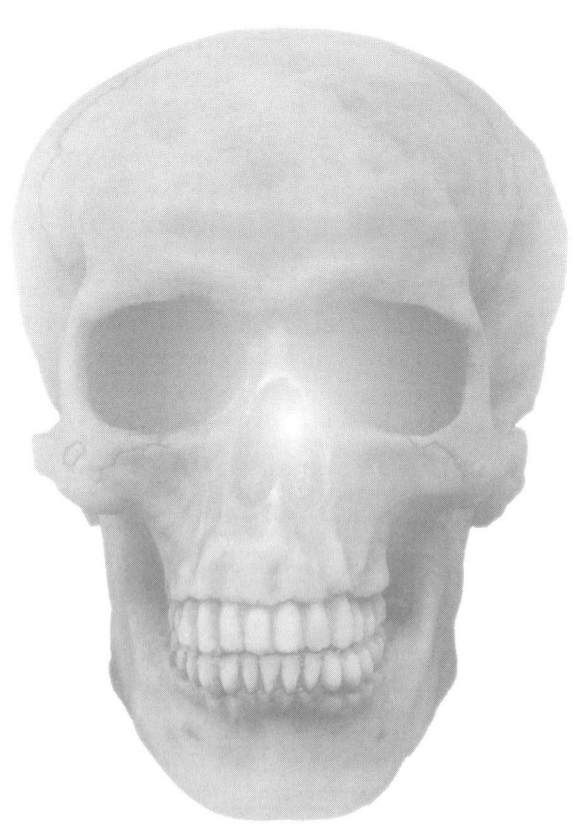

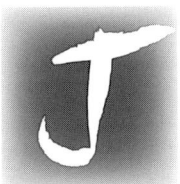

Joyita
Santa Catalina Island

"One often hears of a horse that shivers with terror, or of a dog that howls at something a man's eyes cannot see, and men who live primitive lives where instinct does the work of reason are fully conscious of many things that we cannot perceive at all. As life becomes more orderly, more deliberate, the supernatural world sinks farther away."

—William Butler Yeats

A ship fitter of Portuguese descent fell from the ship *Joyita's* structure just days before she was to be launched. The man died instantly of a broken neck. His widow came down to the Wilmington Boat Works yard and claimed that work on the ship had been rushed and this had caused her husband's death. She placed an ancient Portuguese curse on the *Joyita*.

Roland West, a Hollywood director and producer, was the owner of the *Joyita*. Unaware of the curse, he experienced it first hand on the maiden voyage when a fire broke out in the engine room. The *Joyita* had to be towed back to shore. Misfortune also followed West ashore, when his relationship with Jewel Carmen ended.

Retiring from show business, West went into a restaurant partnership with his ex-wife, Jewel Carmen, and his mistress, Thelma Todd. When Thelma Todd was found in her car, dead of carbon dioxide poisoning, many believed her death was not accidental. They thought Roland West had a hand in her murder. The two were spotted arguing earlier that day. Another theory is that he murdered Thelma Todd on the *Joyita* and placed her body in the car. Thelma Todd's murder is still listed as unsolved. Did the curse of the *Joyita* continue?

The *Joyita* was later sold to a charter service where it was popular with celebrities, Mary Pickford, Douglas Fairbanks, and Ronald Colman. Nothing further odd happened aboard until the fateful day Humphrey Bogart and Errol Flynn decided to sail the boat before buying it. The first part of their cruise was without incident, but sometime between leaving port in Los Angeles and arriving in the waters off Catalina Island, one of their guests disappeared. The men never bought the boat.

During World War II, the *Joyita* was used as a patrol boat; no incidents were reported during wartime—all reports were vetoed. The curse would strike again in 1947. A caretaker died on board after he was overcome with battery acid fumes.

If you need more proof of the curse, in 1955 the entire crew and passengers of the *Joyita* went missing in the South Pacific. {23}

Location

Web site: www.catalina.com
Web site: www.visitcatalina.com

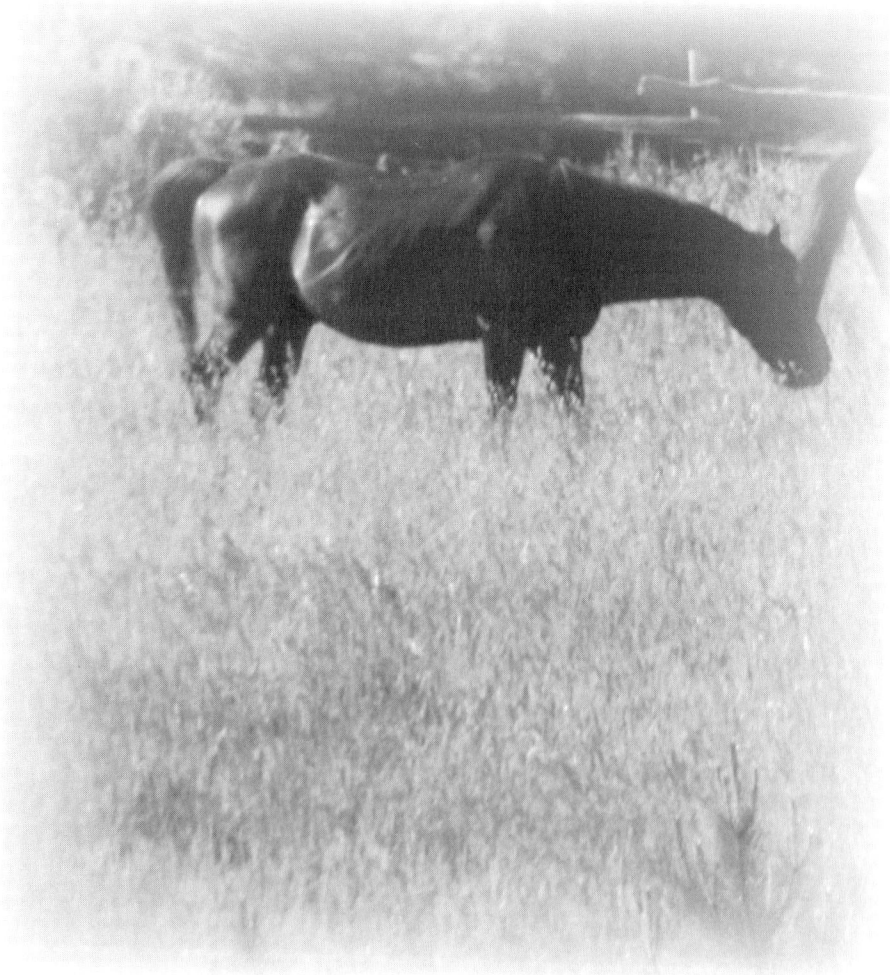

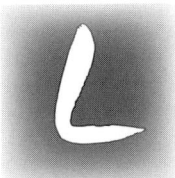

La Casa de Estudillo
San Diego

Captain Jose Maria de Estudillo built the home between 1827-29. Today, outfitted with period furnishings, it feels as if the Estudillo family never left. And some say they didn't!

The home has been featured on shows such as *Ghost Hunters*. The television show was able to capture a few diaphanous forms. One of the spirits at the casa is Father Antonio Ubach who was featured in the novel *Ramona* by Helen Hunt Jackson. This spirit is seen in the house's chapel and the priest's bedroom. The priest also makes his presence felt as pages of the book on a small altar turn by themselves. Though we heard no prayers, visitors have been known to make out the faint echo of prayer. Not all sounds at the adobe are soft and sweet mind you; the heavy doors sometimes slam shut with a tremendous bang.

On the day of our visit, one person swore they briefly saw the image of a small girl kneeling by a cradle of dolls. (For a picture of the cradle, turn to the bibliography.) Later we learned a phantom girl is sometimes seen in the velvet chair in this same room!

In addition, in the dining room, a semi-transparent man and flashes of a mysterious yellow light have been reported. The dining room was one of the most curious rooms we visited. All in the group felt as if the seats around the table were occupied by unseen figures. It was a very uncomfortable experience. Though the day was very warm in this section of the casa, the temperature was noticeably lower.

The Casa de Estudillo is an extremely active site worth investigating over and over again.

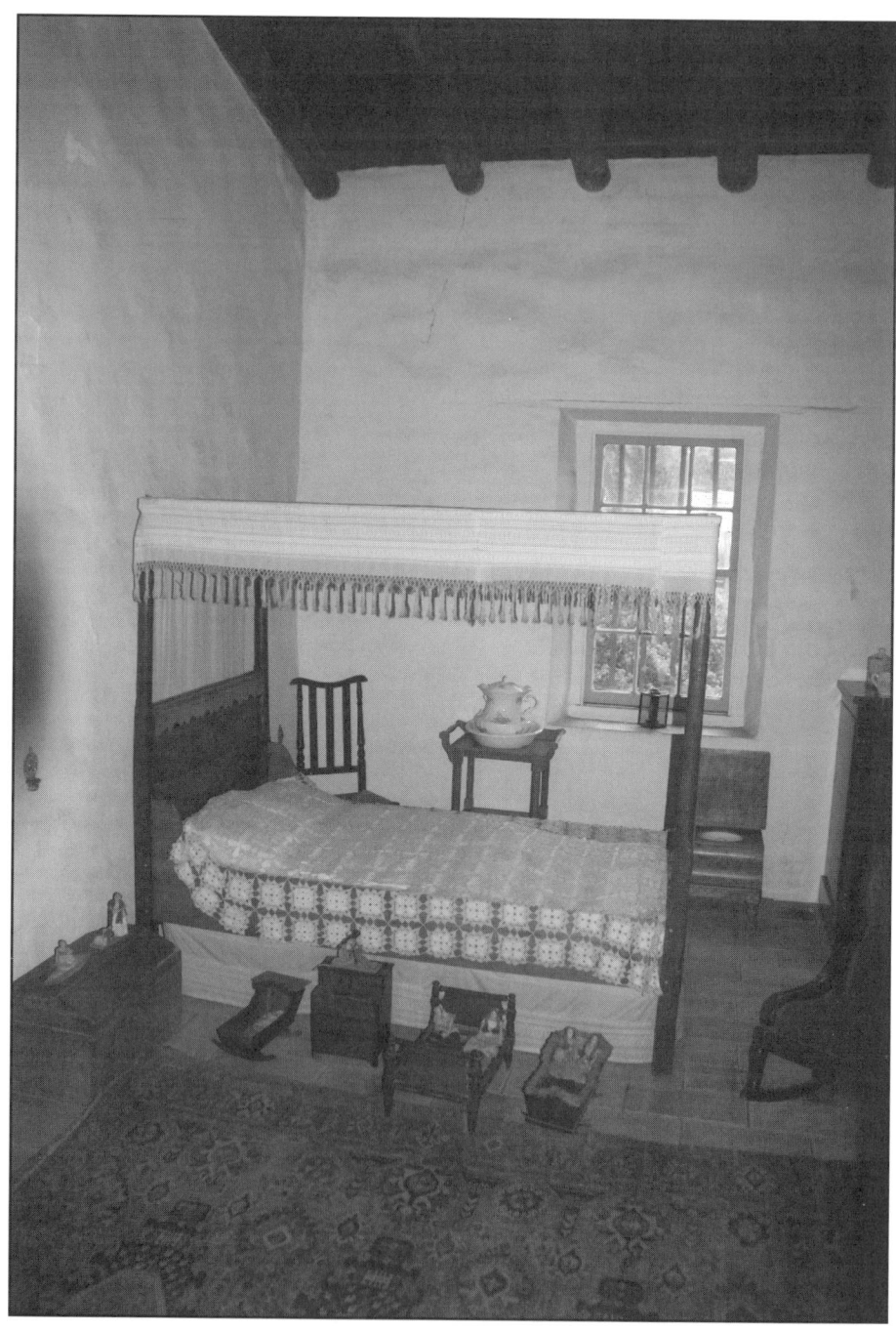

La Casa de Estudillo. Helen Hunt Jackson's book Ramona may have been inspired by this home. After the book was released, the home was known as "Ramona's Marriage Place."

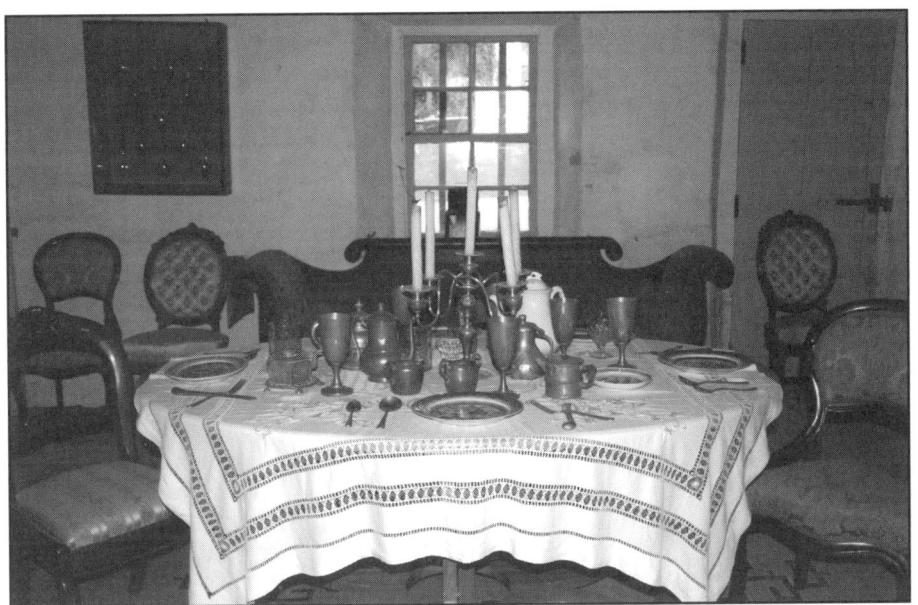

La Casa de Estudillo, Old Town San Diego

Location

Old Town San Diego
4001 Mason St.
San Diego, CA 92110
619-220-5422
Hours: 10 am to 5 pm daily

La Purisma Mission
Lompoc

*"So do we pass the ghosts that haunt us later in our lives; they sit
undramatically by the roadside like poor beggars, and we see them only from
the corners of our eyes, if we see them at all.*
—*Dark Tower IV: Wizard and Glass*, Stephen King

Stories of phantoms haunting the Mission date back to its
earliest days. It was a vibrant community with livestock and
crops being raised and many Chumash Indians living on
the grounds. In 1812, many of the structures at the Mission were
destroyed during a large earthquake. Before this earthquake, the

61

Chumash had suffered the loss of one third of their population to smallpox and other European diseases.

One visitor to the Mission had a very unusual encounter in the weaving room. Today, a large primitive loom dominates the room. There are a few spinning wheels, benches, and bowls creating an authentic re-creation of what the room was like when it was an essential part of Mission life. The lady was one of the first visitors that morning at the Mission. Upon entering the room, she felt a slight chill and looking over to the loom, she saw what looked like fog. It lasted seconds then vanished; puzzled, the woman waited to see if "it" would reappear. But soon the quiet room was the scene of much excitement as a school group came in.

In addition to this phantom in the weaving room, a phantom padre is said to haunt the padres quarters, ghost dog, gardener, soldier, a woman in the church, and music have also been reported. Richard Senate writes of his experience of the ghostly music at the Purisma Mission in his book *The Haunted Southland*. Park Rangers have spoken of their experiences with closing doors, mystery voices and music, fog-like apparitions, such as the one experienced above. A bed at the Mission which remains unmade, ghostly images of Chumash Indians, Spanish soldiers, and the sounds of galloping horses, have been added to the list of unexplained sightings.

Location

Visit the Web site, www.lapurismaMission.org, for maps and complete information.

Contact (805) 733-3713 for hours at the Visitor Center Complex.

Guided tours begin from the center.

The Mission is open for self-guided tours daily from 9 am until 5 pm.

The Mission is Historical Landmark No 340. It was the eleventh of twenty-one Missions founded in California.

Lady in Pink
Yorba Linda

"Certain I am that the lips of the dead moved, and the eyelids fluttered for a moment like the wings of a wounded bird,.."
—*At Abdul Ali's Grave, E.F Benson*

A lady dressed in a pink gown wanders through the tombstones of the Yorba Linda Cemetery—or does she?

The Yorba Linda lady is one urban legend that attracted so much attention during the 1970s that the poor woman's gravesite was more akin to a street fair with crowds numbering in the hundreds. The lady's real name was Alvina De Los Reyes. She was said to return on June 15th of even numbered years, though no explanation is given for this. Try and imagine an overgrown cemetery on a quiet road with ancient pepper trees suddenly brimming over with families, couples, the curious, and the media, all-trampling around expecting a pink lady ghost. Not surprisingly she never showed up, but this didn't deter people from staying until the cemetery closed.

Linda Lorenzi, an Orange County park ranger assigned to oversee the Yorba Cemetery, said "…(sic) she believes the pink lady legend started in the '40s and turned into an event for the young—spending the night at the cemetery became the daring thing to do."

As the story goes, in 1910, dressed in a pink gown, Alvina De Los Reyes was on her way home from a dance when her carriage was involved in a fatal accident on Kellogg Road. Alvina was thrown to the ground and died of her injuries.

Over the years, there have been reports of cars stopping to pick up a hitchhiker dressed in a pink dress only to see the occupant disappear. Sometimes the hitchhiker is dropped off at an undisclosed address. Inevitably the lady leaves behind a personal object, which the driver tries to return the following day. He is then told the lady in question died a hundred years ago.

In June 1990, *The Yorba Linda Star* interviewed members of Alvina De Los Reyes's family. "De Los Reyes' great nephew, Arthur Peralta, explained the story that Alvina died in childbirth at the age of thirty-one. Another error in the story is, of course, the fact that the High School was built in 1910.

Now, before you dismiss this story completely, it is interesting to examine the case of Psychic Barbara Soblewski who initially was skeptical. She learned of the Yorba Linda lady from a newspaper account. In the early 1980s, she braved the "beer drinking crowds" and was able to contact a spirit at the cemetery. She made a shocking discovery. It was not the ghost of Alvina at Yorba Linda, but a woman called Ellie, dressed in a cream dress. Through two psychic processes—automatic writing and psychic art—she was able to channel the spirit.

She learned there was a woman called Ellie and there was an accident on Kellog Road involving members of the De Los Reyes family, though no one was killed. To learn more about her investigation see her site at www.starmerge.com.

The Yorba Cemetery was part of the Rancho Canon de Santa Ana granted to Don Bernardo Yorba in 1834 by the Mexican Governor of California. The Yorba Family Cemetery is over a hundred years old. It is a short distance from Bernardo Yorba's house, California State Historical Landmark No. 226. He set aside this piece of land as a private family plot and for family friends.

By the 1960s, the cemetery was in ruins due to vandalism and neglect. The Yorba family owned the property, until it was donated to the Los Angeles Roman Catholic Archdiocese in the 1920s. The Archdiocese deeded the cemetery to Orange County in 1967. Only the Mission Cemetery in Capistrano is older than the Yorba cemetery. Due to vandalism and crowds, access to the grave is by appointment only.

Location

Woodgate Park
Yorba Linda, CA 92886
(714) 973-3190

Tours are available on the first Saturday of each month from 11:30 am to 12:30 pm, if staff is available. You will need to phone ahead to see if anyone is available.

Web site www.ocparks.com/yorbacemetery for more information.

Lamar Street
Los Angeles

"I walked through the rooms filled with sensations of the most poignant grief. He had been there; his living frame had been caged by those walls, his breath had mingled with that atmosphere, his step had been on those stones."

—*On Ghosts*, Mary Shelley

Lamar Street in downtown Los Angeles, with the constant hum of traffic, doesn't seem a suitable spot for a spirit. In 1906, one home on Lamar Street made headlines because of its visitor from the astral plane.

Harry, his wife, and their young daughter had lived in the area for less than a year when they noticed their home was not quite like the others on Lamar Avenue. For one thing, Harry was pretty certain other people weren't being awakened by voices in

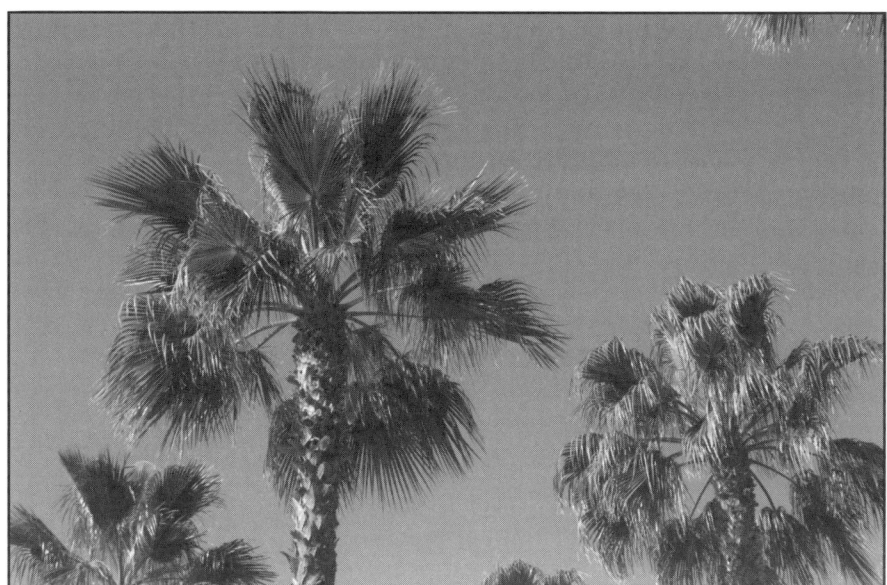

Palm trees Los Angeles.

the middle of the night. Not from the street, but voices above the bed.

Even when Harry was in a deep stupor, he would be aroused by voices or by the rattling of his bed. The unusual activities were confined to the master bedroom. The couple wasn't frightened, but they did want to know why this was happening to them.

Over the course of a few weeks the reasons for the paranormal events became clear. All was not well, as Harry was an alcoholic whose wife had threatened to leave him if he didn't change. While his wife and child were out of town, Harry awoke to a bright white light in his room. He decided the ghost must be an angel sent by God to steer him down the right path.

This wouldn't be the first time Harry's guardian angel had rescued him. In Pennsylvania 1889, he was the only member of his family to survive the devastating Johnston flood that killed over 2,000 people. Since that time, Harry always knew someone was looking out for him.

The white light would pay Harry one last visit in which he "…(sic) was lifted bodily from bed by a dark object which placed me on my feet near the bed and then led me by the hand to the next room and there came around me a brilliant white light…"

When his wife and child returned to Los Angeles, Harry pledged to live a Christian life. The guardian angel of Lamar Street never made the papers again. {24}

65

Location

Lamar Street is a busy downtown street in Los Angeles. The precise location of Harry's paranormal experience is not known.

Le Milagro
Santa Paula

"(sic)...but the rain . Is full of ghosts tonight, that tap and sigh. Upon the glass and listen for reply..."
—*Edna St. Vincent Millay*

On moonlit nights, a cloaked rider on a black horse rides throughout Ventura County. Many have heard the horses hoofs and whinnies, but it moves so quickly, they have never seen it. Native Indians considered it a good omen to hear the galloping of the horse and its master on their moonlit journeys. But who is the ghost rider?

Long ago, Esteban de Villegas came to California from Spain. His ranch was near the modern city of Santa Paula. De Villegas built one of the most successful ranches in the area. It is said he treated all those in his employ with fairness.

One of his favorite employees he had brought from Spain. This man was called Khim and he was groom to the Master's favorite horse, Le Milagro. Khim and Le Milagro were inseparable. Local Indians were in awe of horse and the rider. Khim never used a saddle or a bridle when he rode Le Milagro. The horse seemed to gallop without touching its hoofs to the trail.

Life at the ranch ran smoothly until the day De Villegas hired another groom to help in the care of his ever-increasing stable of horses. This groom became jealous of Khim's talents and of the horse, Le Milagro. One day, Le Milagro went missing. The entire household went into a frenzy looking for the horse. Khim was beside himself as the horse was his best friend. It was soon discovered that the new groom was missing. It didn't take long for the two events to be connected.

Khim rode off in one direction of the canyon and the other men went in the opposite direction. What transpired between Khim and the other groom is not known, but the bodies of Khim and Le Milagro were discovered a few days later.

Shortly after their deaths, Indians claimed they saw Khim and Le Milagro on one of the mountain peaks. Are Khim and Le Milagro still riding in the Santa Paula region?

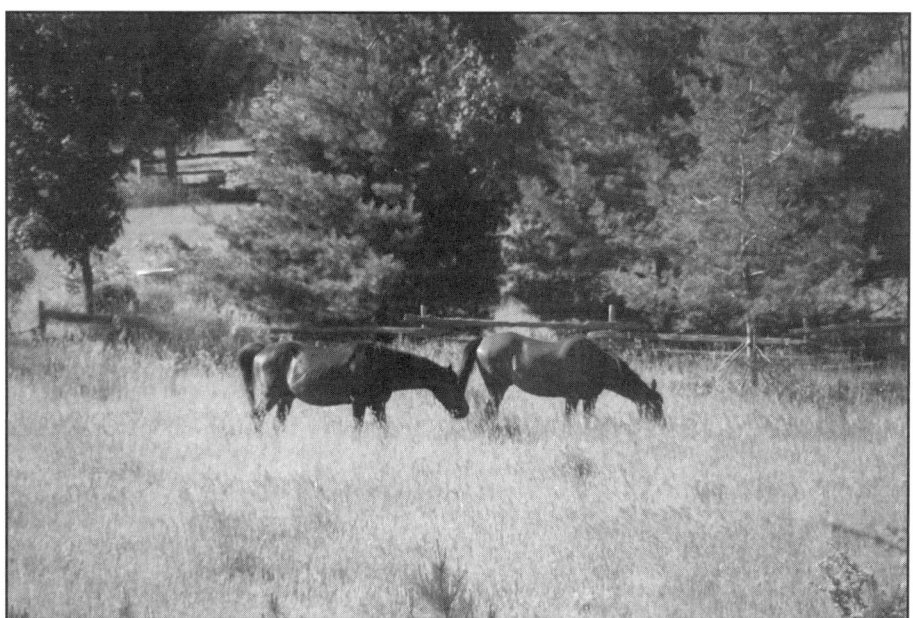

Will these horses riders also return?

One evening, a man waiting for a tow leaned against his car and prepared for a long wait. He heard a noise further up the road. He assumed it was the tow, but as the sound got louder, he realized it wasn't a car but a galloping horse. He could hear its hoofs pounding the dirt. Straining to see down the darkened road, no rider or horse ever came into sight.

The wind picked up and the man felt as if every nerve was alive. He decided to wait in his car before the evening got any "stranger." Moments later, the tow did appear. The man asked the driver if he had seen a horse, but the driver shock his head. "Who would be crazy enough to ride at this time of night," he said.

Well we know there is one rider and horse that would ride through Santa Paula at full moon...

Location

For information and maps of historical sites in Santa Paula see the Web site at www.discoversantapaula.com.

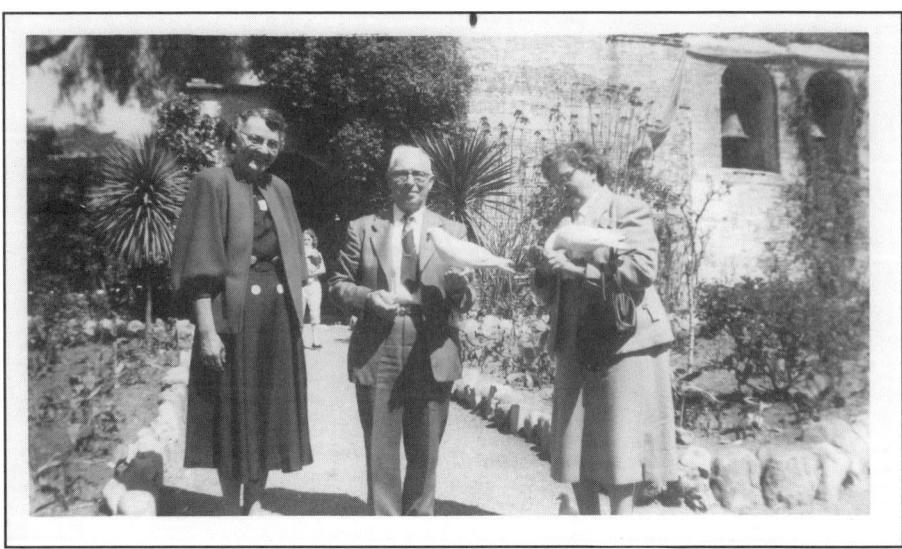

Vintage photograph of a couple with the famed swallows of Capistrano.

Legend of the Swallows
San Juan Capistrano

"The Shades addressed her; she answered them. She knew by intuition what tongue they spoke; it was the Language of the Dead; and, by passing that portal with her two companions, she had herself become enabled both to speak and understand it."

—*Wolverden Tower,* Grant Allen

The swallows are coming. The swallows are coming! Flags and banners are strung through the downtown Capistrano. Parade floats are in position. Happy, but probably tired, faces crowd around. Everyone in the town becomes part of the celebration. Activities continue for a month with the parade as culmination of all the effort.

For hundreds of years the swallows of Capistrano have arrived at the old Mission around March 19th, St. Joseph's Day. They would nest in the ruins of the old chapel. Many saw the swallow's arrival as a religious miracle. The return of the swallows was a day of celebration in the town drawing visitors from far and wide.

The swallow's mystical journey was highly publicized in papers. When the swallows departed, where they were headed was equally a mystery. They always left on the Day of San Juan, at the end of October. Today, it is known the birds travel to Goya, Argentina,

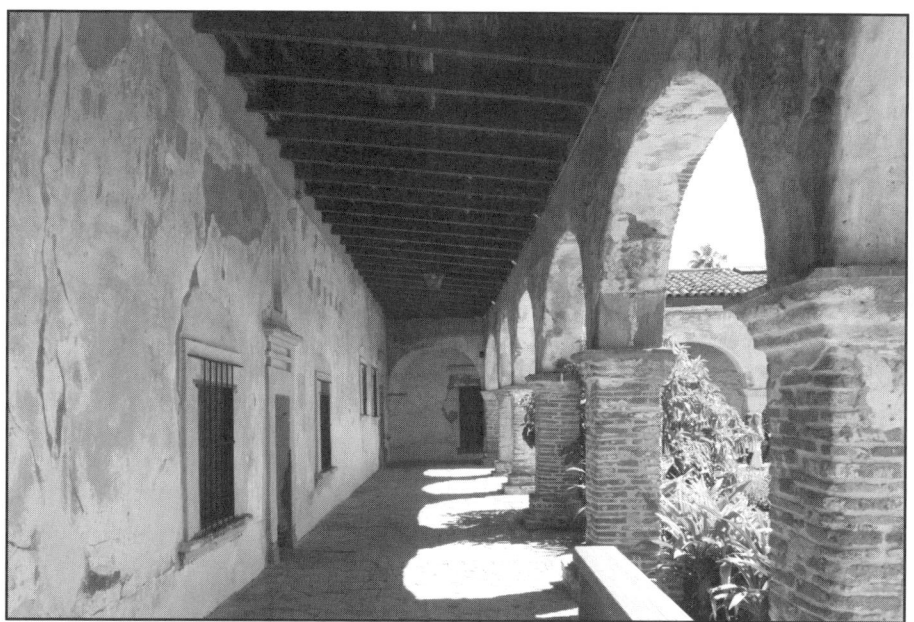

San Juan Capistrano.

a trip of 7,500 miles or 12,000 kilometers. Mission Priests such Arthur J Hutchinson, back in the 1930s, said it was, "not a religious miracle but a coincidence," but people still believed God guided the swallows.

In 1915, the legend was brought to a wider audience when an article about the swallows appeared in the magazine *Overland Monthly*. In the 1930s, Father St. John O'Sullivan and Charles Saunders published the "Legend of the Swallows Return" in the book called *Capistrano Nights*. The story attracted attention forcing Father Hutchinson to stress that the story was interesting, but not a religious miracle.

No matter what you believe, the swallows simply add another mystic layer to this interesting site.

> **Note:** If you want to attend the annual Swallows Day celebration check out the Web site www.swallowsparade.org the parade or the "Fiesta de las Golondrinas" started as a school carnival in the 1930s, celebrating the swallows return.

Leonis Adobe
Calabasas

"For him the universe with all its inhabitants was a great machine, governed by inexorable laws. To such a man the idea of a ghost was simply absurd—as absurd as the assertion that two and two make five, or that a circle can be formed of a straight line. Yet he had a kind of dilettante interest in the idea of a mind which could believe in ghosts."
　　　　　　　　　　　—*The Shadow in the Corner,* M.E. Braddon

Admiring recent renovations, a group of local Calabasas residents followed their tour guide through Historic-Cultural Monument #1—The Leonis Adobe. They were impressed with the work that had made this moment possible and, of course, with Kay Beachy who fought hard to preserve the home. Once a crumbling site almost hidden behind a tangle of vines and pepper trees, the Leonis Adobe was in danger of being razed to the ground in order to make way for a parking lot. Carefully, the group climbed the creaky staircase to the second level of the adobe. As they climbed, the scent of perfume grew stronger. In one bedroom, they took note of the many period furnishings used by the Leonis family. They were returned to the adobe by relatives when the home was restored. The longer the group spent in the adobe, the more they felt the Leonis family had never left.

As the guide, a notable historian and author, led the group to another section, a loud rapping sound was heard at a window pane. The group went quiet, waiting expectantly for another sound or an explanation. When no explanation seemed forthcoming, a man in the group asked her about the noise. The guide, without hesitating, told the assembled group it must be the ghost of Miguel Leonis rapping his approval. A few people chuckled, but others felt uneasy.

Who was Miguel Leonis? During the1870s, until his death, he was the "King of Calabasas" or "The Big Basque" as he was called. Miguel Leonis, was a nineteenth-century Basque who owned most of the land in the San Fernando Valley, extending north into what is now Ventura County. He obtained the land when he married a widowed Indian woman named Espirtu. The adobe in Calabasas was their home. Miguel Leonis had many enemies who resented his wealth and his means of enforcing property boundaries through the courts and with guns. In 1889, he was killed when his wagon overturned in the Cahuenga Pass. His wife, Espiritu, would die seventeen years later.

The Leonis Adobe was neglected for years. In 1961, Mrs. Walter Beachy who wanted to preserve it as a historical monument purchased the house. She then sold the home to the Leonis Adobe Association of which she was a member. It was restored and opened to the public in 1969.

After the first few tours ghost stories emerged from the home, Miguel Leonis and Espiritu were rumored to be still "residing" at the adobe. The author of *The Last Days of the Old West*, Laura B. Gaye, spoke to a reporter about her incident in 1969 at the home. Mrs. Gaye was conducting one of the first tours through the newly refurbished home. "During the first tour when I got ready to leave the bedroom," she said, "there was a rapping on the window, right here where these steps are." Mrs. Gaye believed it to be a sign from the ghost of Miguel Leonis. Mrs. Gaye went on to say, "There are many ghost stories associated with the house. Once an adopted grandchild of Espirtu Leonia in that room one night she heard a voice which may have been that of her dead grandmother."

Reports of unusual activity continued after full-time custodians were installed at the adobe. Robert and Carol Fuller and their son lived in the home during the early seventies. They were interviewed by Eric Leach for his article aptly titled, "*Web Around Leonis Adobe Spun by Ghostly Stories*." Fuller said it took him many months to sleep comfortably in the home. With every creaking floorboard he expected to see a ghost. His wife seemed more practical and simply thought living at the adobe a great experience and settled down to create a home.

In a 2007 article for the *Los Angeles Daily News*, Carol Bidwell writes of Diane Ramadan, the ranch manager who believes "(sic)... the couple's spirits still inhabit their two-story adobe." Ramadan's unusual experiences in the home included smelling a floral perfume near the top of the stairs when no one nearby wore perfume. The perfume is believed to be a signal of Espiritu Leonis's presence.

"I was in there two weeks ago and somebody was walking around upstairs," said Ramadan, who manages the ranch. "But there was nobody upstairs. Maybe it was Miguel Leonis' footsteps. Some people claim he's still here. It doesn't bother any of us, though. It doesn't seem to be a scary ghost."

In another amazing incident a volunteer was saved from injury when invisible hands pushed her to safety as a railing collapsed. The volunteer thought it had to be Miguel Leonis as he was rumored to be very strong. Visiting schoolchildren have claimed to see a large man, dressed in black and wearing bandages, lying in the room where Miguel Leonis slept. A similar repost appears in Richard Senate's book, *Ghosts of The Haunted Coast*.

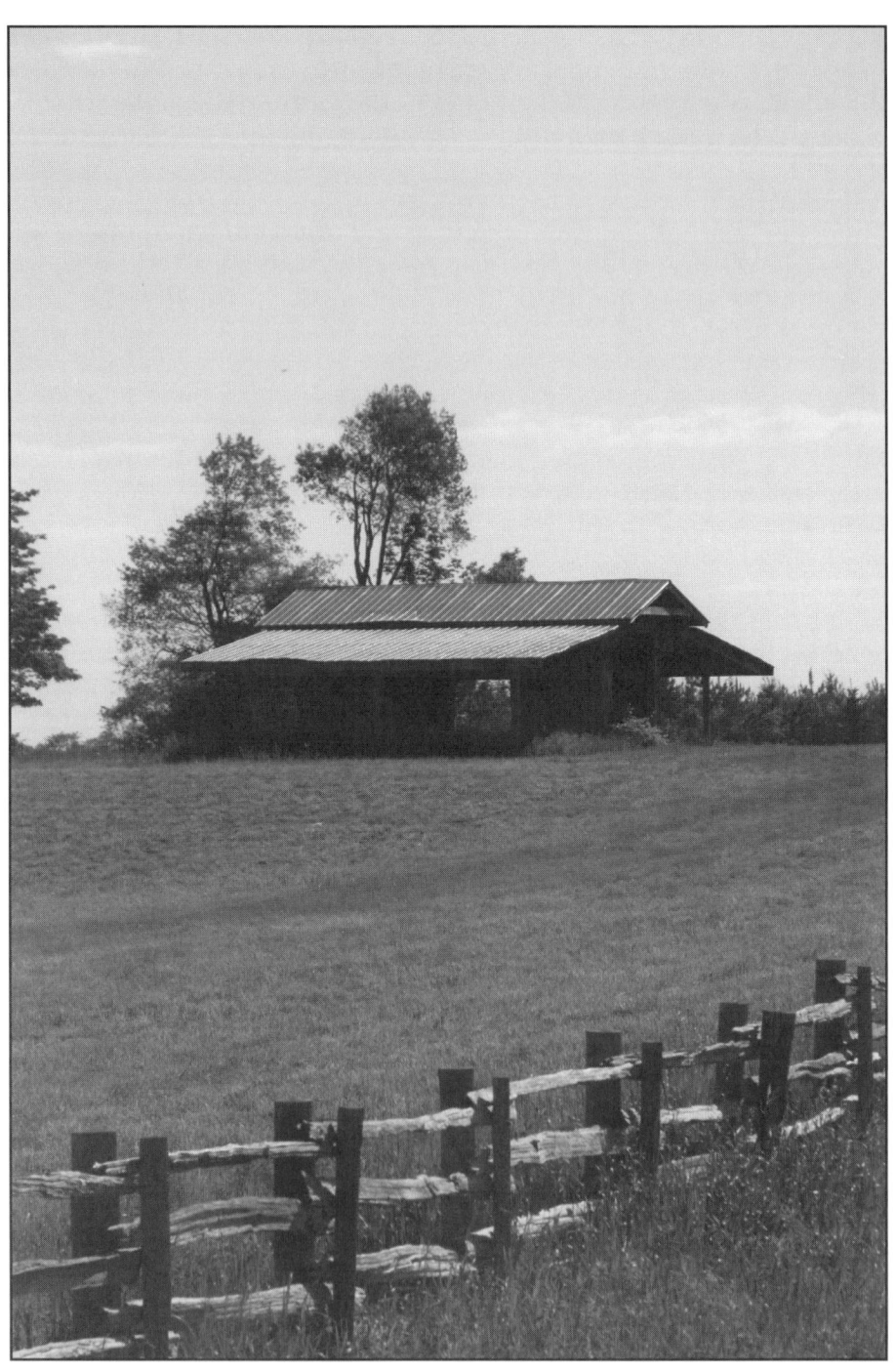

An empty horse shelter.

On my recent trip to the adobe, our small group didn't encounter anything out of place, but as Mrs. Gaye Stated back in 1969 "…guides don't promise a lively ghost each tour; they do promise a brief jaunt into the old West." {25,26}

Location

223537 Calabasas Road
Calabasas, CA
(818) 222-6511
Consult the Web site for hours of operation & tour information.
Web site: www.leonisadobemuseum.org.

Lord Harry
Santa Barbara

"She herself is a haunted house. She does not possess herself; her ancestors sometimes come and peer out of the windows of her eyes and that is very frightening."

The lady of the haunted house, **Angela Carter**

Doctor Samuel Brinkerhoff helped to transform Brinkerhoff Avenue in Santa Barbara from a country lane into a grand street of Victorian Homes. The transformation began in 1857, only five years after the Doctor moved to Santa Barbara from New York State.

Brinkerhoff Avenue is now known for its antique shops. Tourists come to the area not only to step back in time but also to find a memento to take home. Some Santa Barbara memories are not confined to priceless jars or antique chairs. Memories are tucked tightly into the gabled roofs of Brinkerhoff Avenue, memories of the original settlers to the area who made their way by land or sea around Cape Horn.

In the early 1970s, Mr. and Mrs. O were thrilled to be moving into their stately Victorian on Brinkerhoff Avenue. Like most new homeowners, there were pictures to be hung and furniture to be placed. Days were busy but happy as the old house slowly transformed into their vision of a home.

Soon after renovations were in full swing, they realized the home had come with an extra occupant. This occupant was a ghost they would later affectionately call Lord Harry. During renovations to a room on the upper level, Lord Harry made his presence known. Mr. O had retired leaving his tools and work unfinished. The project could wait another day, he thought. The next morning when he went back to work on the room, he was amazed to find several wooden panels nailed into place. Mr. O was certain he hadn't done them before going to bed—and so who did? No workman had been hired for the project and no one had access to the room except for the owners of the home. Most puzzling was why the sound of hammering hadn't awakened either Mr. or Mrs. O.

The identity of the ghosts was revealed to Mr. O by chance. During a stop at a local bookstore, he was drawn to a photograph of a group of men standing by a blacksmith's shop. He purchased the photo and later a friend identified one of the men in the picture as being the original owner of Mr. O's home. His name was Harry Hawcroft, originally from England, who was called Lord Harry in the area due to his fancy attire. White shirt with cuff links were not considered everyday wear for a blacksmith, but that didn't stop Lord Harry from dressing himself out in a fine fashion. He must have been quite the local character. Had the ghost drawn Mr. O to this image?

Mr. O now knew the identity of the ghost, but never saw him. The closest he came to meeting Lord Harry was when he found his gold cuff link in his garden stamped with the date '86.

A friend of the family did however meet Lord Harry. A Ms. M was staying in the home alone while the owners were away. Getting up one morning, she went to the kitchen. Who should be there but Lord Harry himself dressed for breakfast in a black tuxedo. He looked directly at the woman before vanishing right before her eyes.

The ghost of Lord Harry is not only the consummate gentleman and handyman, but also lends a hand when anything goes missing. If all ghosts were so handy more homeowners would invite them to stay! Lord Harry is not content to stay at home, but has even been seen strolling down Brinkerhoff Avenue.

While enjoying the sights of Brinkerhoff Avenue, keep an eye out for a well-dressed gentleman. He might just help you load your purchases into your vehicle, then vanish into the Santa Barbara air. {27}

Location

From U.S. 101, exit northwest on State. Go left at Haley Street, then 1 ½ blocks to Brinkerhoff.

Or take the shuttle which leaves Stearns Wharf daily. Off Cota Street, between Chapala and De La Vina.

Brinkerhoff is also known as Antiques Alley. There are many homes here designated as "structures of merit" by the city of Santa Barbara.

See the Santa Barbara Web site for details: www.santabarbara.gov.

Mission San Fernando Rey De Espana
San Fernando

"For my own part, I never saw a ghost except once in a dream. I feared it in my sleep; I awoke trembling, and lights and the speech of others could hardly dissipate my fear."

—*On Ghosts,* Mary Shelley

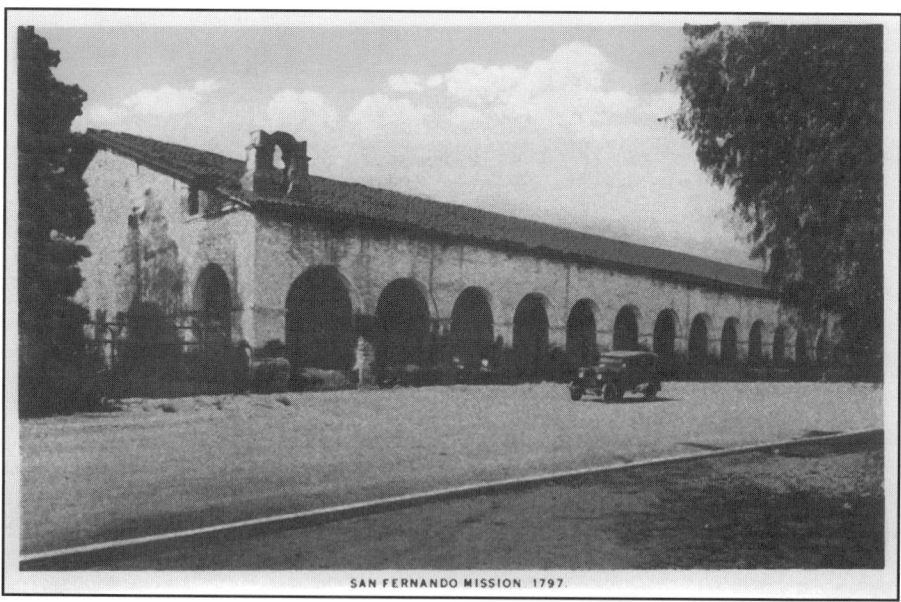

SAN FERNANDO MISSION 1797.

Mission San Fernando, vintage postcard. Produced by Western Publishing & Novelty Co., Los Angeles, California.

The Mission, founded in 1797, is famous for a female ghost who reportedly wanders the halls with a bunch of cats following.

Several spirits walk the Mission grounds. One visitor to the Mission watched in amazement as the image of a monk appeared. He took a few steps towards her and then disappeared. There have been reports of a headless monk, though there is nothing in any historical documents about why a monk would be decapitated.

Other spirits have been seen or felt near the Mission's cemetery where over 2,000 people were buried. Is it any wonder those attuned to the psychic world have felt the presence of spirits? The ghost of an Indian is said to wander at a nearby school, which was once a seminary. A popular rumor, but leaning towards urban legend, is that the ghost of Ritchie Valens keeps this Indian spirit company. Ritchie Valens was killed in a 1959 plane crash in Iowa. Ritchie doesn't seem to mind his early death as he wanders around the cemetery humming a cheerful tune. He was buried in the San Fernando Mission Cemetery, so perhaps this is where the tale began. Also there is a La Llorona story with a woman looking for children killed in a crash. This ghost appears punctually at midnight.

History

Most visitors to the Mission will hear about the Mission's history and see several rooms set up to recreate the Mission period. Father Fermin Lausen founded the Mission in 1797 on "The Feast of the Birth of Mary." The building was damaged during the 1812 earthquake, and later, vandals dug up the church's floor in search of gold—no gold was found, but the damage was done. The building was later sold and, during the late 1800s, the Mission was used as a station on the Butterfield Stage Lines and, in 1923, once again became a working church. The church was restored in the 1940s but later was destroyed again by an earthquake. In 1971, it was completely rebuilt and is known as California Landmark 157.

The ghosts of the monks seem to date to when the Mission was first founded. If you do hear humming you will know whose grave it is coming from.

Location

15151 San Fernando Mission Blvd.
Mission Hills, CA 91345
Hours: 9 am to 4:30 pm
Closed Thanksgiving & Christmas
(818) 361-0186

Mission San Juan Capistrano
San Juan Capistrano

"Spiritualism is associated in the popular mind with the phenomena of table rapping, rope tying, automatic writing, and various forms of physical manifestations of an invisible force. This view of the entire scope of the spiritistic movement is wholly unjust and unauthorized."
—Dr. McIvor-Tyndall's discourse on spiritualism 1905

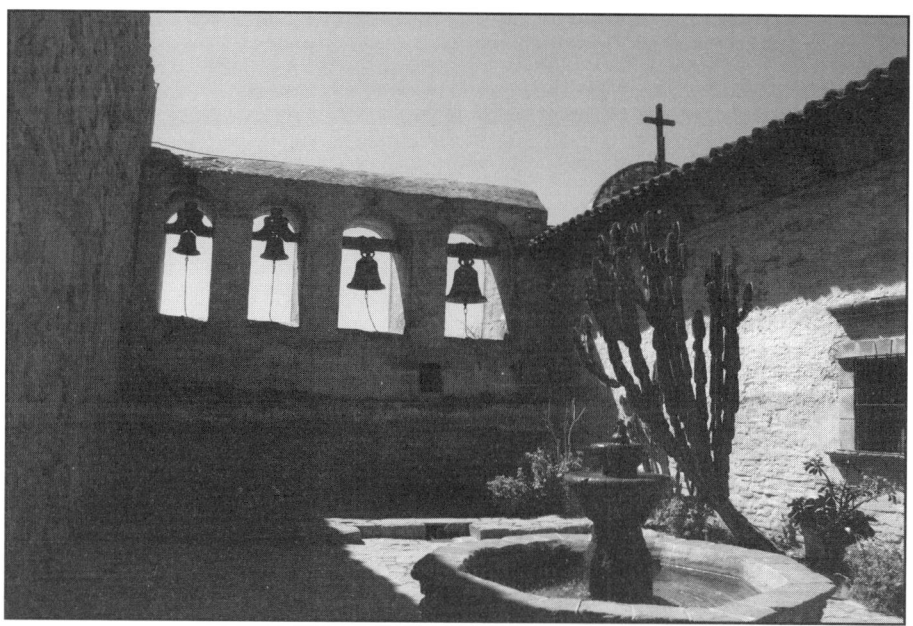

The bells of Mission San Juan Capistrano.

The pride and joy of Mission fathers was Mission San Juan Capistrano. The church designed by Spanish architects was built in the shape of a cross. It was built by Indian craftsmen and was considered a marvel, its seven domes and bell tower visible from ten miles away. For 1806, it was an incredible architectural feat.

December 8, 1812, much of the church building came tumbling down, when an earthquake occurred during morning mass. Forty people died in the rubble. One of them, a young girl carrying a lighted candle, is said to revisit the ruin as a ghostly apparition from time to time.

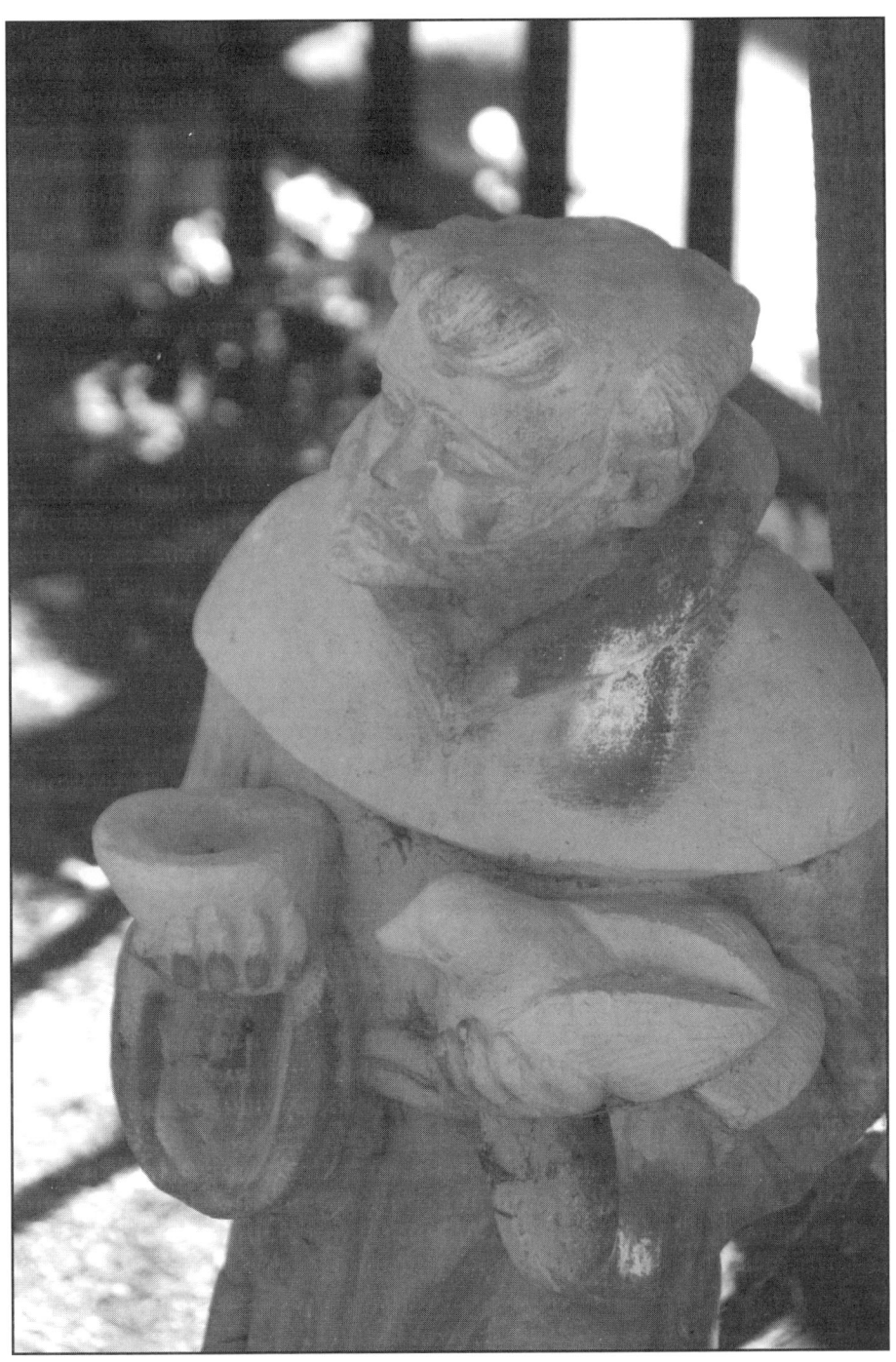

Mission San Juan Capistrano.

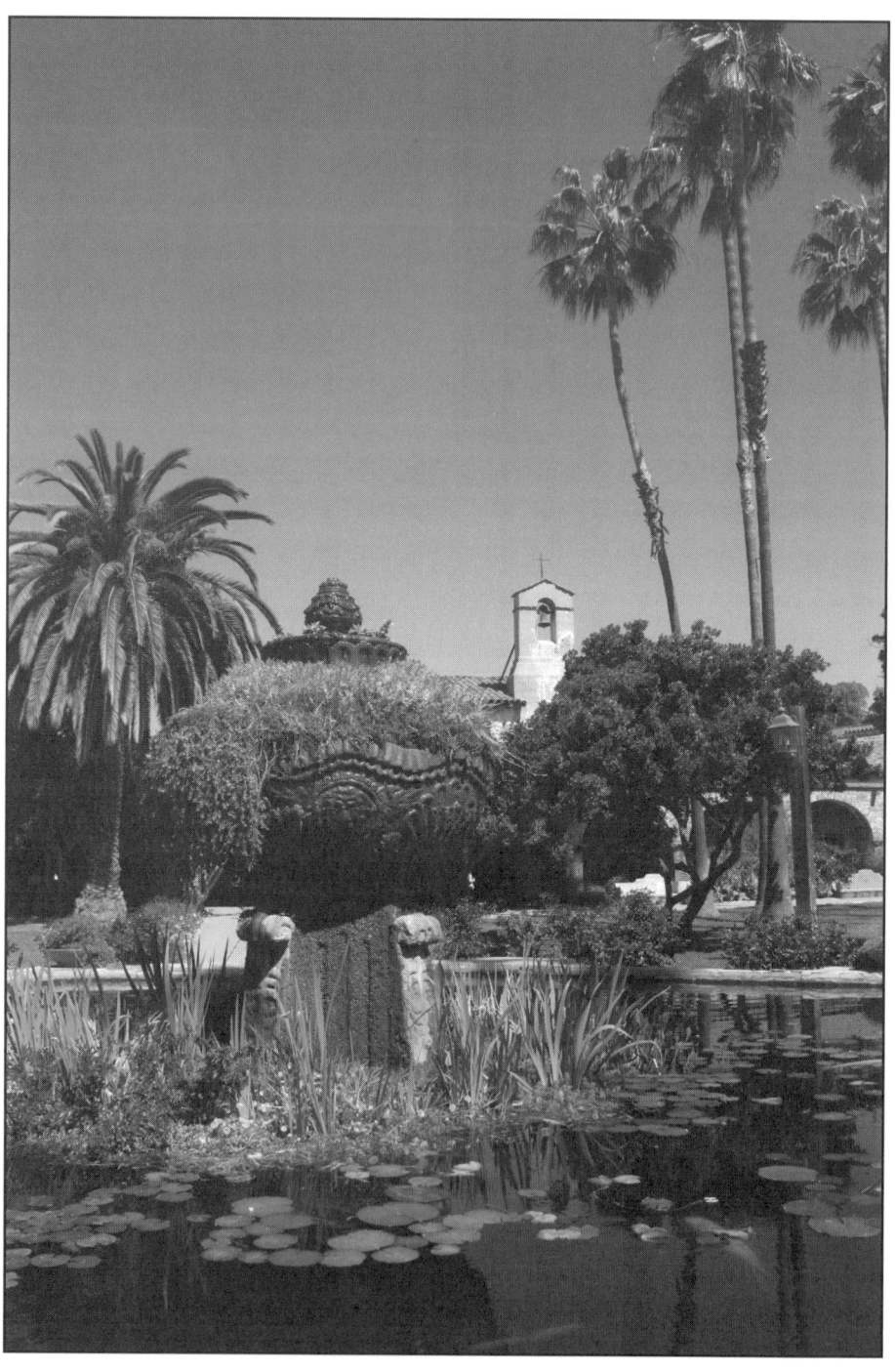

Mission San Juan Capistrano.

The ghost of Magdalena appears in the chapel ruins in the early hours of the evening. She sometimes appears as a very faint image and at other times she seems as solid as the rocks around her. There are also reports of her face peering from the highest window of the church ruin.

There is yet another legend associated with her. Upon her death, so the rendition goes, the Mission bells sounded, untouched by human hands. Later, it was said the sound was not of Mission bells but bells ringing in heaven welcoming Magdalena. Sometimes on still nights the sound of bells echo through the Mission. Reports of voices, chanting and

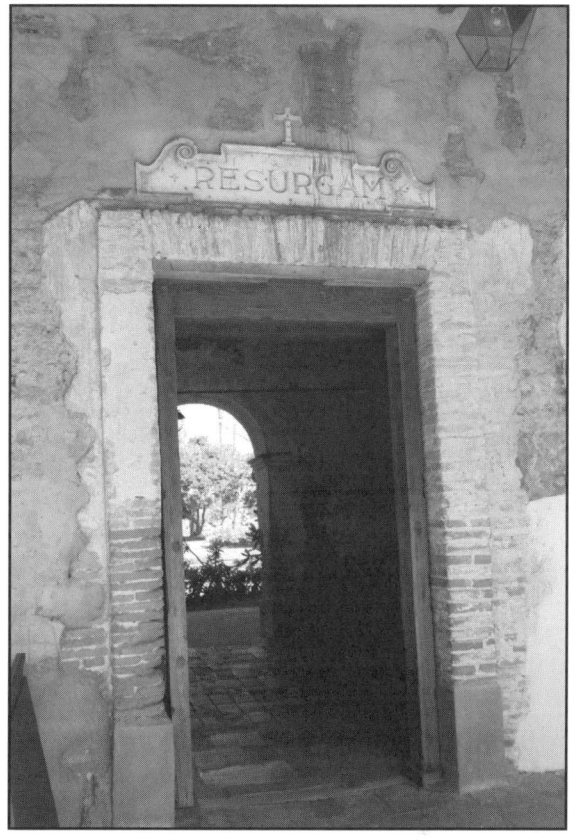

Doorway at the Mission San Juan Capistrano.

even cries for help from the graveyard have been noted in a few books. On the day we were at the Mission, there was no unusual activity, simply a peaceful setting. The only voices heard were from the exurberant children on a school trip.

Location

26801 Ortega Hwy.
AdMission: $9 Adults/ $8 Seniors/ $5 Children 4-11
The adult adMission includes a great audio tour.
Web site: www.Missionsjc.com.
Hours: 8:30 am to 5 pm daily, except Thanksgiving, Christmas, and Good Friday afternoon.

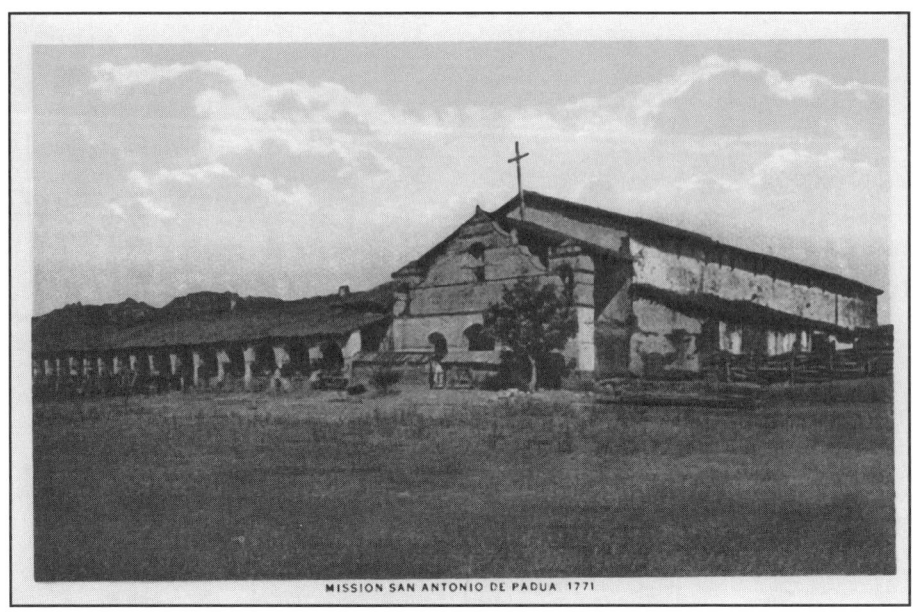

Mission San Antonio De Padua, vintage postcard. Produced by Western Publishing & Novelty Co., Los Angeles, California.

Mission San Miguel
The Wishing Chairs

"We know so little what nature comprehends—what are powers and limits—that we can scarcely speak of anything that happens as beyond it or above it."

—Thomas Street Millington

The *Wishing Chairs* of two California Missions attracted believers from far and wide. In the shade of the long colonnades of the Mission San Miguel, were two huge old chairs fashioned of oak and carved leather. These were the famous wishing chairs, one was brought from the ruins of the San Antonio Mission. Though both were capable of granting wishes they were limited in their power.

The Mission chair from San Antonio was said to be instrumental in saving the Mission from a raid by a band of Indians. A Spanish army Captain is said to have sat in the chair a week before the raid. At that time he received a cryptic message that his services would be needed in the future. On the day of the raid the Captain knew he was needed at the Mission. The Captain and his men arrived just in time to defend it. The chair was also thought to grant good fortune. People would sit on the chair and pray for a good crop, general success, etc.

The Mission San Miguel's chair was more restricted in power. Its occupant could wish for only one thing—the heart of their beloved. Suitors traveled across California to wish for their heart's desire. Long ago, a man named Ramon Vallencia, the owner of a ranch near El Paso del Robles, fell in love with a neighboring ranch owner's daughter. He courted her for months, but the girl was indifferent to him. Ramon traveled to the Mission San Miguel and asked the chair for his heart's desire. Within days, Ramon had secured the girl's hand in marriage. That evening, he rode back to the Mission and destroyed the chair so that no other could sit in it.

No one knows what became of the chairs. Reports of the chairs were published up until 1910. When you visit the Mission, you can see if there are any wish granting pieces of furniture around—you never know! {28}

Mission San Miguel Archangel

"...certain forms of hallucination not only demand, but are actually receiving, a thorough and totally novel scientific investigation. The investigators, indeed, are men who do not believe in ghosts; but they are also men unwilling to accept the cut-and-dried explanation of all visual or auditory hallucinations by nervous disorder."

—*A Ghost Story*, Lafcadio Hearn

The line up at the cash register was quite long one summer day. The young girl asked her mother if she could play outside, her mother consented. Moments later, the girl came back crying that there was a boy outside bleeding from the neck. When the gift shop worker and the mother went out to investigate, no one was there. Was he the ghost of the Reed's son, the murdered family who once lived at the Mission?

The boy's ghost is not the only one said to be at the Mission. There is also the white lady ghost who may be Mrs. Reed. She is sometimes spotted in the courtyard. While some locals believe this is just a tall tale, many will tell you of unusual occurrences at the Mission, unexplained cold spots, a child crying and the sound of objects dragged around. The horrible events of December 5, 1848, have left a scar on Mission San Miguel.

In olden times, San Miguel Mission was used as a halfway house on the journey from San Diego to San Francisco.

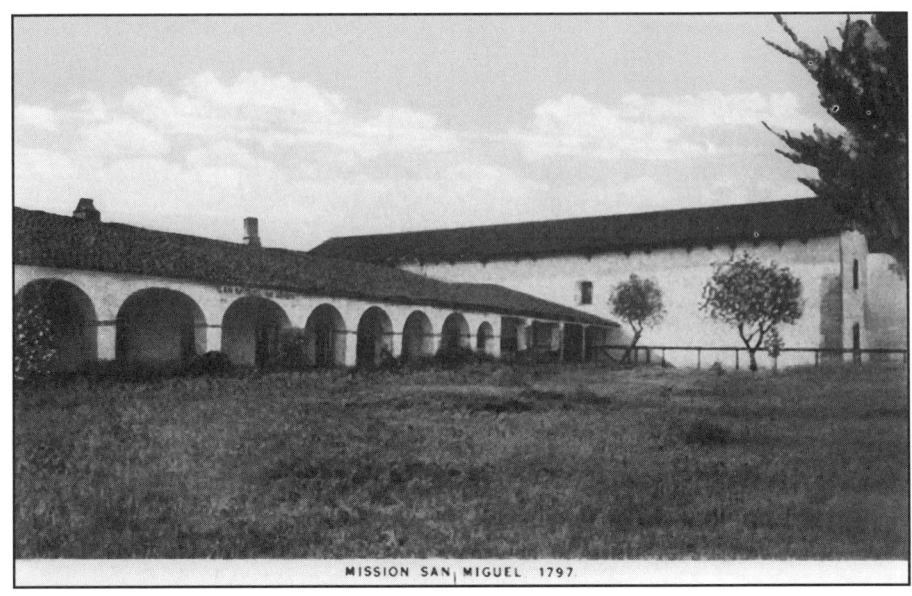

MISSION SAN MIGUEL 1797

Mission San Miguel, vintage postcard. Produced by Western Publishing & Novelty Co., Los Angeles, California.

History

Mission San Miguel was the last of the Missions to be sold. William Reed and Petronillo Rios, his wife's uncle, bought it for $600. William Reed, his wife, Maria, and Uncle Petronillo lived in the original friars' quarters. They ran the entire Mission as an inn and raised sheep on Mission lands. The Reeds were able to make money by selling supplies to miners. They also sold their sheep to the miners who were in need of food.

Reed is said to have boasted about how much gold he made selling his large flock. Two miners with a murderous past, Peter Raymond and Joseph Lynch, overheard. The two men had already killed two other miners for their gold. If only Mr. Reed had known, he wouldn't have uttered a word.

Raymond and Lynch would travel to the Mission along with three other men who had just deserted their ship. The sixth man with them that night was an Indian named John from the Soledad Mission.

Mr. Reed opened the inn's doors to the men and it is believed the men stayed up late telling stories. Mr. Reed is said to have boasted to the men that he had bags of gold dust so heavy his own child could not lift the sack. In the morning the men left. The bandits believed Reed's story of gold dust. They returned axes in hand and slaughtered Mr. Reed, his pregnant wife, Maria, their son, Maria's brother, the midwife,

Mrs. Olivera, her daughter and grandson, the Reed's Indian servant, his grandson, and the cook. Ten people cold murdered for gold.

The bodies were found by Jim Beckworth, the mail carrier. In some reports, he is said to have found one of the children hiding nearby who told him what had transpired. Others say this did not happen.

The Sheriff and a small posse went after the bandits as they fled towards Santa Barbara. The two groups met near Summerland. After a gun battle ensued, Raymond and two other bandits were killed and one of the Sheriff's men. The men were later tried and hung in Santa Barbara on December 28, 1848. Mr. Reed's gold was never found and some stories suggest one of the bandits dove into the ocean with it.

The bodies of those murdered that evening were placed in unmarked graves next to the Mission Chapel. Is this why the ghost of Mr. Reed is seen at the Mission? Still protecting his gold? A ghostly figure dressed in white has been seen floating in the halls of the Mission. Could it be Maria Reed frantically trying to protect her family? {29}

Location

775 Mission Street
San Miguel, CA 93451
* Due to the 2003 earthquake, much of the Mission is closed to the public. Contact the Parish office before planning your visit. (805) 467-2131
Web site: www.Missionsanmiguel.org.

Mission Santa Barbara
Santa Barbara

"Do you know, sometimes on still, quiet evenings like this, I almost get a creepy feeling that they will all walk in through that window ..."
—*The Open Window*, H.H. Munro

A man named Brother Angelo was attached to the Mission. He was once a famous singer in Italy. The lady he was to marry ran off with another and so he became a priest. He asked for a foreign placement to be far from the woman. He was placed in the Mission Santa Barbara where he sang at Mass. It was said when he sang, Heaven's Gates would open.

One day, a man came to the Mission and told Brother Angelo that he was wasting his life. He should return to Europe and earn riches

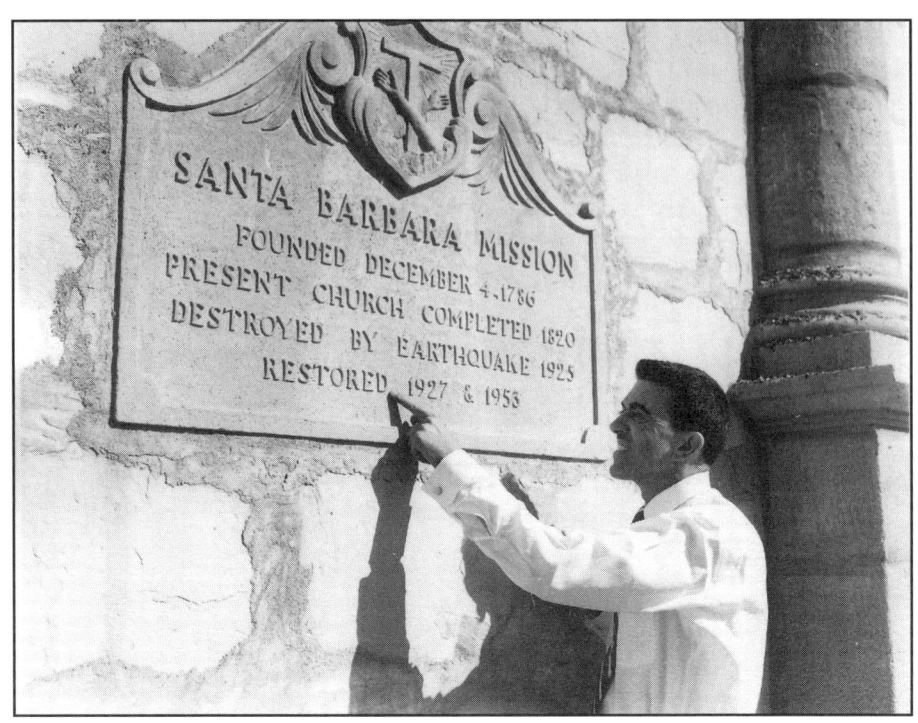

Vintage photograph at the Santa Barbara Mission.

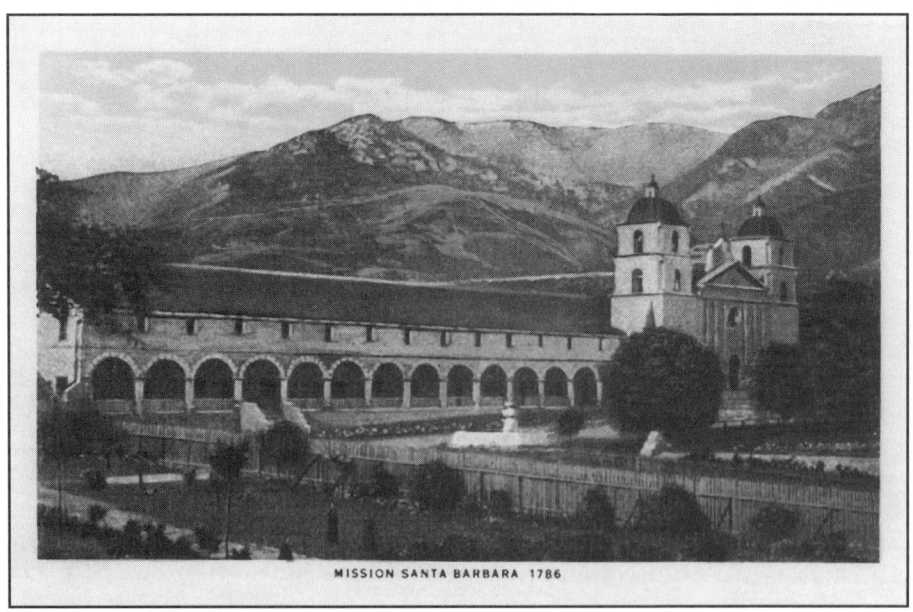

MISSION SANTA BARBARA 1786

Santa Barbara Mission, vintage postcard. Produced by Western Publishing & Novelty Co., Los Angeles, California.

singing at court. Brother Angelo rejected the man's offer, but the man persisted until Brother Angelo changed his mind.

The stranger told him of a ship sailing the next day and Brother Angelo was determined to be on it. The two men set out for the ship, but no sooner had they left the Mission, then the stranger was shot by an arrow. Thinking him to be near death, Brother Angelo poured Holy Water on the man. There was a terrible howl as the stranger vanished in a cloud of smoke. Angelo then realized it had been the devil sent to tempt his soul.

From that day on, Angelo sang joyously at the Mission, eventually taking his vows.

Location

2201 Laguna Street
Santa Barbara, CA 93105
(805) 682 4149
Hours: Daily from 9 am to 5 pm, except Thanksgiving, Christmas, and Easter
AdMission: $5 adults/ $1 children ages 6-12
Web site: www.santabarbaraMission.org

Mission Santa Ines Ghosts
Solvang

"People with eyes such as those that can look into futurity, ought not surely to shrink from a mere gate like death! For death is but a gate—the gate of life in its fullest beauty."

—Wolverden Tower, Grant Allen

The following humorous ghost tale is from the 1920s.

A loud knock at the door roused the Padre from his after-dinner sleep. Opening the door, a peddler asked the Padre if he could spend the night at the Mission to which the Padre agreed. In return for food and shelter, the peddler offered the Padre any of his wares. The peddler proudly pulled out remnants of lace, fine bone buttons, and he would have continued, but the Padre stopped him. He said, "There are no women here except for a cat, so put away your things and rest by the fire."

After the peddler had seen to his horse, he joined the Padre in the large adobe room. He inquired if the Mission was haunted as he had heard rumors. The Padre nodded and said, "There are

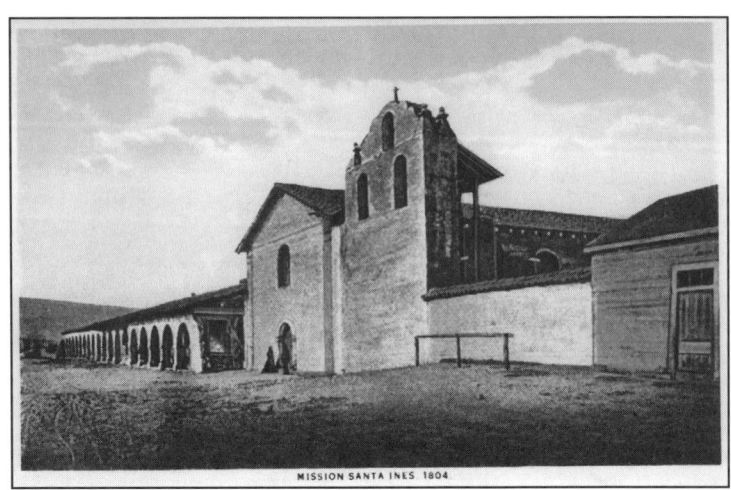

Mission Santa Ines vintage postcard. Produced by Western Publishing & Novelty Co., Los Angeles, California.

MISSION SANTA INES 1804

many ghosts here at Mission Santa Ines. You have your pick of horse thieves, murderers, and even lunatics." The peddler was intrigued, "Go on," he said. The padre obliged and told him there where seven haunted rooms at the Mission and agreed to show each one to the peddler.

With candle in hand the Padre lead the way. The first room he pointed out had a ghost who pulled fingers and toes. In the next room a poor traveler had stayed and then disappeared leaving behind a shoe. The third room was so cold, guests couldn't stand it for more than a few minutes, even if a small fire was burning. There was the room of a Padre who died quite insane, a room where an Indian would slowly materialize out of the floor, and lastly the room of a beheaded robber looking for his head.

The peddler told the Padre, ghosts didn't scare him and he would gladly sleep in any of the rooms. So the padre took a large key from the chain around his waist and opened a door.

Hours after the Padre had gone to bed, he awoke to hear the Peddler crying out for help. "Someone has my toe," he screamed. The Padre, candle in hand rushed down the corridor but the peddler had already fled leaving his horse behind. The Padre peered into the room the man had selected and suddenly remembered he had set a mousetrap in that room!

Location

1760 Mission Drive
Solvang, CA
(805) 688-4815
Web site: www. Missionsantaines.org

88

Mission Santa Ines Legend
Solvang

"It is, alas, chiefly the evil emotions that are able to leave their photographs on surrounding scenes and objects..."

—Algernon H. Blackwood

In an old story from the 1920s, the ghosts of Mission Santa Ines are said to be sociable and never harm as long as they are well treated. No further explanation is given into what exactly "treating a ghost well" could mean. As this is a Mission, perhaps the author is suggesting no exorcism.

The 1812 earthquake destroyed the Mission established in 1804 by Father Estevan Tapis. Some buildings were rebuilt, but after the dismantling of the Mission system, it fell into disrepair. Imagine a 1920s Mission without electricity or even modern plumbing. The full restoration of the Mission wouldn't begin until 1947.

Every evening, the Father would wake up to the moans and whispering from the room above him. To call it a room was kind. The Father slept in a large adobe room formerly used as an office. Above this was a storage room but no staircase as it was destroyed years earlier, and the only access now was by ladder. Naturally, the Father wanted to explore this space to investigate these unusual sounds but he was much too old to climb-up.

Over the course of a few weeks, the Father began hearing the sounds night and day. Now the very walls of the Mission seemed to be whispering to him. One evening when the Father was lying in bed he heard footsteps above him. He got out of bed knelt down and prayed.

After many nights, the Father thought of a plan. He called out to the ghost to confess his sins. The ghost materialized to reveal a Padre who passed away a hundred years previously. He confessed he had fallen asleep and forgotten to say Mass. An earthquake struck and he was unable to say his last Mass. With that, the phantom Padre disappeared. The next day the Padre of Mission Santa Ines said a Mass to the dead on the Padre's behalf. He never heard any unusual sounds again.

Location

1760 Mission Drive
Solvang, CA
Web site: www.missionsantaines.org

Modjeska House
Ventura

She... "brooded over the thoughts of the thing she had seen, firmly believing that she had looked upon the shadow of the dead, and that there was some purpose to be fulfilled by that awful vision."
—*John Granger,* Mary E. Braddon

Nestled in the foothills of the Santa Ana Mountains is the home of actress Madame Helena Modjeska and Count Bozenta. They lived there for eighteen years. The home stands in a live oak grove on the banks of Santiago Creek in Modjeska Canyon. It is a designated National Historic Landmark.

Originally from Poland, Madame Helena Modjeska was one of the greatest dramatic actresses of the day. When she came with her husband to Orange County in 1876, she was already an established actress in Poland. Through ambition and perseverance, she established herself on the North American stage in the Shakespearean role of Rosalind.

Though she died in 1909, some say Madame still haunts her house in the Modjeska Canyon, roughly thirty-two miles east of Long Beach. Today, a bronze historical marker honors the late actress. The stone home has many unusual features, including a long tunnel dug into the hillside. It led from one bedroom into a kitchen cupboard. The purpose for such an unusual tunnel is not known. Residents of the home have experienced cold spots, mysterious sounds, and an uneasy feeling of being watched. It is not clear who haunts the home. She is also said to haunt the Calumet Theatre in Michigan, where her presence is felt in the actors' dressing rooms.

Perhaps the unease people feel in the home is due to the site itself. The canyon was the home of the Shoshone Indians, before Madam Modjeska purchased it in 1888. In 1857, it was the scene of violence when a posse led by General Andres Pico routed out rebel Juan Flores and his gang. Two of Flores' men were hanged from an oak tree on General Pico's orders.

After Madam Modjeska's death, the land was subdivided and Long Beach banker B. F. Tucker purchased a portion of it. Following the death of his wife, Dorothy May, he established the Dorothy May Tucker Memorial Bird Sanctuary.

29042 Modjeska Canyon Road
Modjeska Canyon, CA 92667
(949) 855- 2028
Tours are available on the second and fourth Saturday of each month from 10 am. Reservations are required.

Montanez Adobe
San Juan Capistrano

"The numbing and sickening effect on me of the touch of the object I had not seen was not to be shaken off at once. Indeed, I felt as though my hand were contaminated...."

—*A Dead Finger,* Sabine Baring-Gould

The Montanez adobe, built around 1794 and on the National Historic Register, is one of the most historic homes in San Juan Capistrano. It is named for one of its owners, Dona Polonia Montanez (1827-1917) who lived in the adobe for most of her married life. Today, the home is open to the public with guides more than happy to discuss Dona Montanez's contributions to the San Juan Capistrano community, but don't expect stories of ghosts.

On a cool March day, a visitor to the Montanez adobe may have met the spirit of Dona Polonia Montanez herself. She had been to the adobe several times taking guests with her whenever they were in the area. Nothing out of the ordinary had ever occurred on any of these trips and, as such, she wasn't expecting the next happening.

Within seconds of stepping through the front door, she felt an odd sensation; she felt tiny goose bumps up and down her arms. She tried to ignore the odd feeling and continued looking through the small home. There were no other guests inside the home during her visit. While admiring the living room (sala), out of the corner of her eye she saw a small ball of light. She turned and saw the light slowly travel across the room before disappearing. The whole experience lasted seconds but it felt as if time had stood still.

Local residents and visitors to the Montanez Adobe have reported small balls of light and flickering lights. Believers in the paranormal insist these occurrences signal the former occupant, Dona Polonia Montanez, has retuned. Dona Montanez was a vibrant part of life in San Juan Capistrano instructing children at her home. For a short time, her residence was used for prayer services as San Juan Capistrano was without a resident priest.

Could the prayer services have attracted spirits to the home? Perhaps, but no psychic researcher has yet tried to contact them.

If it is the spirit of Dona Montanez, maybe she returns to visit a place and people she loved.

Location

> 31745 Los Rios Street
> San Juan Capistrano, CA 92675
> For hours of operation, contact the San Juan Capistrano Historical Society at (949) 493- 8444 or call (949) 493-8444.
> The society also offers a walking tour every Sunday at 1 pm and a ghost tour before Halloween.

Morey Mansion
Redlands

"For a little I heard him stumbling after me, breathing heavily and with short broken cries. I ran with the speed of fear, for till I was within my own doors I could feel no security."

—*The Watcher*, John Buchan

"**A**merica's Favorite Victorian House," as it is known, may be a haunted Victorian. The sunny facade and manicured gardens don't seem to say ghost—not the cinematic stereotype of darkened windows and gloomy caretaker. No, this Victorian has been featured in commercials and television such as HGTV where restoration work by current owner Janet Cosgrove was highlighted.

Several stories in the *San Bernardino Sun* have mentioned the benign haunting at this home. M. Frye for *The Sun,* in 2006, interviewed Ms. Cosgrove. This is what was written, "While owner Janet Cosgrove has never seen or felt anything spooky, for the last eight years acquaintances and strangers have recounted paranormal experiences about the house that sometimes coincide with one another..."

A few guests have sensed the presence of both David and Sara Morey in the Blue Room, the couple's former bedroom. Sadly, Sara passed away in this room and David, distraught over her death, later killed himself in San Diego. Now, whether guests were told the history of the home, or knew it before staying in the room, is not known. For Carol Lombard fans, they will be disappointed to know though she spent many summers at the Mansion then owned by her Aunt; she has never been spotted! But of course guests and fans can still enjoy the home as she did.

Who were the Moreys? David Morey was a skilled ship builder. With his wife, Sara, they started the first orange seedling nursery in Southern California. They ran the nursery for eight years. After the business was sold, in 1890, they built the mansion overlooking the San Timoteo Canyon. {30}

Location

The Morey Mansion is privately owned. It operates as an upscale inn with three guest rooms. The owner is quoted as saying she has never felt or seen anything unusual in the home.

190 Terracina Boulevard
Redlands, CA
1-866-990-1890
Web site: www.moreymansion.com

San Timoteo Canyon is a new State Park not yet opened to the public.

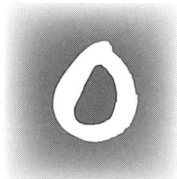

Old Cemetery
San Juan Capistrano

"When we are alone for a long time, we people space with phantoms."
—The Horla Guy de Maupassant

The ghosts of Capistrano wouldn't be complete without at least one La Llorona ghost. San Juan Capistrano is home to several phantom ladies but none so sad as La Llorona.

Walking in the Los Rios District, you have decided to take in a ghost tour. You're a little early, so you do a little exploring on your own. The night is cool, and as time ticks by, the mist seems to be getting thicker. Out of the corner of your eye you sense movement. Turning to look, you see a woman dressed in white. Thinking she may be going on the tour, you wave, but then see with growing horror that she isn't quite like you. She doesn't need to walk on the street; she is floating above it. Before you can scream, she has disappeared. The others in the tour gather but there will be one story you don't need explained; it is San Juan Capistrano's La Llorona.

The weeping lady is seen in the evening hours in the Los Rios District, near the old cemetery, not open to the public.

Location

Consult the San Juan Capistrano Web site at www.sanjuancapistrano. org for a guide to city trails.

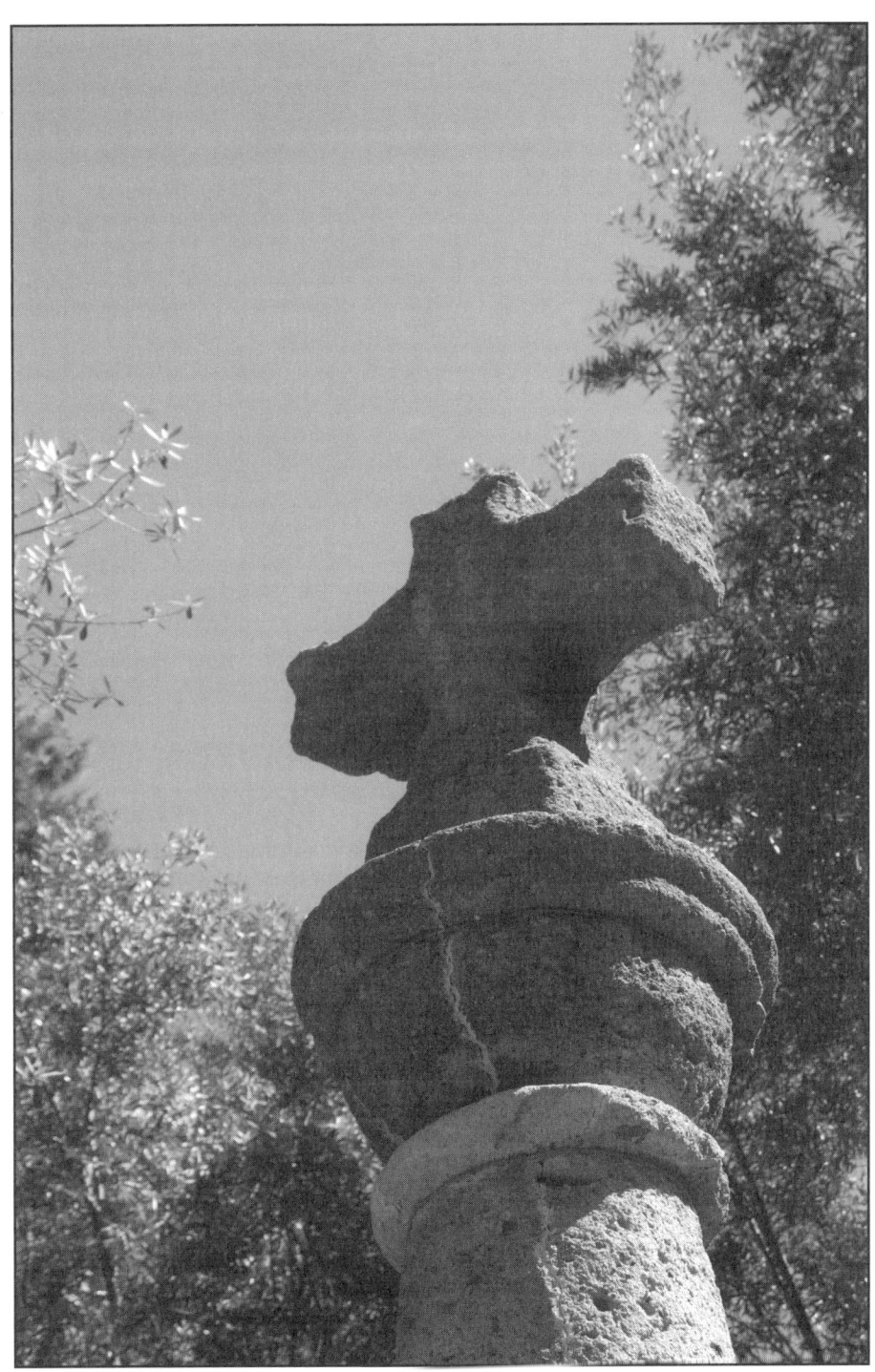

The Mission San Juan Capistrano Cemetery.

Old Fort Tejon
Grapevine Canyon

"It's written that the ghosts of old long abandoned Army posts can be clearly heard through the mists of time and decay...the charge of cavalry with thundering hoof beats, clanging swords and sharp commands of officers ..."

—This quote is from R. Conrad's 1970s article on Fort Tejon

Even thirty-years ago, if not longer, Fort Tejon has been considered a fort with more than one military ghost. The sights and sounds of fort life are faithfully reenacted at Fort Tejon during the year. In the bark of the 400-year-old trees and the walls of the restored adobes, echoes of past sounds can be heard.

One day at Fort Tejon, a window into its past opened long enough for a visitor to experience the fort as it was. After the drive to Fort Tejon from San Diego, the man's wife and children were more than happy to stretch their legs. As they went off to pay a visit to the "facilites," the man began wandering around the Fort. With his back against the barracks, he shut his eyes feeling the sun on his face. His quiet moment was shattered by the sound of hooves. He opened his eyes expecting to

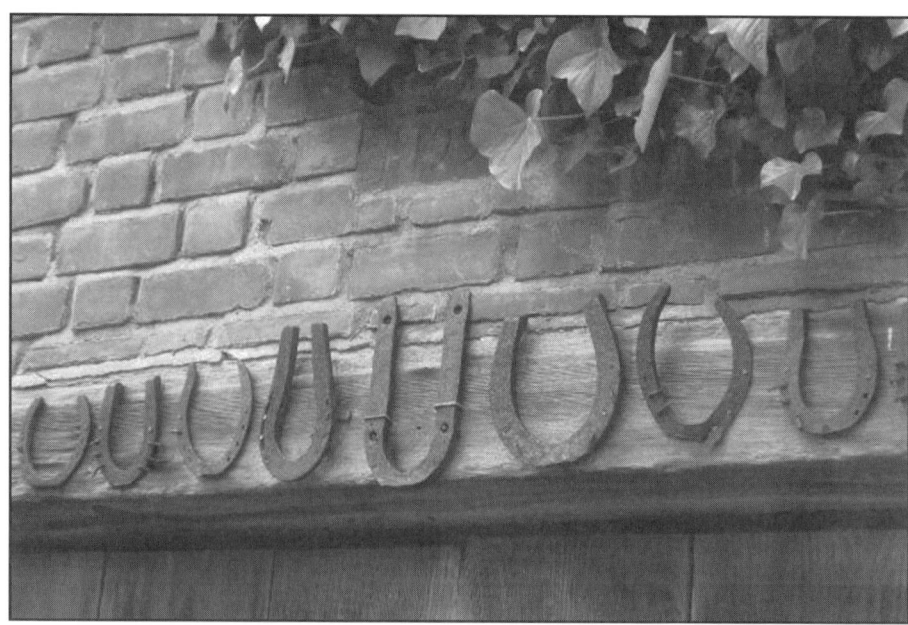

Lucky horseshoes.

see horses, but didn't. The sound got louder and louder, mixed with men's voices; then just as quickly, all was quiet.

Upon seeing the ranger, he went over to inquire when the horse show would begin. The ranger looked puzzled—there was no scheduled reenactments that day. The man then asked where the horses were kept, thinking he'd take his children over to see them. He was informed there were no horses on the premises. Feeling foolish, he briskly thanked the ranger for his time and went to meet his wife and children. The man is still not sure what to make of his experience at Fort Tejon, but he is certain of what he heard. The sounds lasted for about a minute and were as sharp and clear as a radio signal.

The history of the fort goes back to 1854, when it was used by the United States Army, only to be deserted ten years later. A large restoration project began in 1949. The barracks buildings and officer's quarters were completed by 1957.

If you go to Fort Tejon, look for the headstone of a French trapper called Peter Le Beck who was killed by a grizzly bear, or X bear, as they were once called. He was buried by a large oak tree, but Peter Le Beck's body was later exhumed and placed in a cemetery. Written on the tree: "Peter Le Beck, Killed by a X Bear Oct, 17, 1837."

There have been sightings of both the spirit of Peter Le Beck and Chief Black Bear near this oak tree. These incidents are noted in two books: Dennis William Hauck's *Haunted Places Directory* and Richard Senate's *Ghosts of the Haunted Coast*. {31, 32}

Location

Seventy miles northwest of Los Angeles, near Grapevine Canyon.

(661) 248-6692

Web site: www.parks.ca

The Santa Clarita history Web site contains a few pictures of Peter Le Beck's epitaph. www.scvhistory.com

Restoration began in 1949—200 acres were purchased in 1954, and the barracks building and officer's quarters were structurally completed in 1957.

Ghostly Camels

"If a 'ghost' is seen hovering about a grave it is the etheric body or shell of a newly buried person."

—AHT 1908

Driving in the desert, a camel suddenly appears on the horizon. "Oh look," says your passenger, "There's someone riding on it."

Intrigued, you speed up. It's not every day you see a camel. As the car nears, your passenger lets out a blood-curdling scream. Yes, it's not every day you see a headless corpse riding a camel.

From 1856 to 1857, a total of seventy-five camels were brought to America as part of an Army experiment under the direction of Jefferson Davis, the secretary of the war. They were to be used in "The Great American Desert."

"The advantage in substituting these animals for horses and mules over the desert country was that they did not require anything like the care of a horse or mule; that they could go for days without water and would subsist on the coarsest of grass and the sprouts of young trees." (*History of Arizona* by Thomas Edwin Farish 1915.)

According to the Fort Tejon Historical Association Web site, the camels were only on the base a mere five and a half months. The entire camel program was abandoned in 1864.

In the years after the program was disbanded, stories circulated in the Southwest of phantom camels—the most famous being the "Red Ghost," which tells of a headless corpse attached to the back of a camel. This crazed camel was also said to have attacked ranchers and prospectors. Tamer stories tell of camel sightings from Arizona to San Bernardino County. To this day, some people will tell you there are wild camels somewhere out there. There are no known tales of Fort Tejon camel ghosts.

Old Point Loma Lighthouse
San Diego

"The dark was dying silverly, that strange, still hour when Earth is falling toward the day—that hour of spacious silence and delay when all things poise upon the hinge of change."

—Edwin Markham

Thick fog rolls in and once again the Point Loma lighthouse is obscured. This was the reason the lighthouse was only in operation for thirty-six years, as the fog would obscure the light! Definitely not a good thing when your function is to guide ships around this treacherous piece of land.

One summer morning, a man was looking forward to taking in the view from Point Loma. He was one of the first people through the Navy gate that morning. After taking photos of Cabrillo

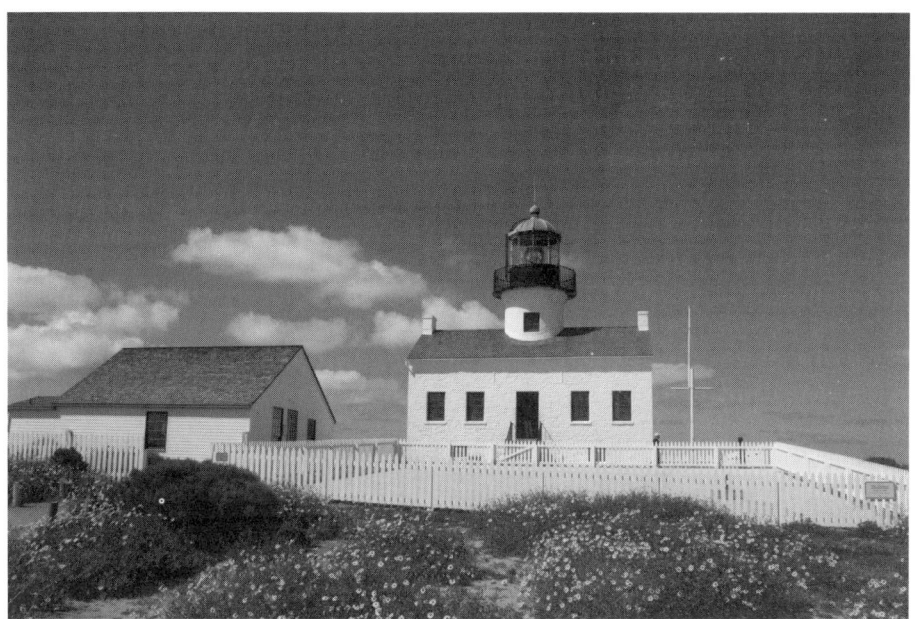

Old Point Loma Lighthouse, San Diego, California.

monument, he headed up to the lighthouse thinking the park would fill up quickly in the summer months. While looking through the glass of the light keepers parlor, he heard footsteps coming down the winding lighthouse steps. As the steps were narrow, he waited for the person to descend. A few minutes went by and no one materialized; he called up the stairs but no one answered. He decided the person must have stopped on the level above and started to climb the narrow staircase. When he made it to the next level, no one was there. Puzzled, he then thought the person was on the level above. Looking into one of the rooms, he once again heard footsteps coming down, glancing over his shoulder, he again saw no one. As he walked over to the stairs to investigate, the temperature suddenly dropped. Up until then he had been feeling quite warm in the confined space. Within moments, the sensation passed.

The visitor to the light doesn't know what happened that day, but he feels someone is still in the tower, although it has been out of commission since 1891. Who is the spirit at the lighthouse? Some believe it is the former keeper Captain Robert Decatur Israel and others have even suggested it is the spirit of Juan Rodriguez Cabrillo. This Portuguese explorer in 1542 claimed this coast for Spain and the monument is named after him. He is also said to haunt one of the Channel Islands.

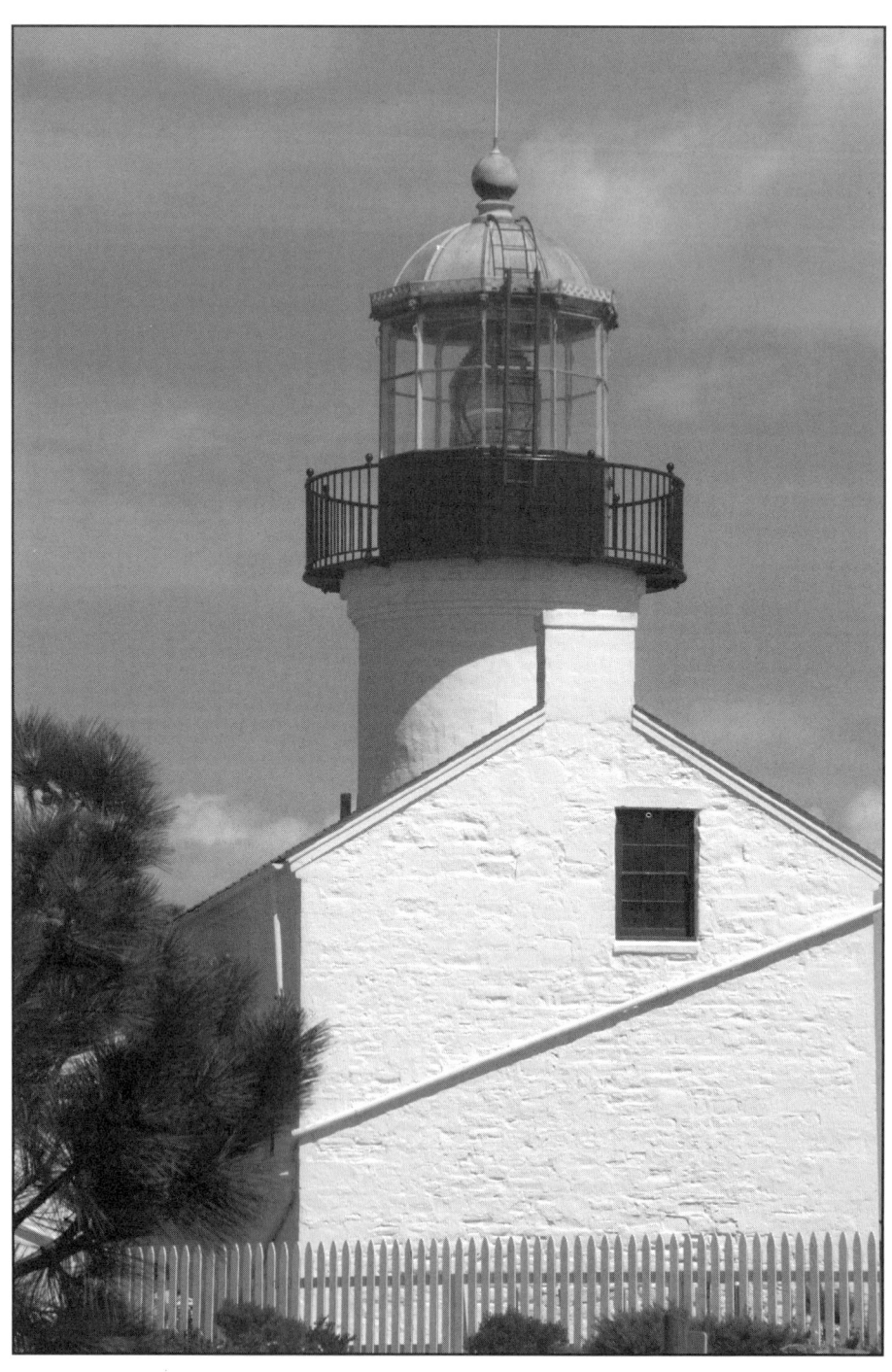

Old Point Loma Lighthouse, San Diego, California.

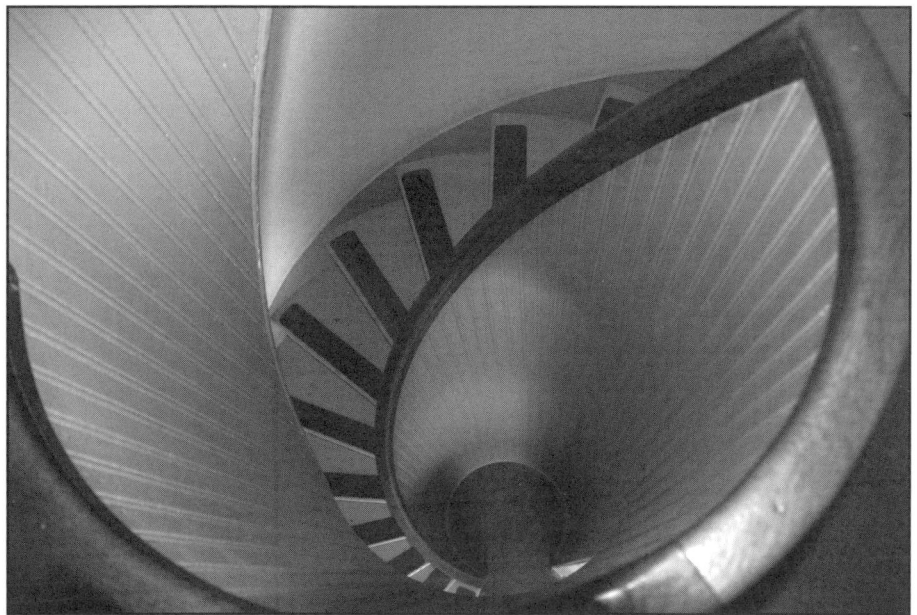

Old Point Loma Lighthouse, San Diego, California.

Construction on the Old Point Loma Lighthouse began in 1851. The lantern wasn't lit until 1855. Soon after the lighthouse was activated, a monumental flaw in its design became evident. Though the lighthouse was built 422 feet above sea level, when fog and clouds rolled in, the light became obscured. The station was abandoned in March of 1891, and a new lighthouse was built on the southwestern top of Point Loma.

Location

Cabrillo National Monument

For complete directions and maps see the NPS governments Web site at www.nps.gov/cabr.

The Cabrillo National Monument is open 365 days of the year from 9 am until 5 pm.

A few of the trails close earlier, so it is best to check the site before heading out. For all those ghost hunters who believe ghosts only come out when it is dark, they will be disappointed that sunset visits to the park are no longer available.

Olivas Adobe
San Luis Obispo

"The old spiritualism represents the phenomena seeker—the person who becomes so absorbed in manifestations that he neglects to look for the truth of which the manifestations are merely the shadow."
—Dr. McIvor-Tyndall's discourse on spiritualism, *1905*

Don't be surprised if upon visiting the Olivas Adobe a pair of icy hands pull at your clothes. Perhaps it is Theodora still wanting you to spend time at her beloved home. You felt her as soon as you entered the home, didn't you? She is said to wander the long covered porch, peer through an upstairs window, and even step foot into the kitchen.

California Historical Site 115 is a popular destination with school groups, tourists, and residents of Ventura, California. The beautiful adobe is meticulously maintained. It is not uncommon to see school children stomping in mud, learning how adobe bricks are made, and others still helping to preserve the home in a program called the "Adobe mud slingers," part of a national preservation initiative.

The beautifully restored home of Raymundo Olivas is a monument to the rancho period of California history. Born in 1809 in Los Angeles, Raymundo was the seventh child of a poor family. He joined the Mexican Army in California at the age of sixteen and was assigned to the Presidio of Santa Barbara. He met his wife, Theodora, in 1832 and married. Theodora bore twenty-one children.

In return for his service to the State, Raymundo Olivas and his friend, Fleipe Lorenzana, were granted 4,670 acres by the Mexican Governor Juan B. Alvarado. Raymundo began ranching in 1847. The home was expanded using Chumash Indian laborers. It was one of the few two-story haceinedas in Southern California—and certainly one of the most impressive homes in the Santa Clara River Valley. For many years, the Rancho prospered, but droughts in the 1860s and the death of Raymundo in 1879 was the beginning of the end for the Olivos fortune. The house was sold in 1899, but the spirit of Theodora or maybe one of her daughters has never left.

The home was bought by yeast King Major "Max" Fleischmann who restored the building in 1927 and built the distinctive archway. Upon Fleischmann's death, the adobe was given to the city of Ventura and it opened as a museum in July 1972. Many visitors admire the herb garden and others enjoy the open courtyard.

In 1837, when the adobe was built, it was the center of a 4,500-acre ranch. Ten years later, in 1849, Don Raymundo Olivas, a cattle rancher, would renovate the ranch to suit his ever-growing family.

A large wall built around the home unfortunately did not keep robbers at bay. It is perhaps this incident that Dona Theodora is replaying from time to time in her ghostly world. Her husband was a wealthy man rumored to keep treasure hidden somewhere on the property. Some put the sum of gold coins around $50-75,000, which is not a small sum even by today's standards. One evening, a group of bandits rode up to the home and threatened harm to the family. They terrorized the family, ripping the gold earrings from Dona Theodora's ears.

The story of Don Raymond's treasure has many versions. In one, a trusted servant escapes from the home and successfully buries the coins. Upon his return the bandits kill him. The inept bandits then realize that the slain man was the only one who knew where the gold was hidden. In a rage, they shoved Theodora to the ground and robbed her of her jewelry.

In yet another version, the bandits are successful, robbing the Olivas of the gold coins and making a quick getaway. Though the Sheriff captures some of the gang, not all are rounded up and the treasure is never found.

Much has been written on the adobe, from the mystical qualities of the herbs grown on the compound to the Mission-style renovations and the ghostly inhabitants documented by Richard Senate and his paranormal investigators. Choose the version you prefer.

Halloween is a great time to take part in a tour of the adobe, if not sooner. You will be thrilled with stories of murder, treasure, and ghosts of course and perhaps Theodora's hand will keep you from exiting the building. Bring your camera, for you never know, you might capture her image.

From time to time, the image of a woman dressed in an 1800s-style dress has been seen at the adobe. She is sometimes pacing on the large verandah and at other times peering out of a second-story window. The window was part of Theodora's former chapel.

Don Raymundo died in 1879, just before his 70th birthday, leaving the adobe and his lands to his wife. The property was divided among their children after Dona Theodora's death, and eventually much of it was sold off. The adobe structures were turned into a dairy farm for a time. Then they were purchased by yeast tycoon Max Fleischmann and turned into a gun club. Fleischmann donated the adobe to the city of Ventura in the 1950s.

Location

Olivas Adobe Historical Park
4200 Olivas Park Drive
Ventura, CA
Open daily; free tours are given from 10 am to 4 pm Saturday and Sunday.
(805) 658-4728.
Web site: www.olivasadobe.org

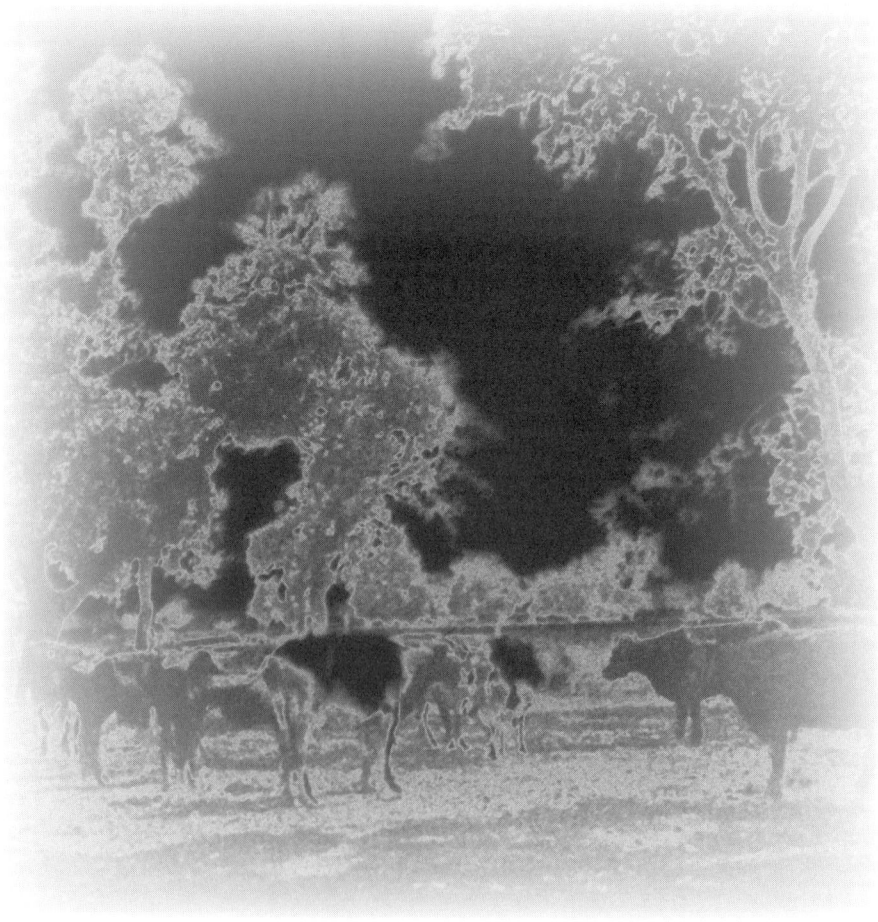

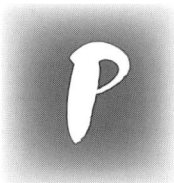

Paso Robles Inn
Paso Robles

"Yet call not this long life; but think that I am, by being dead, immortal; can ghosts die?"

—John Donne

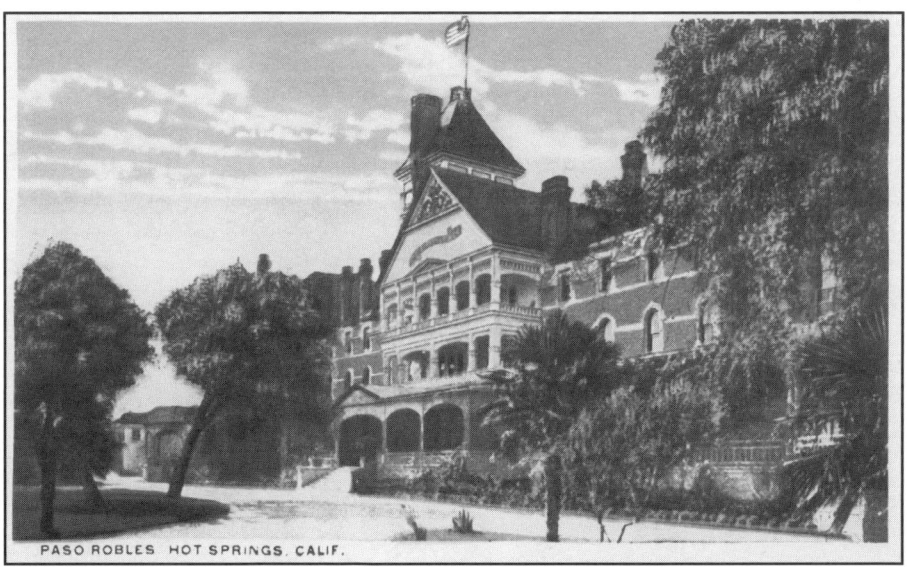

PASO ROBLES HOT SPRINGS, CALIF.

Vintage postcard of the Paso Robles Hot Springs. The inn was established around 1891. It is still in operation today.

It's just after 2 am at the Paso Robles Inn and all is quiet. The night clerk nervously eyes the phone, waiting. Waiting for what, you ask? Why, for the Room 1007 to ring the desk. Within seconds, the telephone rings causing the clerk to jump although he was expecting it. His hand slowly reaches for the receiver. With heart pounding he listens, but like every other night, no one is there. Of course no one is there; Room 1007 is empty. Well, empty of the living.

On December 19, 1940, J.H. Emsley, the night clerk, discovered a fire on the second floor of the hotel. He wasted no time in sounding the alarm. Thanks to his efforts, all the hotel guests were safely evacuated. Sadly, one person didn't survive. Night manager Emsley suffered a massive heart attack, moments after the alarm sounded.

It is believed his spirit is responsible for making the mystery phone calls from Room 1007. He doesn't just make calls to the front desk but he dials 911 as well. Is the ghost of Emsley still trying to evacuate the hotel and save all the occupants?

The Inn's phone service was inspected, but the phone company said it was in fine working order. There seems to be no mechanical reason for this odd occurrence. Staff went to the room to look at the phone, and while they were in the room, it mysteriously lit up again and dialed out. "Wallace [General Manager] said he had no idea why a ghost would choose Room 1007. But he noted that the façade of the new wing was built with bricks from the original hotel." Did the spirit of Emsley somehow become absorbed into them? Maybe...

The Paso Robles region was known for its mineral hot springs. It was a rest stop for travelers along the Camino Real trail. The springs have been a popular local attraction since the late eighteenth century, when Franciscan padres from nearby Missions began using them. Brothers Daniel and James Blackburn and Drury Woodson James founded the Paso Robles hotel. The brothers bought the Paso Robles land grant in 1844, and sold one half interest in the El Paso de Robles Hotel to Drury James in 1867. The hotel had a seven-acre garden and nine-hole golf course, a library, salon, barbershop, billiard, and lounge rooms. The hotel offered a hot springs plunge bath along with individual bathrooms. The plunge bath was thought to be the best in the U.S. and often compared to famed San Francisco hotels. {33}

Location

1103 Spring Street
Paso Robles, CA 93446
(805) 238-2660
Web site: www.pasoroblesinn.com

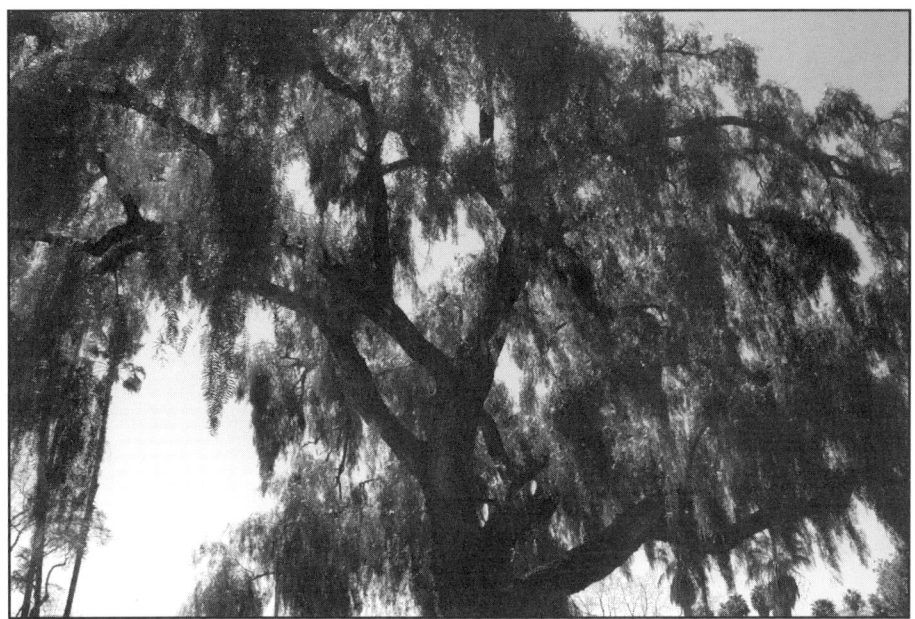

Does a ghost lurk near this tree in San Juan Capistrano?

Pepper Tree Legend
San Juan Capistrano

Why would a ghost no longer communicate with someone? According to Dr. James H. Hyslop in 1909, a spirit told him, "The effort to transmit thought to my fellow workers is causing me trouble and loss of spiritual privileges."

A lady in a long white dress materializes out of the fog in the Los Rios District. She is not a sad spirit and laughs mischievously at those she has startled. The lady never says anything. She lingers for a few minutes before disappearing.

The old pepper tree is the site of one of the most famous hauntings in San Juan Capistrano. The white lady of Capistrano has been seen for almost one hundred years.

Another legend concerning the Pepper Tree is the story of the ghost who is said to linger at the tree. In this version, the ghost is one of the builders of the Mission who was an Aztec and secretly placed an Aztec symbol above the door which led into the stone chapel. During his time building the chapel, he had fallen in love with an Indian girl. The priest had given his blessing for them to be wed. Their wedding was to be held in the Spring.

107

One day, a monk caught the man worshipping the symbol above the door. The padre instructed the man to cease at once and to take out the offending stone. The man refused and the padre swore he would never allow the man to be married at Capistrano. The angered Aztec strode into the church, interrupting Mass, and grabbed the young woman saying he would take her with him to Mexico married or not.

At that exact moment, a large tremor was felt and before they could escape, the entire building collapsed. The maiden is said to have gone straight to heaven and the man is forced to wander the grounds near the pepper tree.

Background: On the morning of December 8, 1812, while a service was being held at the church, an earthquake happened. The congregation was buried under the wreckage of beams, tiles, and stones.

Pierpont Inn
Ventura

"A ghost is someone who hasn't made it—in other words, who died, and they don't know they're dead."

—Sylvia Browne

A scent of flowers fills the air. The air becomes heavy and sickly sweet. A woman working at the hotel feels nauseous as the scent envelops her. This is the first signal that one of the spirits of the Pierpont has returned—but whom? Could it be a previous owner who loved fresh flowers in her hotel? This is one of many puzzling questions about the Pierpont.

The ghost of Emma Darling is but one phantom said to be there. Emma frequented the Inn, and after her death, reports of her ghost returning to the site began. Why exactly is not known. Her family's wealth came from investments in gas drilling in Summerland. Spiritualists settled Summerland and after the discovery of gas, there was conflict between the two groups. There is a suggestion that this lingering conflict is the reason why her spirit has stayed.

According to Pierpont spokeswoman Denise Bean-White, through the years, guests have reported seeing a woman dressed in early black twentieth-century clothing near the Pierpont parking lot and near its cottages. After a long shift, one man encountered the lady in black as he made his way to the car. Looking back towards the Inn he saw a transparent woman in black beckoning to him.

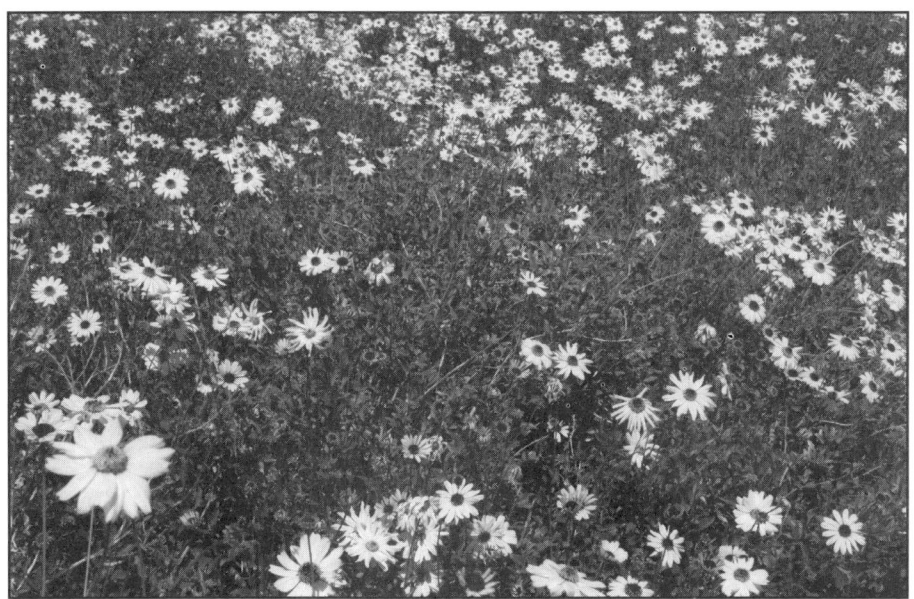

The smell of flowers at the Pierpont Inn, Cayucos.

He got in his car, started the engine, and looked back up at the image. Much to his relief, it was gone.

Emma Darling has company at the Inn. Apparitions of a little girl, a man in a top hat, and even a ghostly card party in the St. Miguel room have all been reported. At least the ghosts are friendly. The ones having a party gestured to the shocked maintenance man, to join them but he chose to leave the building instead!

An area of activity is a former linen room, now a supply room. Voices echo in this part of the Inn, unexplained noises of chambermaids from the past still going about their duties.

The night auditor, John Mork, witnessed quite a few paranormal happenings. He has heard the sound of glasses and bottles clanking—the sound so persistent, he tried to drown it out by turning up the radio. On occasion, he has heard his name spoken, but not one living person is around. One of the creepiest things was when a guest asked for a wake up call. Another guest phoned the front desk complaining about a faulty heater. Off he went to fix it and when he got back to the desk it was 4:30 am. He had missed the requested four o'clock wakeup call. He called the room to apologize to the guest. No apology was needed as a woman called the room and woke the guest. Mr. Mork was working alone, so who called the room? Did the ghost of Emma Darling place the call for him? Perhaps...

109

Socialite Josephine Pierpont-Ginn opened the Inn on September 6, 1910. It was her hope that the Inn's convenient location on the coast would attract the new automobile tourist. Local Ventura residents Mattie and Gus Fleishmann eventually bought the Inn. Mattie was known for running a top quality inn and filling it with flowers. Though her family strongly believes Mattie is at peace, there are those who believe that the scent of flowers at the Inn is an indication of her presence.

As for the image of the young child, she has been described as mischievous with curly hair, between the ages of eight and ten. One guest claimed that one night she pulled the covers off him. Another employee at the Inn saw a fellow worker coming down the hallway holding a little girl's hand. She didn't pay much attention to the event and returned to work. A short time later, the man exited his office alone, so the woman inquired what had become of the little girl. The man didn't know what she was talking about as he had been alone the entire time. {34}

Location

500 Sanjon Road
Ventura, CA 93001
(805) 643- 6144
Web site: www.pierpontinn.com
Ventura County Landmark No.80

Pirate Lights
Smuggler's Beach

"I figure I basically am a ghost. I think we all are."

—John Astin

After a long day of hiking, a couple decided to rest on the beach at Smugglers Cove. Sandwiches were shared and water bottles drained. As the couple relaxed with the sound of the waves, small flickering lights under the water's surface caught their attention. They got up to investigate. The couple watched in amazement as far below the water a row of lights moved slowly out to sea. Then, all was dark again. The man thought maybe the lights belonged to some species of phosphorescent fish, but his wife wasn't so certain. Years later, reading an old history book, they would learn of the pirate lights of Smugglers Beach.

Long ago, a pirate named Hippolyte de Bouchard came to Ventura. History will tell you the padres and their followers at the Mission fled into the hills with precious relics from the church. This legend tells a different version of the story. The pirates sought shelter at the Mission of Buenaventura and were given food and anything else they might need. Though the padres pleaded with the men not to take the scared objects from the chapel, the pirates helped themselves. One Padre, who tried to prevent the pirates from taking the pearls draped around the Madonna, was struck down and killed in the chapel.

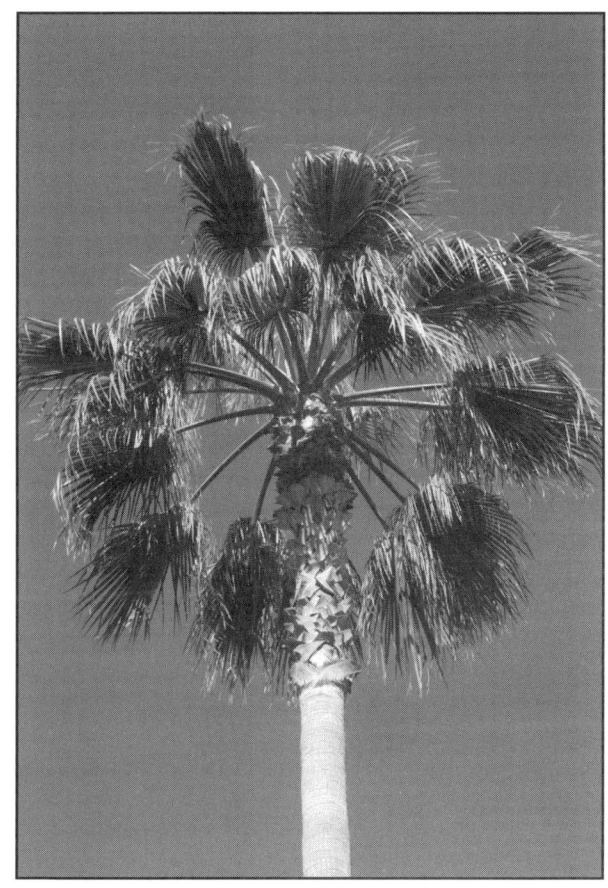

Is Hippolyte de Bouchard's treasure buried under this palm tree?

As the morning sun filtered through the clouds, the pirates placed their stolen treasure on the Mission horses and headed for the beach. The pirates dragged out their hidden rowboat from under the brush and loaded it with the valuables. As they worked, their lanterns bobbed up and down in the first light. How pleased their captain would be to see this loot they thought. They pushed their boat out into the water and made it past the breakwater. Suddenly, a storm was upon them.

The small craft pitched violently as it was unstable due to the amount of treasure it held. Wave after wave hit the craft until it capsized, throwing the pirates and the valuables into the water. Indians from the Mission claimed to have seen "angels riding the crest of the waves." The men perished and the treasure was never found.

Legend has it that those who camp out on the beach can see the lights from pirate lanterns. After checking out *google* maps, wear a hat

111

and a good pair of hiking shoes, as a rocky beach awaits you. If you are there in the hours just before sunset, you might catch a glimpse of pirate lights. The lights are said to streak across the waves or appear as dots as the ghostly pirates walk along the bottom of the sea.

Location

Smugglers Cove is located between Inspiration Point to the east and Portuguese Point toward the west.

The Mission is open daily except on major holidays. Hours of operation are Monday to Friday 10 am to 5 pm; Saturday 9 am to 5 pm and Sunday 10 am to 4 pm.

Web site: www.sanbuenadventureMission.org. The site also provides a link to a detailed map.

Pisgah Grande
Santa Susana Mountain Park

"I see the state of all of us who live, nothing more than phantoms or a weightless shadow."

—*Sophocles*

The 3,200-acre ranch "La Quinta," historically known to several generations as Pisgah Grande, is on the fringe of Eastern Ventura County. Ms. Hinkston, founder and president of the Santa Susana Mountain Park Association, is quoted as saying, "I can feel the presence of ghosts of Indians who walked here."

At one time, Pisgah Grande near Santa Susana was Dr. Finis Yoakum's retreat for the downtrodden and oppressed. Dr. Yoakum was seriously injured in an accident involving a team of runaway horses. He attributed his full recovery to his strong belief in God, and to show his gratitude, in 1908, he climbed Mt. Pisgah. He then devoted the rest of his life to helping the sick and the poor. In some newspaper articles of the day, he is credited with providing over 350,000 free meals to the poor.

Those who wished to join the colony, gave away all their belongings in return for prayerful guidance. Daily prayer and meditation were two requisites of Pisgah Grande. Devotees had to be ready to build their own accommodation, making bricks from clay dug out from nearby hills. They constructed a two-story brick prayer tower, built a road down the canyon, dug irrigation ditches, a school, Mission headquarters, dining hall, post-office, and an orphanage. Pisgah Grande even had a third-class post office. After the commune was abandoned, more than 5,000 letters containing handkerchiefs requesting blessings were found.

With the death of Dr. Yoakum in 1919, the sect's California location disbanded, but a Tennessee location still exists. In local papers, it was touted as a place of unusual interest to motorists. C. Ray Miller bought the ranch in 1938. Later, Bob Hope may have owned it. In order to prevent people from trespassing, the area was closed and protected by a full-time caretaker. The fire of 1970, which surrounded Simi Valley, destroyed some of the land but an earthquake on February 9, 1971, did more damage destroying many of the structures, leaving behind piles of red bricks.

In the years after Dr. Yoakum died, Pisgah Grande was considered a ghost town. Tales of eerie sights and sounds haunting the mountaintop made their way into local and State papers. To this day, reports of a white lights moving through the area and the deserted structures exist. You might be tempted to think these lights are from modern ATVs patrolling the property, but remember, reports of lights and unusual sounds were reported in the 1920s when the property was deserted. In a *Twilight Zone* twist, some wonder what happens to prayer letters left unanswered. {35, 36}

Location

Santa Susana Park. www.parks.ca.gov
Web site: www.pisgah.com
Pisgah Grande stood at the head of Las Llajas Canyon.
For more information on the Simi Valley see *Simi grows Up*, by Janet Scott Cameron, *Early Days in Simi Valley* by R.E. Harrington, or Book *California's Utopian Colonies* by Robert V. Hine

---

Plummer Auditorium
Fullerton

"Without the utopians of other times, men would still live in caves, miserable and naked;…utopia is the principle of all progress, and the essay into a better world."

—Anatole France

The tunnels that run underneath Fullerton are accessible from the auditorium and other spots in the city. Ghosts apparently haunt these tunnels. One such ghost is the spirit of a gentleman from World War II who it is said follows visitors, then vanishes when they reach the exit lights.

Could Fullerton be one of the most haunted cities in Orange County? There are many people who believe it to be and they have made the annual Haunted Fullerton Walking Tour a huge hit. The ghost of Louis Plummer is said to wander the dark corridors of the catwalk, along with the spirit of a dead electrician and a female spirit who is unidentified.

Odd occurrences include melting light fixtures, people being pushed against the wall, and chandeliers stopping in mid swing. To this day a "ghost light" is placed on stage.

Tony Gonzalez, a manager at Plummer Auditorium, in a 2005 interview said, "He ran one time when he saw one of the large chandeliers moving. He knew all the chandeliers were connected and one can't move if the others aren't moving." He ran to get another manager but when they got back, it had stopped moving. Tony also told of the mirrored disco ball on stage spinning wildly when no one was near it. {37}

Location

218 W. Commonwealth Avenue
Corner of N. Lemon Street and E. Chapman Avenue, Fullerton, CA
Web site: City of Fullerton; www.ci.fullerton.ca.us

The auditorium is named for Louis Plummer. He was the superintendent of schools from 1917 to 1941.

Tour Details: The tour through the Fullerton Museum Center runs from September until November. For exact dates, it is best to check with the museum. The tour is so poplar that tickets often sell out months in advance.

Point Vicente Lighthouse
Palos Verdes

"No ghost was ever seen by two pair of eyes."

—Thomas Carlyle

Perched on top of a cliff, on the tip of the Palos Verdes peninsula, this white plaster and concrete lighthouse was built in 1926. The lighthouse affords the visitor with amazing views of the Pacific Ocean.

After countless maritime disasters around this point, a lighthouse was installed. Sixty-seven feet high, the eight-sided tower rests on a stone

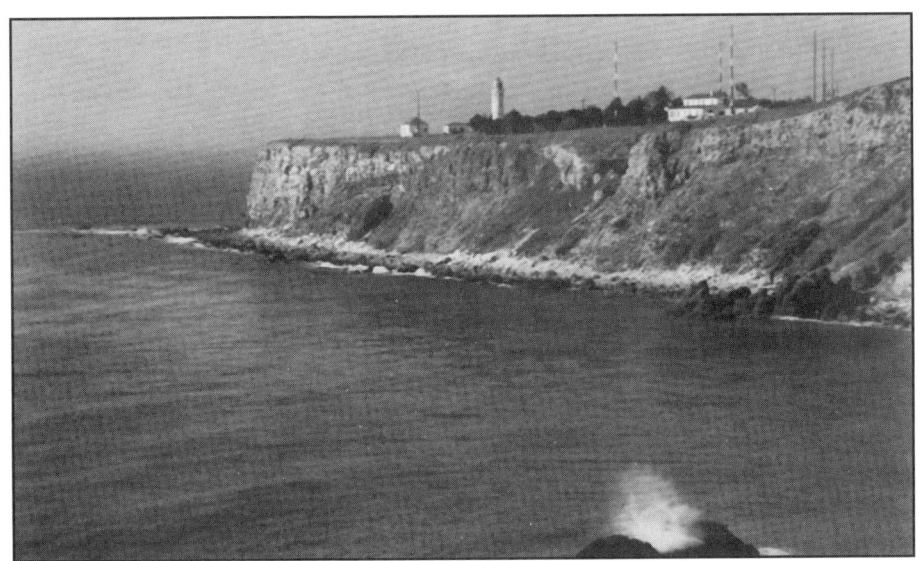

Vintage photo postcard of the Point Vicente Lighthouse at the tip of Palos Verdes Peninsula.

foundation. Past light keepers climbed a steep, almost perpendicular staircase with a total of seventy-five steps twice daily. Until 1939, a civilian lighthouse keeper manned the lighthouse then the U.S. Coast Guard became responsible for its operation. The keeper's job was demanding, covering 365 days a year, twenty-four hours a day. In 1971, the keeper was retired and the light automated.

The tower is capped by an iron lantern and balcony painted in the familiar lighthouse red. The Fresnel light was made in Paris in 1886, and first used in Alaska before being brought to its present location. Vessels are able to steer a safe passage around the point thanks to the main beam of light, which can be seen twenty miles out to sea.

Another car slows down and parks in view of the Point Vicente Lighthouse. Couples have staked out this road for years in hope of seeing the white lady—that is if their windows don't steam up first! Of course, there may be a dedicated ghost hunter or two in the line up.

On moonless nights, the phantom lady is said to walk the narrow platform near the lantern. She has waited a hundred years for her husband's return. She watches over the Catalina Channel hoping his spirit will come sailing home. Another legend told of the ghost lady is that, distraught over her husband's death at sea, she hurled herself from the top of the tower. Yet another tale tells of a young lighthouse keeper's wife stumbling over the cliff to her death.

For years this yarn has been spun in the San Pedro area, with reports of unearthly wails and unusual light activity by the tower.{38}

31501 Palos Verdes Drive W., Rancho Palos Verdes, CA 90275
(310) 541-0334

It is open to the public every second Saturday of each month from 10:00 am until 4:00 pm. AdMission is free.

Next to the lighthouse is the Point Vicente Interpretive Center. It is a great spot for whale watching. Open to the public daily from 10 am to 5 pm year-round. (310) 377-5370

Possessed Bridge
Pasadena

Can we prove ghosts exist? "…(sic) the popular notion of what constitutes scientific evidence is sadly in error—great masses of the people have only a vague conception of what is meant by proof."
—Los Angeles Herald August 11, 1907

Could the ghost of an unnamed construction worker killed while building the Colorado Street Bridge in 1913 be coaxing people to jump? The Crown City's Colorado Street Bridge is better known by its sickening nickname: Suicide Bridge. If you are under the impression this is a new nickname, then you are mistaken. As early as 1932 it had been called Suicide Bridge by the press.

According to legend, a man fell into a cement mixer and was ground into the cement. Tragically, the man wasn't missed for quite some time. When it was discovered he had never finished his shift, it was too late—much too late. The menacing ghost still stalks the bridge, calling to the lonely and distraught that have taken solace on its upper deck above the Arroyo Seco River.

Soon after the bridge opening, people began using it for a purpose never foreseen by the city planners. One of the earliest suicide reports was in 1915, a mere two years after construction when an unidentified young man leaped from the bridge rails. He fell 150 feet to his death. There were no other identification marks.

By 1929, suicide prevention nets were considered. They were first suggested by Chief of Police C.H. Kelly. "Nets have been installed beneath a bridge in Rome, from which more than a hundred persons have leaped to death," said Chief Kelley in *The Oakland Tribune*, "I believe we can put a stop to suicides on the Colorado Street Bridge by the same method."

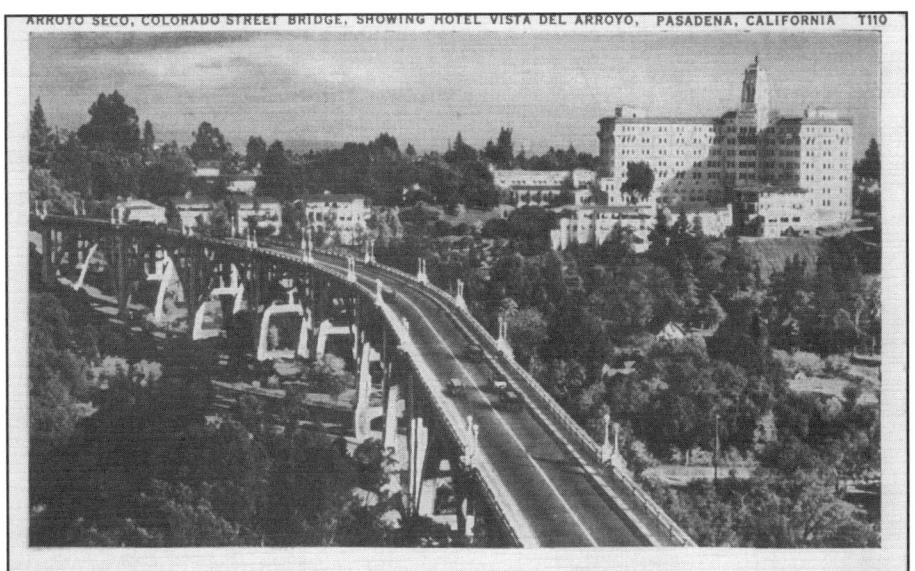

ARROYO SECO, COLORADO STREET BRIDGE, SHOWING HOTEL VISTA DEL ARROYO, PASADENA, CALIFORNIA   T110

Vintage postcard of the Arroyo Seco, Pasadena California. An exert from the back reads, "..Etched on the camera's plate; this magnificent view across the Arroyo Seco Bridge shows the Vista del Arroyo Hotel & Bungalows...) Produced by Ticnor Art Company LA.

In 1933, it was falsely hoped "(sic)... that the demands of the ghost that stalks over this bridge at unseen hours have been appeased at last..." Why was this? Exactly thirty-nine people had leapt to their deaths, and there was a theory that this number was significant. The unnamed construction worker had died on the thirteenth of the month and three times thirteen is thirty-nine. The superstitious say, "(sic)... that the demands of the ghost have been satisfied."

This was not the case,however, as a few years later the number reached seventy-five with one man trying to drag his wife with him. Calls to make the bridge suicide proof were heard and money set aside by the State Highway Commissioners, but nothing, it seems, deters those wanting to jump. No one knows if the ghostly legend is merely superstition, as those who encountered the ghost are not talking now! {39}

Location

171 South Los Robles Avenue
Pasadena, CA 91101
(626)795 9311
Web site: Pasadena Convention & Visitors Bureau; www. pasadenacal.com

Possessed Rail Car
Long Beach

What would happen if the police gave chase to a ghost? "...(sic) while the policemen entered the building and pursued the spook through the corridors and up stairs. They could not catch sight of the ghost, but plainly heard its footsteps." The police were, as you have already guessed, unsuccessful at apprehending the spook.

—*Los Angeles Herald.* Anonoymous. December 16, 1905

Next time you are in a traffic jam on the 101 with nothing but containers to look at, think about this story. Fifty years ago, rumor had it that one Los Angeles freight car was unlike the others. It seemed to have a mind of its own or an evil presence attached to it. The men in the yard kept the car's break on at all times as it would mysteriously jump the track.

The stories of at least three murders are attached to the car. Originally, the car had come from Boston loaded with antiques and other furnishings for a new hotel in Sacramento. The first half of the journey was uneventful and the car was securely locked when checked. Somewhere in Nevada, two tramps forced the door and enjoyed a "private" car all the way to California. Workers realized the door had been forced, but for some reason, did not evict the tramps. When the hotel staff came down to the yard in Sacramento, anxious to get the furnishings from the car, they were shocked to discover the body of one of the tramps. His throat had been slit and the other tramp was never found.

For three months, the car sat in the yard in Sacramento. Railroad workers avoided it, saying the spirit of the dead tramp was still there. One night while it was at the depot, two-railroad hands decided to play cards in it. Many rounds of poker were played, and sometime after midnight, one of the men, John Dewey, stabbed his friend. He would later claim it was in self-defense, but the jury didn't believe him and sentenced him to San Quentin.

The third murder occurred in El Paso, Texas. Italian laborers boarded the car during a strike. Again a quarrel broke out and one was beaten to death.

It was rumored the car was pure evil. Evil influenced anyone who dared enter the car. When the car returned to Long Beach, it was pulled off the rails because it would move even on a level track. Workers claimed to hear moans from inside. Is this proof it was haunted or were the murders just coincidence? {40}

118

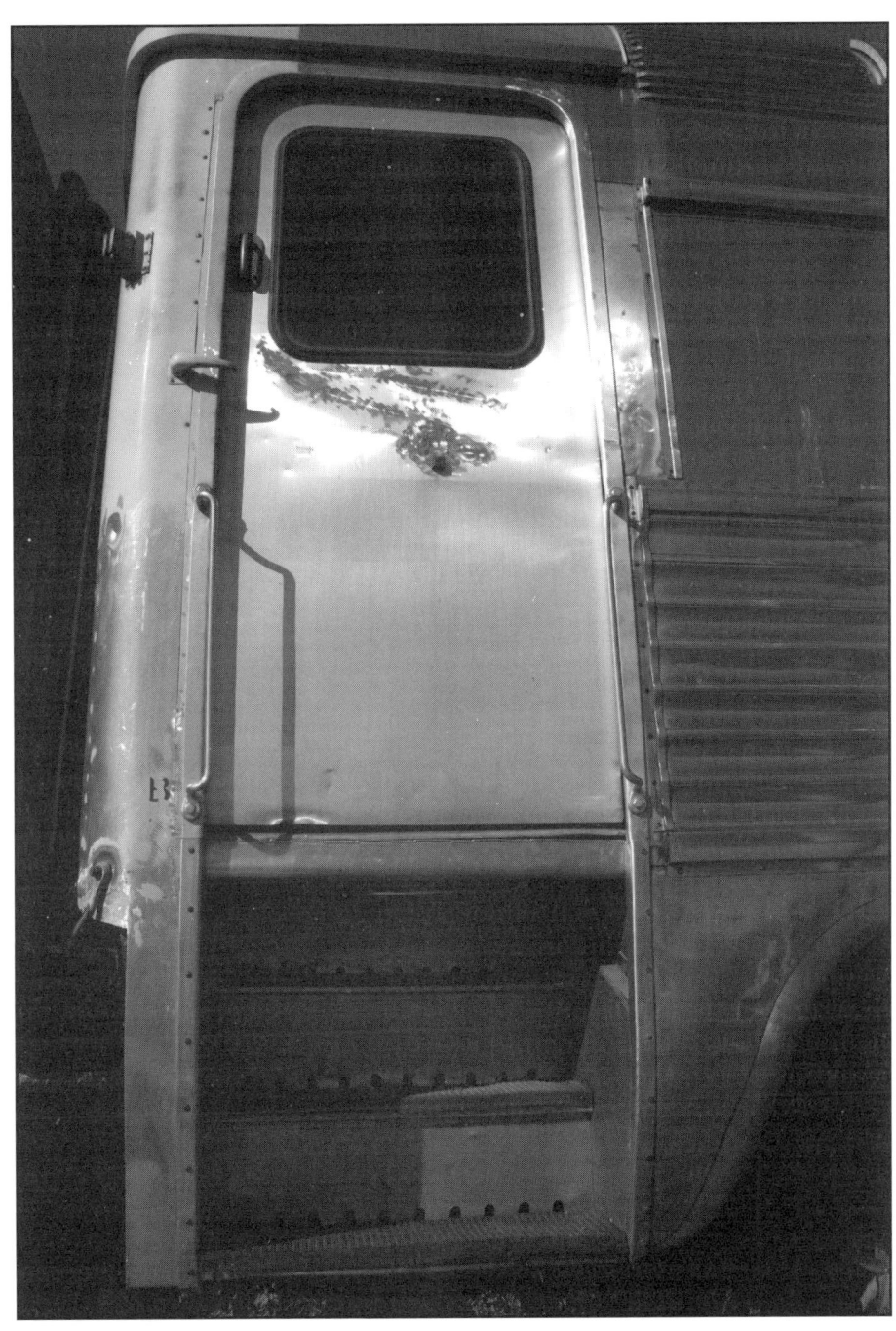

Are there ghosts aboard?

Queen Mary
Long Beach

"Curses are like chickens, they always come home to roost."
—Robert Southey

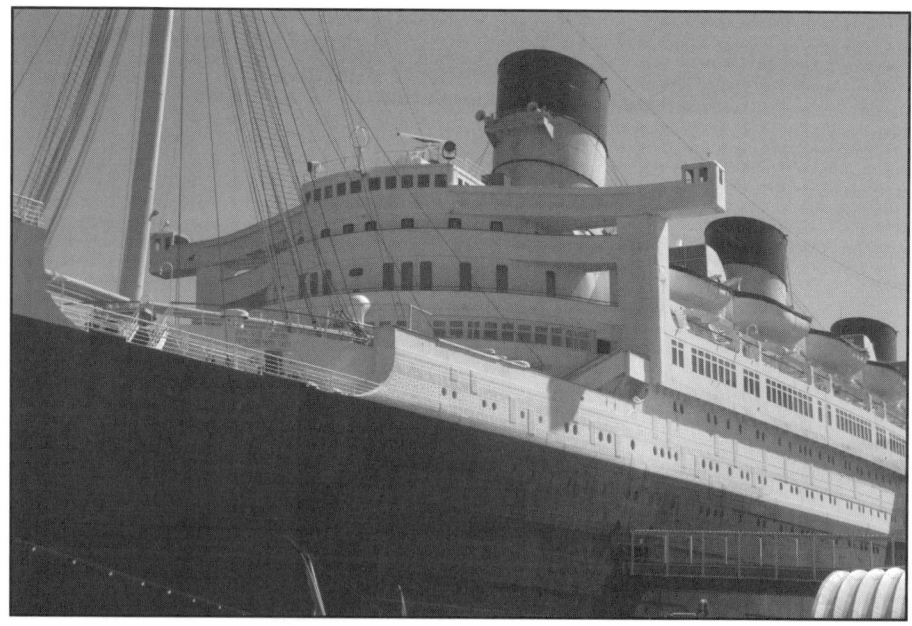

The *Queen Mary*, **Long Beach.**

ndrew and James were thrilled to be upgraded to the King George Suite on the *Queen Mary*. They had convinced their parents to stay on the ship when planning the trip from London to Los Angeles. There hadn't been time to take the tour of the *Queen Mary* but the boys didn't care. "Ghost tour," (Honestly hadn't their mother something better to do?)

Exhausted from walking all day around Knotts Berry, the family went to bed by 9 pm. Once tucked into bed, their experience on

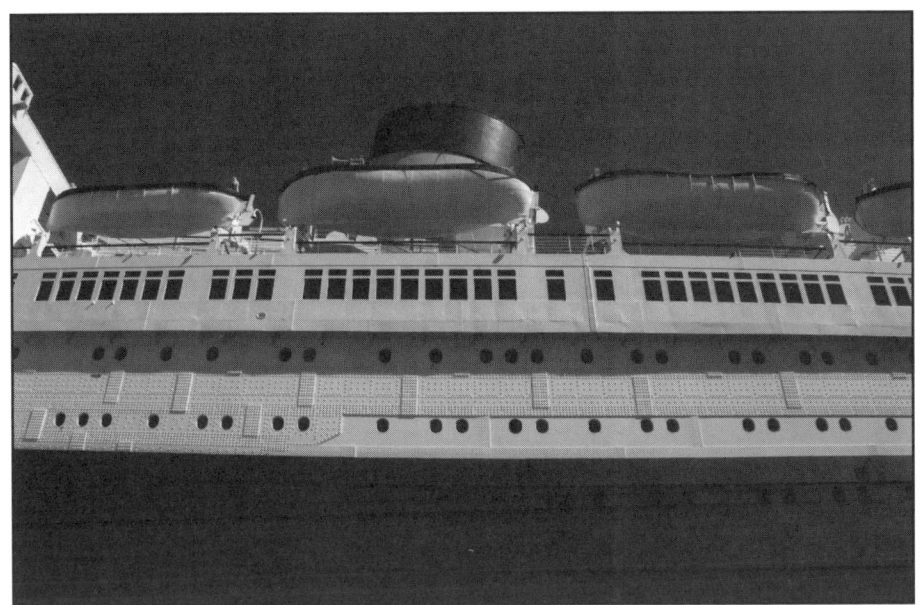

The *Queen Mary*, **Long Beach.**

the *Queen Mary* entered into another realm. First Andrew woke up; he could distinctly hear two people engaged in an animated conversation. Feeling a little sleepy, he thought the voices were in the hallway. He got out of bed to investigate, but when he looked down the corridor, it was empty. Andrew climbed back into bed, and within minutes, the voices were back. To his growing fright, he realized the voices were not out in the hall but in the room. Nudging his brother awake, Andrew told him what had just happened. James was not impressed at being woken up and thought his brother was playing a joke on him. As James struggled to get back to sleep, he too heard the voices. Before either brother could decide what to do, the lights suddenly flickered on, then off, in the room.

The next morning, they told their mother what had happened. She had slept through the entire thing. She did inquire at the desk about the room and learned Queen Mary herself, King Edward VIII (later Duke of Windsor), the Duke and Duchess of York, their daughter Princess Elizabeth, and Sir Winston Churchill, all stayed in the same suite. Who was speaking that night the boys will never know, but they will never forget their night spent aboard the *Queen Mary*.

Painted a military camouflage grey, the Grey Ghost sliced through the dark waters unnoticed. German u-boats couldn't match her incredible twenty-eight and a half knots. So highly regarded was the *Queen Mary*, that it was the only ship Winston Churchill would sail on during World War II. During wartime, she carried thousands of troops from the Pacific theater to North America and to the European theater.

Not all voyages went smoothly for the *Queen Mary*. The worst tragedy occurred in 1942, when the ship was involved in the accidental sinking of *HMS Curacoa*, 338 sailors went to their deaths. The ship was engaged in a standard zigzag pattern, but somehow the *Curacoa* got in the *Queen Mary's* path and was cut in half. The *Queen Mary* was under strict orders not to stop so she had to abandon the crew of the *Curacoa* to the icy depths. The *Queen Mary* sustained hardly any damage to her hull. You can see where the replacement steel was welded on the Ghosts and Legends Tour. It is said in this area of the ship, screams and sounds of metal ripping are heard as if the accident is replayed over and over again.

More than thirty-nine passengers and sixteen crew members have died on-board during her trans-Atlantic crossings. The spirits of those people are now seen on the lower decks, first-class swimming pool, boiler room, and several other locations throughout the ship. The ghosts, oblivious to present day, continue to swim, drink martinis, and smoke cigars as if still passengers on board the luxury ship.

Several séances and professional ghost hunters have explored the *Queen Mary*. Each time, new spirits appear, leading some to believe there is a special vortex on board. The vortex's location is given as

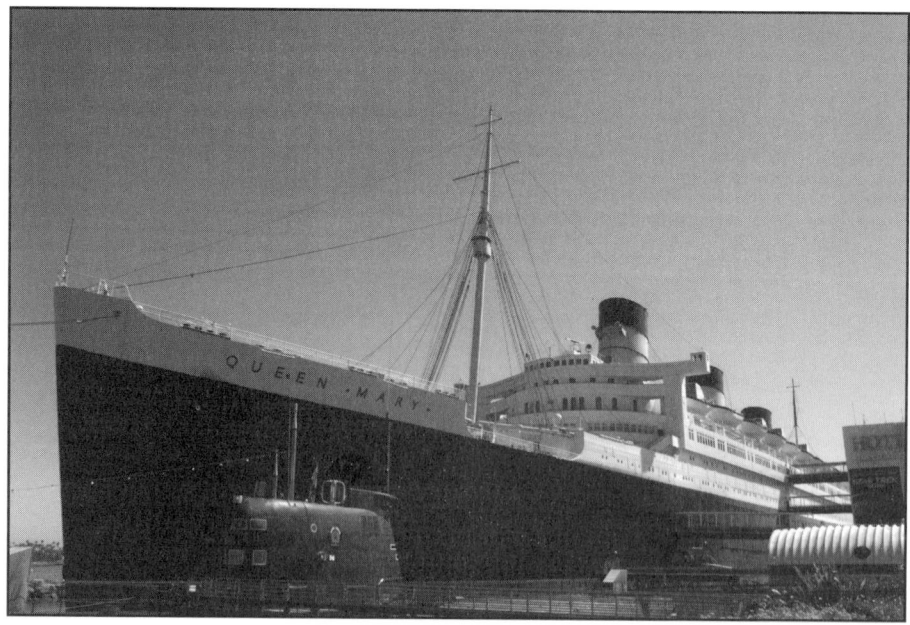

The *Queen Mary*, **Long Beach.**

the Art Deco swimming pool, which according to the ghost hunter medium, acts as a door to the next world. The day we visited, all was quiet, but that didn't stop members of the tour yelling excitedly they could see footprints!

In addition there is a spectral dog whose owner died while on board. The dog waits patiently for his master to come and claim him. There is one room said to be so haunted that no one is allowed to stay. I know of a certain small person who volunteered.

In Lady Mabel Fortescue-Harrison's prophetic words as the Queen Mary was being launched, "Most of this generation will be gone, including myself, when this event occurs. However, the RMS Queen Mary,…will know its greatest fame and popularity when she never carries another passenger."

Location

1126 Queen's Highway
Long Beach, CA
(562) 435- 3511
Web site: www.queenmary.com
Long Beach transit: See http://www.lbtransit.com/Services/Passport.aspx

If coming by car, there is a large parking lot for the *Queen Mary*. Early morning hours are best to avoid congestion. In the week and during off-season, parking isn't an issue. If you are just interested in a photo opportunity of the *Queen Mary*, it is possible to enter through the Gates and park for free, if you stay less than thirty minutes. Check before entering to make sure this is still valid. The ship is parked beside a Russian submarine. Passing by the rousing sounds of Russian music, a large billboard announces the ghost tours of the *Queen Mary*, aptly called Ghosts and legends.

R

Red Lady of Pendleton Road San Bernardino County

"As a ghost hunter, I not only investigate the facts but actively help the creatures of the nether world escape into the "happier hunting grounds."
—Hans Holzer, *Eureka Humbolt Standard*, February 15, 1964

Driving along Pendleton Road late at night, a woman in red may hail your car. You stop to let her in, but as you open the door, the woman disappears. Instinctively, you pull your hand back. Nervously, you look into the rearview mirror, unsure of what to expect, but nothing is there. You pull back onto the road and drive nonstop home. Was it just a figment of your imagination? No, it was the Lady in Red who haunts this stretch of road.

The Red Lady is believed to have died over seventy years ago in a single car crash. The impact of the crash didn't kill her. She slowly bled to death waiting for help to come. In another version of this story, she manages to free herself from the wreck and go in search of help. Along the lonely stretch of road the woman, unable to stand, pulled herself along. For some reason, in neighboring homes, no one heard her cries or the sound of the crash. When a passing motorist finally discovered her the next morning, it was much too late.

Pendleton Road attracts amateur ghost hunters in the evening hours that have managed to photograph orbs and other unexplained lights. Just another urban legend or is something really out there? You'll just have to take the drive and see.

Location

Located in Yucaitpa, just off from Oak Glen Road.
32183 Kentucky Street
(905) 795-3485
Hours: Tuesday to Saturday from 10 am until 3 pm. It is closed on certain holidays, so check before heading out.
Web site: San Bernardino County Museum; www.co.san-bernardino.ca.us/museum.
While you are there looking for the "Red Lady," you can also visit California Historical Landmark #528, the Yucaipa Adobe.

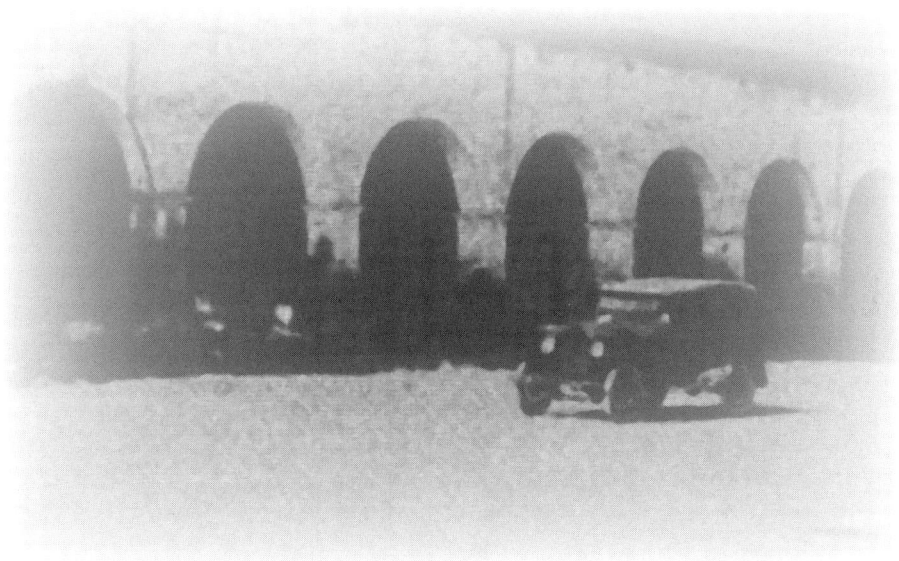

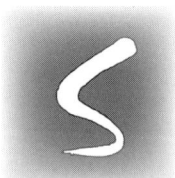

San Bernardino High
San Bernardino

"If you have money you can make the ghost and devils turn your grind stone."

—*Chinese Proverb*

Police are constantly asked to stop trespassers to this area's high school as Halloween approaches. Rumors of ghosts have circulated for more than a decade. One of the spirits haunting the school is that of a girl on her way to a prom. The car she was riding in was involved in an accident and the girl never made it to the prom. This story is very similar to one from San Luis Obispo, but in that case it was a carriage overturning.

You will not meet the spirit of Vicki on the road to school, but she will make her presence known in the school's auditorium. In 2006, Y. Alvarez interviewed a former student for *The Sun*. In the interview, Alexandra Sokoloff, 1980s high school alumna said, "I think the auditorium is home to their spirits. Things actually happened to us when we were there. Lights would go off and on all the time, there were cold spots, I mean, there were some pretty spooky things going on. Sure they were things that could have easily been faked, but they were really scary."

The ghost of poor Vicki is said to appear during prom season or on other social occasions. She is blamed whenever flickering lights or objects go astray.

The janitor also returns to the school's auditorium and makes his presence felt. Harvey is said to have died onsite. He may have died due to a work-related mishap, but this has never been documented. Students have said they can hear Harvey's keys clinking when they are in the building after school. They even hear him walking down the hallways and in the auditorium. Can teenagers hear sounds that adults can't?

The school's history dates back to 1885, which means the halls have witnessed many events. San Bernardino High was the first high school in the country.

When San Bernardino High was the only one in the area, imagine students coming from Rialto, Victorville, Highland, and other areas. {41}

Location

> While the high school is off limits, those interested in the history of San Bernardino should check out The San Bernardino County Museum
> 2024 Orange Tree Lane, Redlands, CA 92374
> Web site: www.sbcounty.gov/museum

San Diego State University
San Diego

"An idea, like a ghost, must be spoken to a little before it will explain itself."

—Charles Dickens

Is there a ghost roaming the halls of a residence at San Diego University? The residence's name means *mysterious*. Back in 1999, A. Osorio interviewed several students for a story on the haunted corridors of this dorm.

San Diego University was first founded in 1897. It is the third oldest university in the California State University system. The ghost that is said to haunt the residence is much younger. In 1974, an undergraduate was murdered in this building, and since then, it has been plagued with rumors of murder, suicide, and haunting. A graduate student interviewed for the article said, "I used to get chills when I was the only one on my floor. I heard so many stories about Zura that I don't know what to believe."

Alone in the fourth floor bathroom, a student was certain he could distinctly hear a man's voice, but no one was in the room. There was no plausible explanation for the sound of the voice, either from a ventilation shaft, open window, or hallway.

Students have reported feeling a presence on the upper floors. Known for the sunset view from the open deck on the ninth floor, some have distinctly felt uncomfortable the higher they climb. Reports include the sounds of marbles dropping in the bathroom and voices on other floors. {42}

Location

Trespassing in dorms is not allowed.
To see the campus:
5500 Campanile Drive
San Diego, CA
92182
Web site: www.sdsu.edu

San Pasqual Battlefield
San Diego

"True love is like a psychic experience. Everyone tells ghost stories, but few have ever seen a ghost."

—Anonymous

From Rancho Santa Fe to the San Pasquel Battlefield, a stallion can be heard racing through the night. Look outside; you may catch a glimpse of a rider dressed in an army uniform riding a white stallion. The moonlight bounces off his lance. Who is the rider? He is Leandro Osuna, looking for his old life, his family, and his land which vanished centuries ago. Who was Leandro?

Leandro Osuna's father was the mayor or alcade of San Diego. The Osuna family could trace its lineage back to Father Junipero Serra. Jose Maria Osuna's father had actually having traveled with Father Serra. After serving with the army he was granted land under General Pio Pico. This was known as San Dieguito, later known as Rancho Santa Fe. Juan Maria Osuna's powers included the approval of land petitions. He approved his own of course for San Dieguito (Rancho Santa Fe).

In December 1846, during the Mexican American War, Leandro's adobe was reportedly used to provision and shelter Californios after the two-day Battle of San Pasqual against Brigadier General Stephen Watts Kearney's American forces. Californios, who ruled California during the Mexican period, was the name used for people with mixed Spanish, Mexican, and native ancestry.

When news reached San Diego of the oncoming invasion of the U.S. Army, Juan Maria's sons, Leandro, Ramon, Julio, and Santiago enlisted with General Andres Pico's fabulous riding unit of 150 skilled lancers called the "Californios" stationed at Rancho San Dieguito. Leandro, leader of the unit, cut a fine figure on his favorite horse, a white stallion named "El Apache."

On December 6, 1846, the Lancers charged the U.S. Army at the Battle of San Pascual. Leandro fought fiercely, killing Captain Abraham Johnston, the first American casualty of the conflict. (Source: *Reflection Fall* 2006 Vol. 37 Issue by Rancho Santa Fe Historic Preservation Committee.)

At the battle of San Pascual, the First Dragoons under General Stephen W. Kearny were exhausted having marched from New Mexico. The Californios were more than ready for them, having rode from the Osuna Ranch. After this battle the Californios would eventually surrender to the Americans. A few days after the San Pasqual conflict, eleven Californios, including Leandro's brother, were captured and killed by Indians. This event is known as the Pauma Massacre in which the eleven men were tortured and killed. "The bodies were piled in a heap while the Indians danced around them in wild triumph all one fearful night." (*San Diego History*. April 1968, Vol. 14 Number 2.)

With the death of his brother, and later his father, events were already put in motion which would lead to Leandro's decline. He took possession of his father's ranch in 1851, but unlike his father, he did not have a good reputation for being a fair man. On the contrary, he possessed a terrible temper. His cruel treatment of the Indians may have led one of them to poison Leandro. Some sources claim he hallucinated, suffered from depression and convinced himself he had been poisoned.

Whatever the case may be, Leandro believed he had been poisoned, and instead of succumbing to an agonizing death, decided to take matters into his own hands. A bedridden Leadro called for his nephew and asked to see the boy's pistol. With this pistol he shot himself in the heart. He was only thirty-seven years old.

Leandro could not be buried in the family plot as he committed suicide. No one is absolutely certain where he was finally buried but he was not laid to "rest."

Not long after Leandro took his own life, rumors surfaced of a ghost carrying a shining lance riding a white stallion. People whispered Leandro rode on El Apache at night because he was unable to find peace. "Soon after his death whispers went about the ranch, concerning strange events that occurred when the moon was full and the wind piped a sad song through the tree leaves."

Leandro Osuna is the best-known and historically documented phantom, but some say the San Pasqual battlefield is home to more ghosts. On certain nights, Leandro has company on the battlefield as the fallen soldiers buried there are said to rise again.

Location

15808 San Pasqual Valley Road
Escondido, CA 92027
(760) 737- 2201
Web site: www.parks.ca.gov/
At time of publication, park was closed due to the Witch Fire.
Juan Maria Osuna Adobe: preserved but not open to the public.

Sea Serpent
Long Beach

"When we are alone for a long time, we people space with phantoms."
—The Horla Guy de Maupassant

During 1907, there was a rash of sea serpent sightings along the Southern Californian coast. From March of that year until December, every old sea salt had either seen one or knew someone that had. Here are a few of the highlights from that year. It is interesting to note that sea serpent sightings further up the coast did not peak until twenty years later.

In March 1907, a peculiar creature visited the Long Beach shore. Three bristling horns emerged from the water as fishermen on the outer wharf caught sight of the creature. Fishing rods were dropped and tackle boxes abandoned as the men hurried to the edge of the pier to get a better look. They reckoned the monster was at least fifteen feet long.

Its long tail was split for a distance of three feet into three sections no less. Incredibly, each end was tipped with a barb! The monstrous creature swam for over an hour near the breaker line in full view of the lifeguard's station. Luckily, the men told the reporter from the Los Angeles paper, no one had yet arrived at the bathhouse. Up and down, the creature jumped in the surf flashing its tail. (Hmmm.....yes very threatening behavior indeed.)

Based on the creature's exuberance in the water, it was decided the men had witnessed a young sea serpent at play. Concerns were raised that the creature might return with its mother. What could anyone do to protect himself from such a creature?

In December 1910, it did return or at least one of its kind. A Mrs. Jessie McDonald was surf fishing in Long Beach when a sea monster grabbed hold of her legs. She struggled with the creature but only succeeded in having her entire body entangled in the tentacles. Her cries brought nearby fishermen to her rescue. They tried unsuccessfully to pull the creature off her. In the struggle, Mrs. McDonald fainted. One man quickly reached for his knife and slashed away at the creature until it let go. Mrs. McDonald suffered from shock, but had no other injuries. She was happy to return to her home in Tuscon, Arizona, and had no plans to ever brave the Long Beach surf again.

Mrs. Jessie McDonald's sea monster might have another name: Giant Pacific Octopus. Its arms can measure up to sixteen feet and weigh around fifty-ninety pounds each. One, according to the National Parks Conservation Association, grew to be six hundred pounds! {43}

Location

There are eleven miles of oceanfront and several beaches to choose from.

Web site: www.ci.long-beach.ca.us

Sea Serpent Ocean Park

"Ye auld fishermen
Need alla be thinkin'
To see me so strong
As I waggle me tail,
Yo billows along."
   —Excerpt from *Song of the Sea Serpent* (*LA Herald* 1907)

The headline "Sea Serpent Nears Shore" blazed from the *Los Angeles Herald* on September 12, 1907. Long before the silver screen would create one, Los Angeles had its own hometown sea serpent.

In 1907, two old-time residents of Ocean Park got the shock of a lifetime when they spotted a sea serpent just off shore. The sea serpent had been seen in this area a few times in the previous five years.

Ed Matthew, a local resident, and George Franklyn, a visitor to LA, were fishing early in the morning when they spied the creature. "The first thing which attracted my attention was when a huge head bobbed up above the surface of the water," said Mr. Franklyn. He described the creature as being stripped and roughly thirty feet long. He also noted a fin on its back and two on the side with which the creature "lashed" at the water. The water around the creature foamed dramatically. Thanks to a pair of binoculars, he was able to see the serpent's details.

Word quickly spread from the docks into the town bringing hoards of people to the shore. Soon "(sic)…the rail of the pier was lined with a curious throng who watched the antics of the huge creature as it swam back and forth on top of the waves." One spectator brought a rifle, but luckily for the "monster," it did not swim close enough to the pier to be shot. The creature stayed for about twenty minutes and then swam out to sea.

The creature never returned to this pier, but was spotted a few more times in the waters off Long Beach. {44}

Location

A neighborhood located in Santa Monica, just north of Venice.
Web site: To read about the very interesting history of Ocean Park see http://oceanpark.was

---

Sea Serpent False Alarm Malibu

"Unfortunately, our feelings do not always respect the law of probabilities and to me that evening, the possible and the impossible were equally disquieting."
—Ambrose Bierce

D id you hear about the sea monster that washed ashore in Malibu in 1963? A resident of Malibu, Carole Richards, hadn't expected to find a creature on the shore. Her hysterical cries alerted another resident, Phyllis Hughes. It wasn't long before the Malibu community was alerted to the fact of a sea monster in their midst.

An unidentified man driving by the beach stopped and decided to investigate. He thought it would be a great idea if he took the creature with him. A small car with a massive creature draped over it catches the attention of law enforcement even in California. He would later claim he was taking it to the proper authorities.

After all this fuss, it was discovered the monster was in fact an eighteen-foot long-rare oarfish. It is currently on display at the Los Angeles County Museum of Natural History.

Location

900 Exposition Boulevard
Los Angeles, CA
(213) 763-DINO
Hours- 9:30 am to 5 pm Monday-Friday
10 am to 5 pm Saturday, Sunday, and Holidays
AdMission is free the first Tuesday of each month.
Web site: www.nhm.org

Spirit of The Rios-
Caledonia Adobe
San Miguel

"A ghost is someone who hasn't made it—in other words, whose dead, and they don't know they're dead."

—Sylvia Browne

The Rios-Caledonia Adobe is a century-old inn and stage stop on the old Mission trail between San Francisco and San Diego. The home was built in 1835 by area Indians. It is located on grounds that once belonged to Mission San Miguel. Many families have lived at this adobe. For a complete history, please see the official adobe Web site given below. Later, it would not only be a residence, but school, post office, and even a dressmaking shop. In 1964, the San Luis Obispo County Board of Supervisors purchased the home.

Since opening as a museum, the spirit of a young boy is said to reside on the second floor. He might be one of the twelve children belonging to the Rios family who lived there in 1851.

"According to Wally V. Ohles, a long-time docent with Friends of the Adobe, he's never seen anything, but many visitors have told stories of seeing the ghost. Since 1971-72, he has worked with friends of the adobes. "This building to me is one of the most interesting places in Northern San Obispo County."

Young visitors report seeing the ghostly child more often than older patrons. Once a couple and their four-year-old boy went up the stairs to tour the adobe. When they turned to leave, their little boy waved goodbye to somebody he saw in the corner of the room. When asked, he said that he was saying goodbye to the little boy. {45}

Location

700 S. Main Street
San Miguel, California
(805) 467-3357
The adobe is open Friday to Sunday from 11 am until 4 pm.
Web site: www.rios-caledoniaadobe.org/
California Historical Landmark No. 939.

Stage Coach Inn
Ventura

"All houses are haunted. All persons are haunted. Throngs of spirits follow us everywhere. We are never alone."

—Barney Sarecky

The stage pulled up in front of El Hotel Grande in Conejo. Many of the weary passengers were grain and cattle buyers visiting the area ranches. A man, named Pierre, without a word to his fellow passengers whom he had grown more than tired of, also stepped off the coach. He paid for a room and trudged wearily up the staircase, noticing the bullet holes as he walked. *Bad luck*, he thought absently.

Sometime between checking in and going to his room, one of those bullet holes in the Conejo Inn staircase would be from the gun which killed Pierre. Whether he had been the intended victim or simply got in the way of a gun battle, the result was the same—Pierre, the stagecoach traveler, lay dead at the top of those stairs.

Of course, we really don't know what Pierre's last day was like or why he traveled to the Inn, but his presence at the original Conejo Inn was authenticated by medium Sybil Leek. In 1966, then curator Dr. Cyrill Anderson invited parapsychologist Hans Holzer and medium Sybil Leek to the Inn to conduct a séance. During this visit, the ghost at the Inn was identified as Pierre Duvon or Duval, a sheepherder. According to Ms. Leek, she felt the man had been shot in 1889. Sybil Leek felt a presence and a great deal of disturbance at the head of the stairs. The stairs in the original building were riddled with bullet holes.

Cold spots always signaled Pierre's presence. Visitors would report feeling uneasy and some rooms became uncomfortable, almost clammy. One well-known incident published in Hans Holzer book, *Ghosts of the Golden West,* occurred when the building was being moved. "A workman was checking to be sure all was secure when a piece of two by four came hurling out of an upstairs window, narrowly missing him." The workman was certain there was an otherworldly explanation for this. No other poltergeist activity attributed to Pierre was ever published.

When fire raced through the structure in 1970, someone took a picture of the event. This photo can be seen on the museum Web site; the address is given below. In the shot, there appears to be the image of a person in the smoke and flames. A few have speculated it is Pierre's spirit, but you will have to check it for yourself.

James Hammel constructed the original Inn, eleven years after the end of the Civil War for the grand sum of $7, 200. He hoped the Butterfield Stage, an overland route from St. Louis to San Francisco, would stop at the Inn, virtually guaranteeing him a lucrative income. This never materialized; instead, only the local stage stopped at his inn. When the Inn opened, it had large balconies on two sides of the way station. It became known as El Hotel Grande or The Big Hotel. It was an elegant lodging house marking the halfway point between Los Angeles and Santa Barbara. Inn patrons were cattle and grain buyers visiting the Conejo's big ranches, homesteaders, and land speculators. From 1887 to 1909, the hotel served as a regular depot for the Coast Stage Lines, which operated thrice weekly carrying both passengers and mail.

Over the years, the inn was rented out as a military school from 1925-1931, a chicken and steakhouse, and clothing store called Tantony's. The Inn faced certain destruction in the 1960s when it was in the path of a new freeway. The historical society managed to secure a lot nearby and arranged for the entire building to be moved. Sadly, the inn burned to the ground, April 1970. Once again, the Conejo Historical Society stepped in and the entire structure was rebuilt. Today it operates as the Stagecoach Inn Museum. {46}

Location

51 South Ventura Park Road
Newbury Park, CA 91320
(805) 498-9441
Hours: Wednesday to Sunday 1 pm to 4 pm
* Closed Easter, Thanksgiving, Christmas, and New Years Day
Web site: www.stagecoachmuseum.org

Stanley Ranch Museum
Garden Grove

"The lawn is pressed by unseen feet, and ghosts return gently at twilight, gently go at dawn..."

—T.S. Eliot,

Stepping inside the Stanley-Ware home, you expect Lillian Agnes Staley herself to greet you. Quite suddenly, the stillness of the home is broken by the soft cries of a baby emanating from the upstairs. Maybe the rest of your group has gone up? But when you try to climb the stairs, you find your legs just won't move. You don't get winded that easily. Before you blame it on lack of exercise, blame it on the ghost of L. Agnes Ware Stanley.

A former curator of the Stanley House was convinced the home was haunted, not just by Agnes, but also by several other spirits, including a crying baby. Agnes Ware Stanley was very ill at the end of her life—so ill in fact, she found small tasks almost impossible to accomplish. One of these tasks, which most people take for granted, was climbing the stairs. Many visitors to the home are overcome with a deep sense of frustration and feel as if they are being tugged backwards as they proceed to the second level of the home. Agnes Ware Stanley, a trained schoolteacher, must have felt her limited mobility to be a deep source of aggravation, after such an active life.

Walking through the home, pay special attention to the pictures. People have noticed the image of Mr. Stanley changing as they watch. Look closely at his mouth; you might see him smile. Other pictures in the home are also known to change, but in a sinister way. Straight out of a B horror movie, a portrait of an unidentified man sports drops of blood around the neck.

The Stanley House was built by rancher Edward Ware. Construction began in 1891, but was not completely finished until 1892. The Victorian-style farmhouse is perfectly preserved thanks to the Garden Grove Historical Society. A small manicured garden with seasonal plantings and an inviting white gazebo speaks of Mr. Ware's interest in horticulture. Edward Ware built the home for his wife, Mary, and their daughter, Lillian Agnes. In 1905, Agnes married Arthur C. Stanley and returned to live in her family home after her parents passed away. After Agnes died, her son, Emerson, in 1971, donated the home to the city. The home presents a small window into Garden Grove's past when it was a farming community. It is located on a two-acre park called Heritage Park.

Location

12174 Euclid Avenue
Garden Grove, CA 92840
(714) 530 8871

Star of India
San Diego

"I saw the pale student of unhallowed arts kneeling beside the thing he had put together. I saw the hideous phantasm of a man stretched out..."
—Mary Shelley

The life of a stowaway was anything but glamorous. The crew's cramped sleeping quarters looked four star to a stowaway. Contrary to storybook images of sleeping under the stars, the stowaway's life was on par with a rat; in fact, the rat might have been better at scrounging food.

In 1884, a boy named John Campbell decided to gamble on an iron-hull sailing ship. He was discovered and put to work. Everybody on board earned their passage, including those not on the ship's roster. John lost his footing when he was working high in the ship's rigging. The crew watched helplessly as he fell 100 feet.

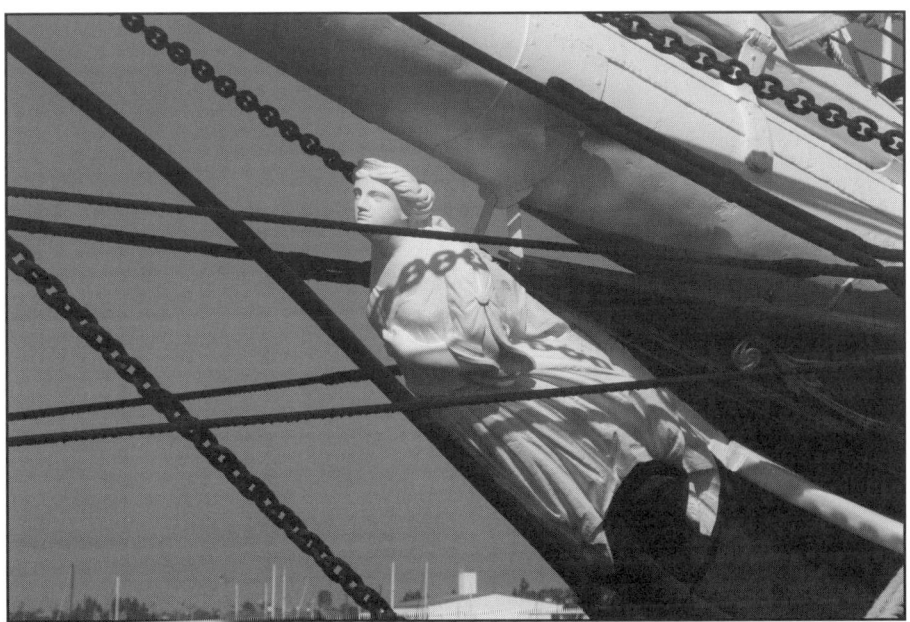

The *Star of India*, **San Diego.**

137

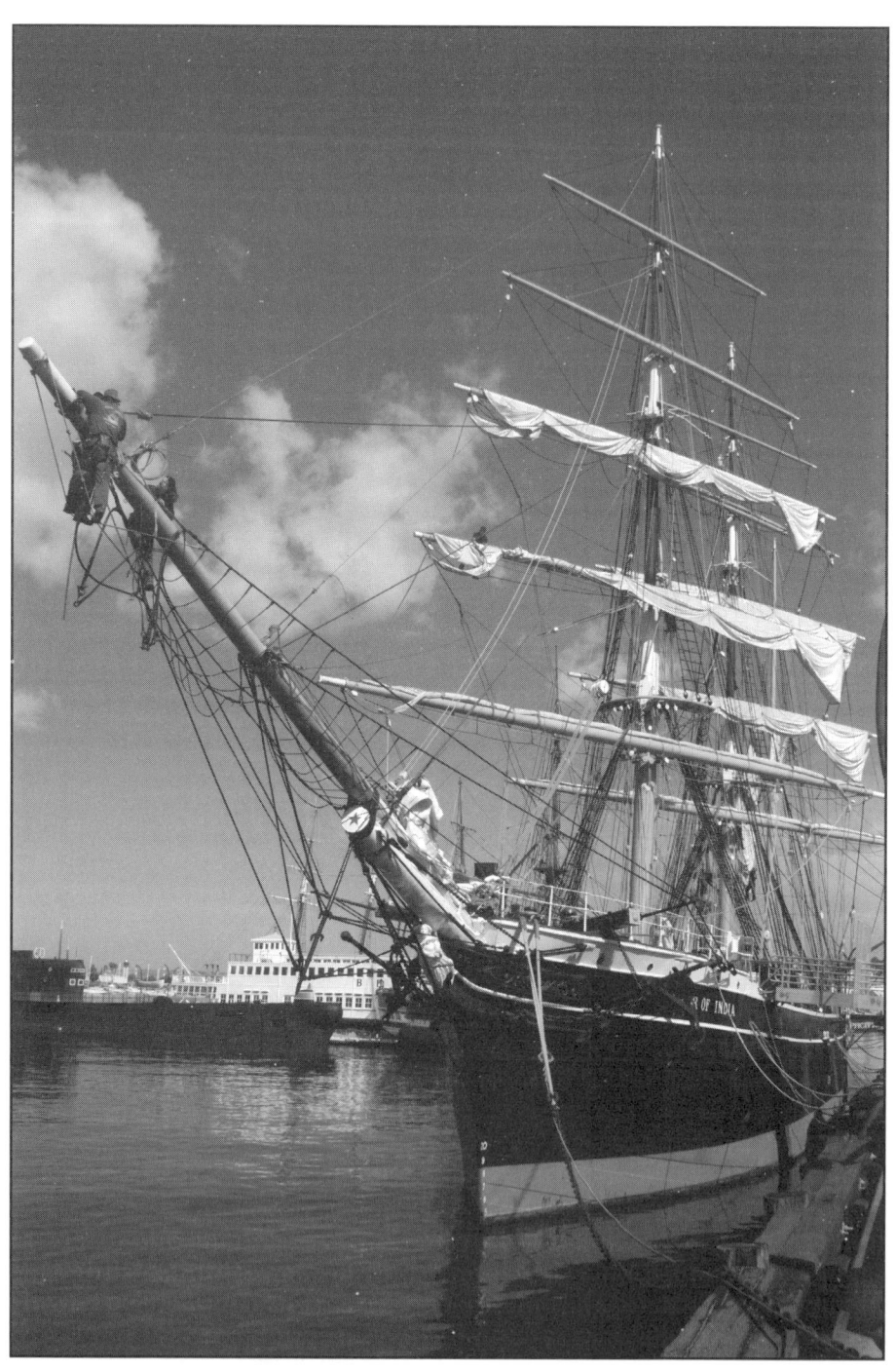

The *Star of India,* **San Diego.**

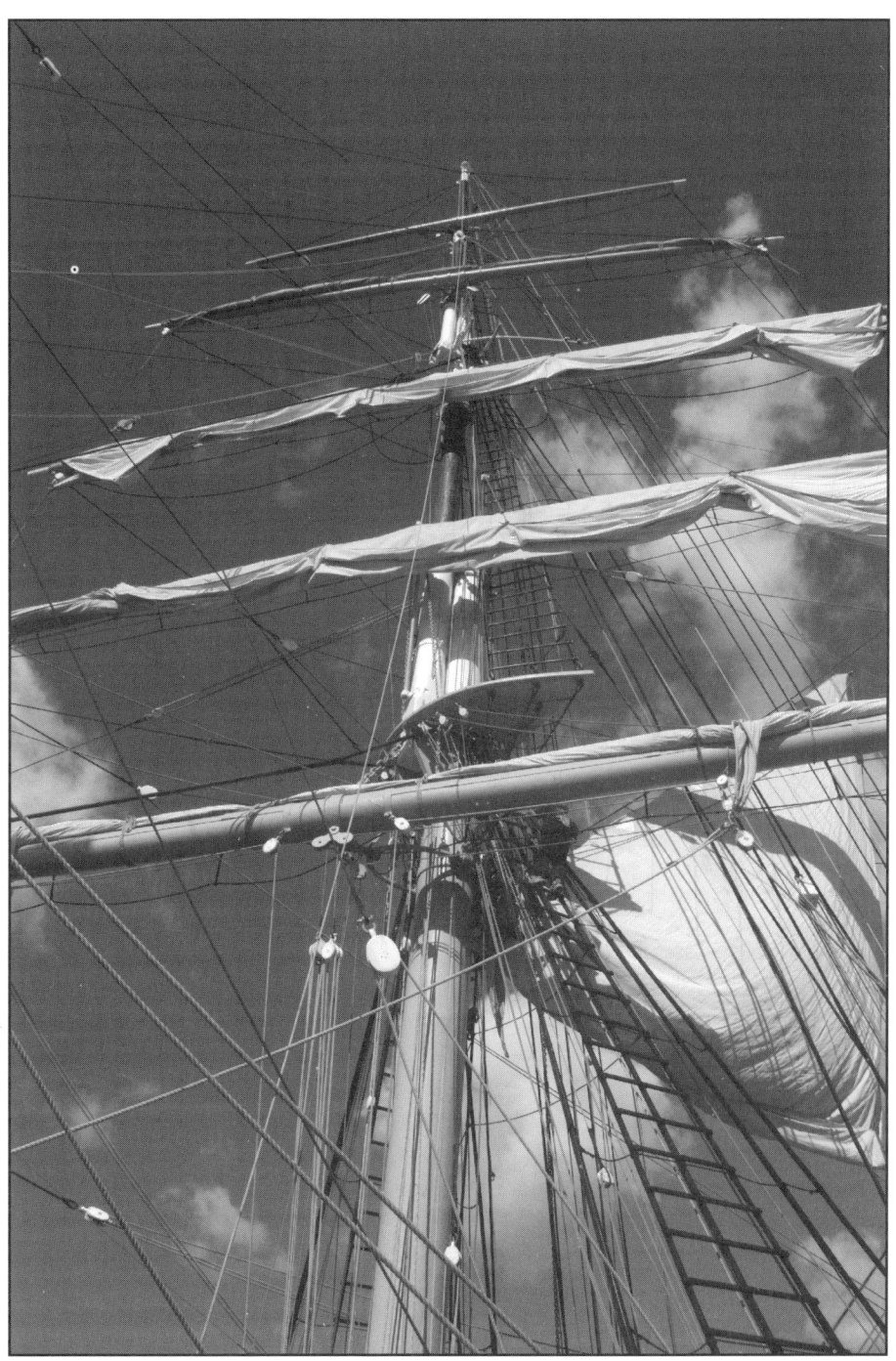

The *Star of India*, San Diego.

John lingered for days before dying. One sea faring custom was to sew the dead man into his hammock, and throw him overboard to ensure his ghost stayed buried. His presence has been detected near the base of the mast where he fell. One lady on a recent visit to the ship was certain she could feel someone by her side. It was such an overwhelming creepy feeling, sending shivers up her arms. It was only after her visit, her daughter informed her of the ghostly legend.

The *Star of India*, was originally the *Euterpe*, a sailing ship launched in 1863 from the Isle of Man. For thirty-five years it sailed under a British Flag before becoming a salmon-fishing vessel in Alaska where it was renamed. In 1927, she sailed into San Diego and became a museum. Badly neglected for years, she was not restored until 1976. Today, the ship is part of the Maritime Museum of San Diego, welcoming visitors onto her deck. On regularly held ghost tours, tourists learn of the ghost of a Chinese man killed when the crew lowered the anchor into the storage locker where he was hiding. Visitors heard pots and pans moving and the smell of baked bread from an unused stove. Remember, according to legend, it takes thirteen stitches with the last one through the nose to keep a sailor down. Obviously nothing is keeping down some former members of the ship's crew.

Location

Maritime Museum of San Diego
1492 North Harbor Drive
San Diego, California 92101
Hours: Open daily from 9 am to 8 pm
Open until 9 pm on Memorial Day through Labor Day
Web site: www.sdmaritime.com

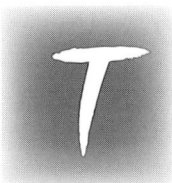

The Bluebird Motel
Cambria

"I'm not afraid of werewolves or vampires or haunted hotels, I'm afraid of what real human beings to do other real human beings."
—Walter J. Williams

A pair of tourists from England spent the day sight seeing in the town of Cambria. It was not their first trip to the town. They had been there the previous year. After a full day in the sun, they were looking forward to their comfortable room back at the Bluebird Motel. They put away their purchases and climbed wearily into bed. In the early hours of the morning, they were awoken by a noise in their room. Peering into the darkness both ladies saw the image of a woman in Victorian dress. Even more unbelievable the phantom woman seemed to be admiring their clothes! The apparition then disappeared.

These visitors were not the only ones to experience something odd at the Bluebird Inn. A worker at the Inn left after six months. Why? The family found it extremely disquieting to have objects move from one room to another by themselves. Also, objects would simply disappear, only to reappear days or weeks later.

The present owners have found the motel a perfect place to live. They have experienced lights turning on and off by themselves and objects moving, but have never seen the ghost who is believed to be Mary Leah Inman Lull.

According to the Cambria Historical Society's site, she was born Mary Leah Barnhardt of Illinois. She married Dolphin Inman in 1854. After his death, she married Vermont native, George Lull, who came to San Luis Obispo County in the late 1850s. The two resided in Cambria where Lull was a partner in a general merchandise store, Grant, Lull and Company, which also operated a store in San Simeon. (This store is still preserved.) It wasn't until George Lull retired that he built Mary her home, today known as the Bluebird Inn.

George, whose spirit has not been sighted at the Inn, died in 1899, aged sixty-eight. Mary has often been spotted in an upper window of the home. Is she still waiting for George to return from the medical treatment he sought in San Francisco for an undisclosed illness? After George's death, Mary sold the home to a woman who turned it into a rooming house. Cabins were later added in the 1930s, and in the 1950s more additions were made.

Mary Leah Inman's spirit is most strongly felt throughout the original home. If traveling to Cambria, look into the upper window of the home; you just might spot Mary looking back. {47}

Location

1880 Main Street
Cambria, CA 93428
1-800-552-5434
Web site: www.bluebirdmotel.com

The Clubhouse at This Old House Cayucos

"My life has been strangely bound up with extraordinary incidents, some of which occurred before I had any connection with the principal actors in them, or, indeed, before I even knew of their existence ."
—*The Poor Clare*, Elizabeth Gaskell

Walking down the corridor, the night manager stopped mid step. He could see the reflection of a man through a glass door—not unusual for a restaurant, but no one was on the other side. As for the reflection, it simply evaporated before the man's eyes. Something is going on at this San Luis Obispo restaurant.

Some things have been reported in local San Luis Obispo papers and television shows. The current owner, Andrew Adams, is quoted in a 2007 October issue of *The Tribune*, "….likes the idea of ghosts in his establishment, in fact, he believes they're guardians because they like what he's doing with the place."

During the renovation process, the spirits made themselves known to Andrew by moving objects in the bar area. He heard a loud crash that turned out to be three smashed wine glasses. They didn't just fall off the shelf, but moved eight feet away from the wall and then fell. Even to the most hardened skeptic that Andrew came across during the renovations is amazing. He found old employee logs from the 1930s, which talked about—what else?—ghosts. The ghosts of The Clubhouse may be connected to when the building was used as a sanitarium for the poor in 1917. Thanks to Andrew's discovery of the logbook, paranormal activity can be dated to the 1930s.

Recently, *The Tribune* invited paranormal investigator Joyce Davantzis to visit the Clubhouse. She felt there was a love triangle at the inn. She also sensed a car crash and a sick child. As of this printing, no one had ever seen the spirit of a child, only its handprints. {48}

Location

740 Foothill Boulevard
San Luis Obispo, CA 93405
Tel (805) 704-6000

The Cursed Ship
San Clemente

"Parapsychology will be an ordinary science in our lifetime."
—Hans Holzer, *Eureka Humbolt Standard*, February 15, 1964

It was 1927, the height of prohibition, when George Michaelis bought the *Grey Ghost*. He couldn't believe how cheap she was—a steal. Maybe George should have looked into her hoodoo history a little more closely, but with big dreams for his business, shipping cases of illegal rum, he didn't bother with details.

Unaware of the curse of the *Grey Ghost*, George set out with her for Point Vicente. He had secured himself a bit of legal business towing a $30,000 yacht. The water was calm and the job routine, but within minutes, things went awry on the boat. It was as if another pair of hands had taken hold of the wheel causing the boat to be grounded. The yacht was completely wrecked. George should have realized something was amiss. But his eyes were still set on rum running. He patched up the *Grey Ghost*.

A few weeks went by without incident and George successfully put the incident out of his mind. While George was lobster fishing near San Clemente Island, the phantom of the *Grey Ghost* struck again. The boat slipped her moorings and left George stranded on San Clemente Island. With no provisions, he decided his best bet would be to climb one of the island's steep cliffs in order to signal for help. While climbing the cliff, he fell and fractured his leg, effectively putting an end to that plan. George managed to stay alive by eating cactus pearls and drinking rain water. Two fishermen discovered George eight days later suffering from blood poisoning and exposure.

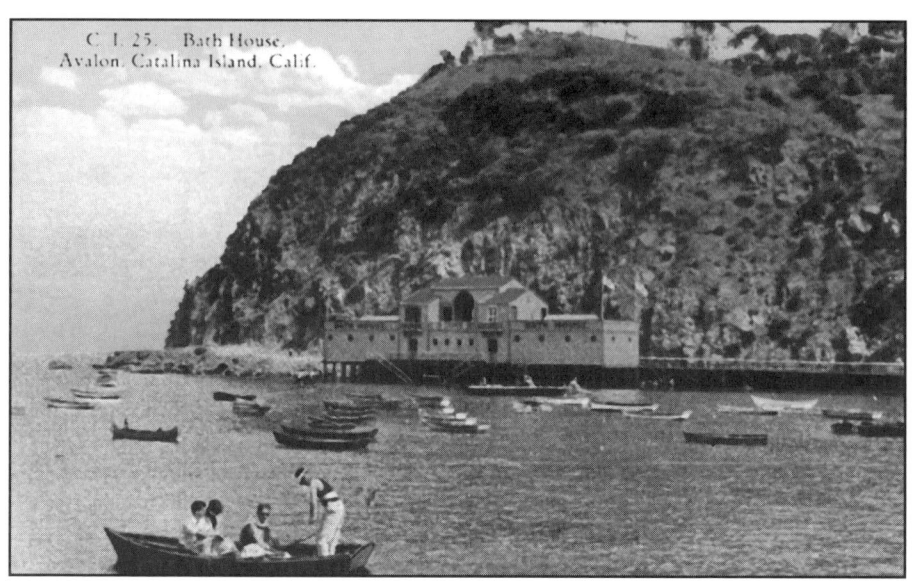

Vintage postcard of the Bath House Avalon, Catalina Island. Published by Western Publishing & Novelty., Los Angeles, California.

After his near death experience with the *Grey Ghost,* her cursed history came to light. Only two months before George bought the boat, a man named Eli Kelly had owned it. Eli Kelly and his fishing partner, James McKinley, got stranded on the island. The men struggled to stay alive. The ordeal would be too much for James McKinley who died leaving Eli Kelly alone. Eli turned to cannibalism to keep from starving. When he was finally rescued, he was completely insane. The mutilated body of his friend, James McKinley was found in the *Grey Ghost.*

After George's near-death experience, talk amongst local sailors was of James McKinley's ghost. The ghost was seeking revenge for what had transpired at San Clemente Island. Who ever owned the boat would most certainly meet with bad luck or worse, death.

As for the *Grey Ghost,* it would appear in the news one last time. Just weeks after George's hospitalization, the *Grey Ghost* blew up and sank off San Clemente with a cargo of rum. Maybe the ghost of James McKinley was finally laid to rest—or are phantom sailors able to sail phantom boats?!

Location

San Clemente is owned by the U.S. Navy and as such is not open to the public.

The Del Coronado
San Diego

"Be silent in that solitude, Which is not loneliness- for then The spirits of the dead, who stood In life before thee, are again In death around thee.."
—Edgar Allan Poe

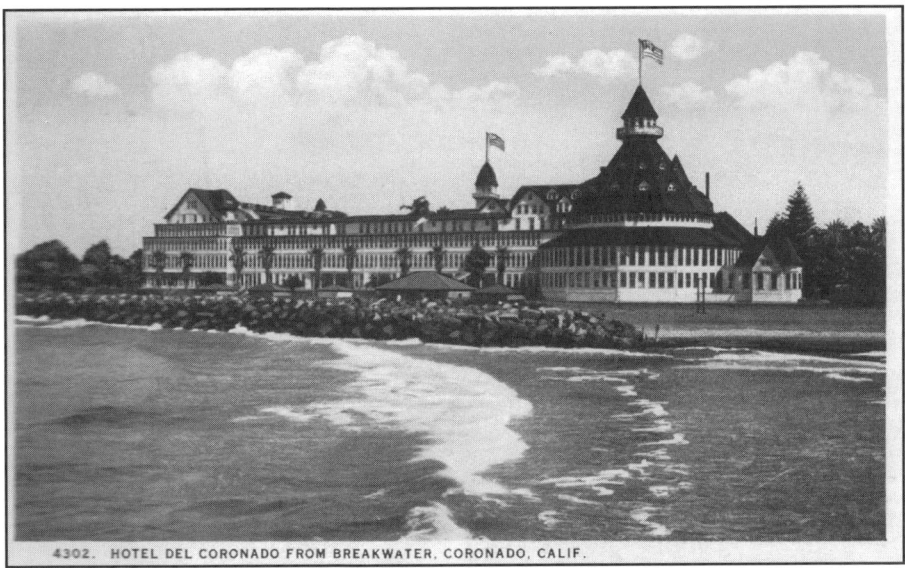

4302. HOTEL DEL CORONADO FROM BREAKWATER. CORONADO, CALIF.

The Hotel Del Coronado, San Diego.

Long before Marilyn Monroe would pose for cameras outside the Hotel Del Coronado while filming *Some Like It Hot,* there was a guest who in death would eclipse even the most famous visitors to the hotel. For over a hundred years, this guest has been the resident spirit of the hotel. Her name is Kate Morgan and she is as synonymous with the Hotel Del Coronado as its trademark red Victorian turrets and first-class accommodations. So entwined with the history of the hotel is Kate, that she is acknowledged on the hotel's Web site, and even in books available in the hotel's bookstore.

But it wasn't always this way. Between checking into the Hotel Del Coronado under a false name and being discovered dead five days later, she was a hotel's worst nightmare. Murdered guests, or guests who commit suicide, are not events which make a public relations department say, "Great, we'll use this in our next brochure." So what transpired over the years from 1892 until the present? Read on...

Kate was born Kate Farmer in Hamburg, Iowa, in 1865. Her mother died in childbirth and her grandmothers raised Kate. Author Barbara Smith writes, "He [her father] taught her how to play poker and not much else." On December 30, 1885, she married Tom Morgan. Though Tom had been a medical student, he pursued his poker "degree" instead. The pair are said to have ridden the rails swindling fellow gamblers using Kate's allure and Tom's skill with cards.

It is only conjecture, but something is believed to have gone very wrong with this pair. When Kate got off the train in San Diego, she was alone. It was almost Thanksgiving and a twenty-four-year old and possibly pregnant Kate made her way to the Hotel Del Coronado. The glamorous resort had only been open four years when Kate picked up the pen at the front desk and wrote Lottie A. Bernard in the register. She told the desk her brother would be meeting her soon and, of course, he never did. Kate was given the key to Room 3312 (Room 3327 today), and for the next five days, she was just another visitor at the Del.

On the fifth day, her lifeless body was found on a staircase leading to the beach. She was dead, a gunshot wound to the head. The coroner would rule the death suicide. The papers had a field day when it was learned Lottie A. Bernard had been a pseudonym. What kind of "lady" checks into a hotel with no luggage and under a different name? Interviews were conducted with staff that said the woman seemed frail and unwell. Medical help was offered but the woman turned it down. She was also remembered as a figure dressed in black, always alone, and at times crying.

When the coroner made a public appeal for help in identifying the lady, one man would step forward to say he had seen her in a heated argument with a man on the train the day she had disembarked in San Diego. This man, whoever he was, was never identified. Was it Tom? There are even more questions. Alan M. May in his book, *The legend of Kate Morgan: The Search for the Ghost of the Hotel Del Coronado*, thought Kate may have been murdered. After exhaustively researching her story, he found out the bullet in her skull did not match her gun.

Today, the spirit of Kate is said to manifest itself in her original room. Guests have experienced flickering lights, televisions that mysteriously turn off, then on and back off again, and scarier are the sounds of footsteps—no, not coming from the corridor, but directly above the room, which is impossible as there is no room above.

Once, she left behind an impression of herself in the bed. This was discovered when a hotel employee attempted to straighten out the bed, but it was as if an unseen body was weighing down the sheets. Even more puzzling are the brief glimpses of a woman with long dark hair wearing period dress seen throughout the hotel. Countless employees, guests, and psychic researchers to the Hotel Del Coronado have seen this apparition.

Kate Morgan's story is just as mystifying today as it was to the public in 1892. Though Kate was an anonymous guest, for those five days at the Del Coronado, now her spirit is remembered.

Location

1500 Orange Avenue
Coronado, CA 92118
1-800-468-3533
Web site: www.hoteldel.com

The Drum Barracks
Wilmington

"I have never yet heard of a murderer who was not afraid of a ghost."
—John Philpot Curran

Standing in one of the mansion's restored rooms, visitors to the Drum Barracks were puzzled when the strong scent of pipe smoke wafted through the room. Surely smoking wasn't allowed on the premises. Thinking it had come in through an open window, they continued to examine the room. One person's attention was diverted by the sound of loud footsteps. Thinking it was a docent, to whom she planned to complain about the smoke, she turned just in time to see a ghostly image of a man disappear into the door frame. No one else saw the image or heard the steps that day.

The ghost of the Civil War soldier is not a lonely spirit. He has quite a bit of company at the barracks. Images of women, men, and children are seen throughout the fort. The Drum Barracks has even been profiled on *Most Haunted*.

The Drum Barracks is named for Lieutenant Colonel Richard Drum (Assistant Adjutant General of the Pacific Department of the U.S. Army in Wilmington). It is the only major American Civil War landmark in Southern California. It was located on sixty acres of land which Phineas Banning, the founder of Wilmington, sold to the federal government for a total of $1. Fort Drum was the military headquarters for the Union's southwestern headquarters. From here, expeditions were sent to Arizona, New Mexico, and troops were even placed on Catalina Island. The camp operated from 1861 to 1871, and closed shortly after the Civil War ended. In the following years, it served as a hospital, a Methodist co-ed college, a private home, and a boarding house.

In 1962, the building was going to be torn down, but concerned citizens and the owners of the remaining buildings organized an effort to save the historic site. On the day a historical plaque was placed at the site by the California State Park Commission, the Knott's Berry Farm Ghost Patrol, attired in Union Army costumes, performed. A dress ball featuring antebellum costumes was also held. Just maybe amongst the crowds were a few of the original occupants of Drum Barracks. In 1987, the Drum Barracks museum opened to the public.

After the barracks opened to the public, visitors and workers reported paranormal activity at the facility. The phantom images date back to when the barracks was a military operation. Women appearing in period dress are seen and heavy footsteps, presumably belonging to soldiers, are frequently heard at the museum. Tobacco smoke is not the only smell indicating the presence of spirits, but also women's lavender perfume. And no, smoking is not allowed. The scariest sounds at Drum Barracks are those of chains being dragged across the floors. When admiring the detailed restoration of Drum Barracks, keep an eye out for its former occupants.

Location

South of Banning Park at 1053 Cary Avenue
Wilmington, CA
(310) 548-7509
For tour times see the Web site.
Web site: www.drumbarracks.org
California Historical Landmark No. 169

The Sirens
Channel Islands

"The dim light of the waning moon shone into the chamber; it fell upon the face of my antagonist, and one glance froze the blood in my veins. It was he!—who I had murdered, glaring upon me with eyes which no mortal could..."

—*The Minotaur,* J.Y. Akerman

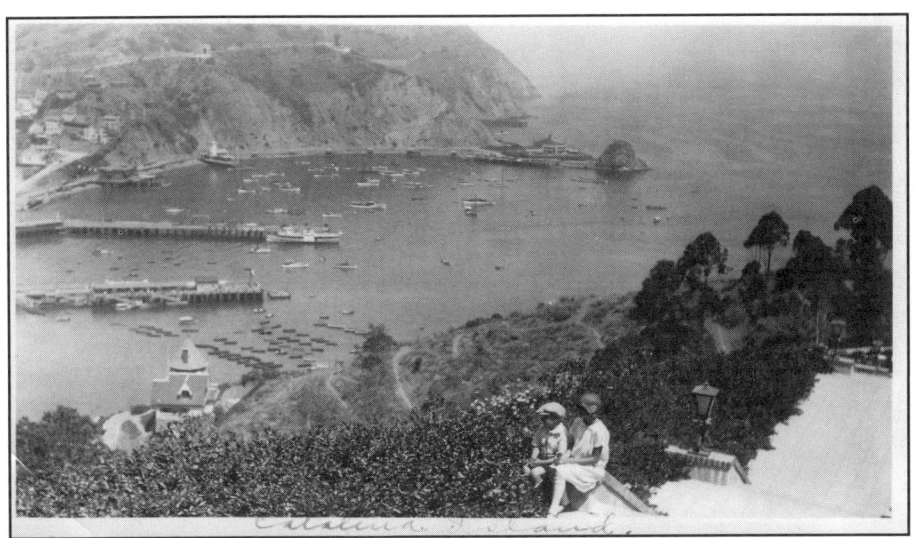

A vintage photograph of Avalon Bay, Catalina Island.

A chain of eight islands off the Southern California coast make up the Channel Islands. The islands are San Miguel, Santa Cruz, Santa Rosa, Anacapa, Santa Barbara, San Nicolas, Santa Catalina, and San Clemente. The first recorded mention of these islands comes from Juan Rodriguez Cabrillo in 1542. According to the Santa Cruz Foundation, for much of the sixteenth and seventeenth centuries, only a few expeditions visited the islands. It was not until 1769, with the Portola expedition, that the islands were claimed for the King of Spain under the Law of the Indies.

What kept sailors away from the islands for so long? Charles M. Skinner mentions one theory in the 1896 book *Myths and Legends of Our Own Land*. The Santa Barbara Islands, as he refers to them, were to be avoided at all costs. They were the headquarters for sea monsters, and worse, sirens. Sirens mentioned in Greek Myths would lure hapless sailors ashore, dooming both the ship and the men who came to their call.

Those who lived to tell of their harrowing experience spoke of yells, screams, and strange songs. The disbelievers blamed the ruckus on a shipwrecked tabby cat, but the cat must have had super-cat lungs to be heard miles out to sea above the sound of the wind and the breakers!

Location

The Islands extend from Point Concepcion to San Diego.
The Channel Islands National Park Visitor information
(805) 658- 5730
The Santa Cruz Island Foundation
1010 Anacapa Street
805-963-4949

Theodore Sparkuhl
Santa Monica

"Man has fettered his powers of spiritual insight till the faculty for using them has nearly atrophied."
—Dr. James H. Hyslop, 1909

Theodore Sparkuhl, known for his work as a cinematographer, built his Santa Monica home in the 1930s. After his death, the home exchanged hands several times until it was a virtual skeleton of its once-grand self. By the time a brave new owner purchased it in the 1980s, it could have served as a location for a horror film. When Mr. P bought the home in the Santa Monica Mountains, he knew the home would require countless hours of labor. To say the home was neglected was an understatement. Many of the windows had been destroyed. The inside of the home was moldy as hundreds of pigeons had taken up residence. The Kanan Fire in 1978 had destroyed the garage and a guesthouse. Mr. P thought with perseverance and help from a home hardware store, the home had potential.

It was this history that Mr. P would reawaken as he patched, dry walled, and finally decorated his new home. In an article written by V. Giraud, Mr. P told the reporter of a visit by the Sparkuhul descendents to the home during renovations. They "(sic)… told him they felt Theodore's intense work on the home might have contributed to his death in the mid-1940s. The cinematographer did not die at this home, but in Santa Fe, New Mexico.

But this home seems to draw him back, or at least it is thought to be his spirit. One evening, the strains of music drifted through the home as Mr. P relaxed. A series of loud bangs at the back door startled him. Investigating, he discovered no one at the door. He went back inside and replayed the song, but just as the tune

150

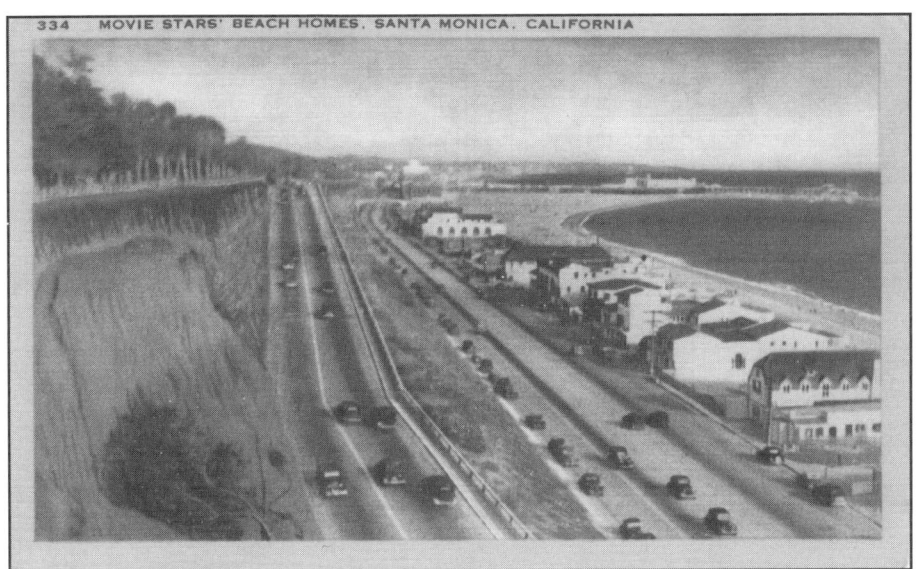

Vintage postcard of Movie Stars' Beach Homes in Santa Monica, California. Manufactured by Longshaw Card. Co., Los Angeles, California. An exert from the back reads, "Many celebrities and screen stars build palatial homes by the sea for their moments of play and relaxation."

neared the same spot as before, the banging started. Mr. P once again checked the doors and windows but all were securely locked. There was just no way it was either a prank or a strong wind. Mr. P played the song eight times and each time the pounding occurred. Which two lines of the song had caused the mayhem?

"No grave can hold my body down; this land is still my home."
—Terence Trent D'arby

No further reports of this home have ever surfaced in the media. Perhaps the ghost of Mr. Sparkhul is at rest. {49}

Story Note

There have been reports in the media about the home but sometimes Theodor Sparkuhl's name is misspelled Spurkuhl. Theodore Sparkuhl was born in Hanover, Germany, in 1891 and died in 1946.

Trained Serpents
Southern California Coast

"All houses are haunted. All persons are haunted. Throngs of spirits follow us everywhere. We are never alone."

—Barney Sarecky

Sitting on their deck chairs overlooking the Pacific Coast, the couple knew California was going to be exotic. They hoped for sunshine, hot temperatures and hours relaxing under palm trees, but they hadn't counted on a sea serpent. The woman's screams sent the other resort guests into a panic. Pails were dropped and lunches abandoned as the lifeguard led the exodus from the beach. As she turned to run, her husband grabbed her arm. "That's no sea serpent," he yelled, "Those are plain old car tires someone lashed together." She took a second look at the object she'd first spotted off from the breakers. "Hmm," she said, "I should have known it was just another resort serpent." The couple had a private beach for the rest of the morning.

The sea serpent used to entice visitors to a resort was a well-used trick in the 1900s. Practically every resort had a lovers leap, a resident ghost, and sea serpent. The sad resorts, which had nothing, needn't worry because one enterprising American was set to solve all their problems. He was going to create homegrown sea serpents.

The wacky headline "Trained Serpents" used at the beginning of the story was real. It appeared in 1907 in *The Los Angeles Herald*. One summer, instead of waiting for a sea serpent to appear off the coast which had become an annual occurrence, an entrepreneur decided to go into the sea serpent business. He was not put off by the obvious danger and difficulty in obtaining the creature. This man whose name was never mentioned decided to make his own.

He decided to import pythons from South America. Now, there is confusion in this story as boas come from South America and pythons from Asia. Though pythons may be good swimmers, they certainly do not live for twenty-four hours in the water, and certainly not in the Pacific Ocean.

The man kept the snakes in a massive tank fed by seawater. He is quoted as saying, "The snakes are fed enormous meals to hasten their growth and each day they are stretched to increase their length."

How did he expect to change the snakes from domesticated pets (that is if they survived the sea water tank) to fierce sea serpents? Why with training of course. "To make them duly ferocious they are urged

152

to attack miniature ships and swallow them whole, at the same time lashing their tails with anger." How the training proceeded was never fully explained.

Needless to say, the reporter was not impressed and suggested that he feed them literature from seashore resorts! No sightings of any "homemade" sea serpents were ever reported. {50}

Note: According to the San Diego Zoo site, pythons do lie beneath water in a stream or slow-moving river to catch prey such as birds or small mammals— but not ships.

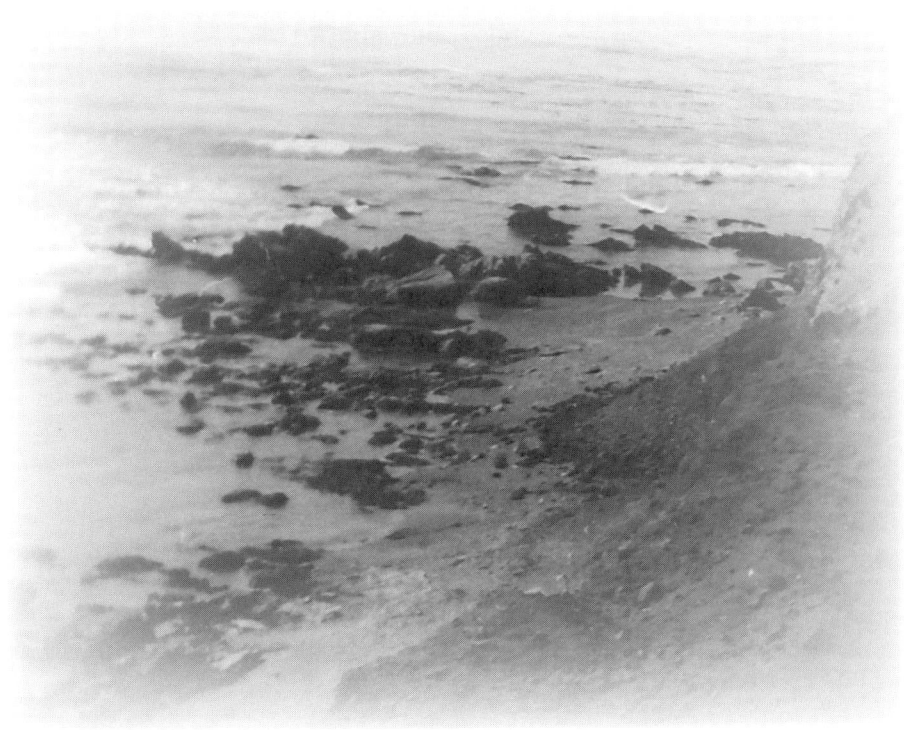

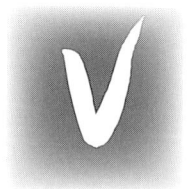

Valentino Hollywood

"Most people who went about saying a ghost had poked them with a brolly would be locked up somewhere."

—Pamela Stephenson

On our visit to the Los Angeles Pet Cemetery, also known L.A. Pet Memorial Park, Kabar, Rudolph Valentino's great Dane did not come and lick our ankles. Milk bone biscuits and calls of "Here Rudy" were of no avail. He was perhaps sleeping as most dogs do, curled up in his spirit-world bed.

But Rudy made a dramatic appearance at a séance held for his dead master back on May 7, 1948. As reported by *The Oakland Tribune* and many other papers, the deceased Rudolph Valentino showed up for his birthday celebration. The headline read, "Valentino greeted by thirty mediums." One can only imagine Valentino's home, Falcon Lair, besieged by mediums, a Buddhist Missionary called Lokanatha, clairvoyants, and countless reporters.

Rudolph Valentino was born May 6, 1895. It was decided that it would be a great time to contact the star. Some of the mediums claimed "…(sic) the departed movie idol floated on a stream of ectoplasm to the minor palace, Falcon's Lair, where he lived when he was just plain folks."

One medium claimed Valentino's dog was sniffing around the room and others saw him lurking in a corner. Another man claimed to have been licked by the dog. Reporters only claimed to see a birthday cake and droopy red roses.

One medium said, "I felt pressure on my shoulder." The table legs tapped sharply which the mediums said meant messages from Valentino. He announced that current movies were lousy, that he had a message of love for humanity, and that he was very glad the newspaper people showed up—there were chants of "Raise the table, Ru-dee dear."

One of the more humorous aspects of the night was the guest of honor, a Buddhist Missionary who was living at the house. He was on a twenty-four hour word fast and consequently said nothing.

One medium, Mrs. Carol McKinstry, said Valentino had dictated an 80,000-word book to her. She said reporters couldn't see Valentino because they were too skeptical.

If you decide to go in search of Kabar bring Milk Bones™ and wear long pants if you don't want your ankles licked. {52}

Location

Los Angeles Pet Cemetery
5068 N. Old Scandia Lane
Calabasas, CA 91372
Hours: Monday to Saturday 8 am to 5 pm, Sunday and holidays 8 am to dusk.
(818) 591-7037
Web site: www.lapetcemetery.com

Villa Montezuma
San Diego

"All houses wherein men have lived and died are haunted houses."
—Longfellows

Villa Montezuma, a few minutes drive from San Diego's bustling Gaslamp District, stands in a world of its own. The beautiful 1887 Victorian home is built in a Queen Anne style. With more than twenty-one stained glass windows, a tower room, and fanciful turrets, you wish you were back in the late 1800s and lucky enough to be invited to a Jesse Shepard private concert. If you were like Jesse, part of San Diego's elite artistic circle lured to the city by real estate developers, entrance to the concert would have been guaranteed.

With the completion of the 1885 railroad, San Diego's population jumped from 5,000 to 40,000 in anticipation of the industry the railroad would attract. In an effort to bring culture to San Diego, civic boosters and real estate developers financed opera houses, schools, and colleges. They persuaded Harr Wagner, editor of a San Francisco literary magazine, *The Golden Era* and his artistic circle of poets, painters, and musicians to settle in San Diego. One of this circle was Jesse Shepard—spiritualist, musician, and author for whom Villa Montezuma was built.

Stepping from your carriage you quickly walk up the steps into the grand home, and your heart skips a beat. Quickly, you are ushered into

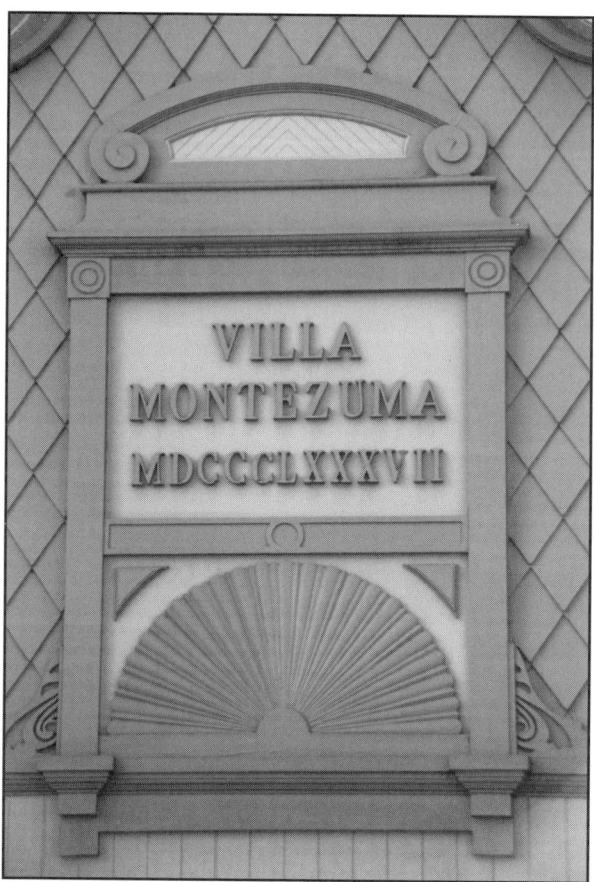

Villa Montezuma Museum, built by Jesse Shepard. San Diego, California.

Mr. Shepard's private music room. Feeling more than a little smug over the invitation, you settle into your chair, discreetly noting who else has been invited. At exactly midnight, the door opens to reveal a handsome young man, dressed in a short velvet coat and a red smoking cap. The young pianist steps onto the stage, briefly acknowledges the crowd, before seating himself at the piano. Dramatically, all candles are extinguished as the first strains of music are heard. This is the man people call "astonishing, brilliant, a prodigious talent."

Jesse Shepard, was a gifted musician, vocalist, and author under the penname Francis Grierson. Born in England, his family came to America when he was an infant. At the age of six, he was giving performances. His reputation at adulthood preceded him throughout Europe and North America. He would say of his own talent that it was directed by no rules, but from inspiration. A reporter once commented, "There is no such music that can be heard or purchased and it has an entrancing effect upon all who enjoy true musical inspiration."

An audience at one of his performances might be treated to a Russian song in which Jesse Shepard could sing both bass and contralto or he might imitate one of the more popular parlor songs of the day. Though he hated crowds, fifty or more people attended his private concerts paying $2 a head. His concerts were advertised in papers. One such headline read, "Jesse Shepard Will Give A Grand Performance."

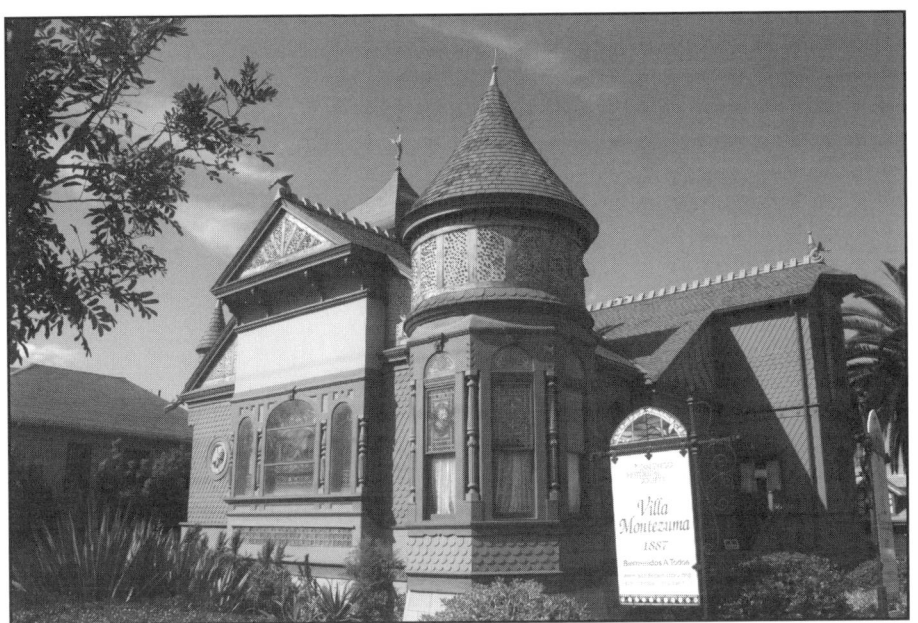

Villa Montezuma Museum, an 1887 Victorian mansion. San Diego, California

It was not only his natural talent which drew people to his concerts, but also his deep interest in spiritualism. This interest in spiritualism would later drive Jesse from his home in San Diego when his "interest" raised the ire of certain society people. Piano is one thing, but someone who openly advertises musical evenings with séances, where guests will witness the "most startling manifestations known in the realm of psychological and metaphysical science" is quite another. He left San Diego for Europe where his interest in both music and spiritualism could be indulged.

In North America, Jesse freely told people that angels guided him. He could in fact channel late and great composers into his own hands. In *The Oakland Tribune,* October 14, 1875, the following was written about one of his performances. "(sic)...the piano made several jumps in the air we are certain. It really seemed to be possessed, animated, excited, mad!" ...instead of being manipulated by one pair of hands, it seemed as if there were a dozen magnetic performers pounding on it."

On May 29, 1927, at the age of seventy-nine, Jesse Shepard announced he was giving his last performance. As the last notes filtered through the auditorium, Jesse Shepard died, still sitting at his beloved piano.

After Jesse returned to Europe, the Villa Montezuma went through many owners. It was sold for a pittance, just $12,000 in

157

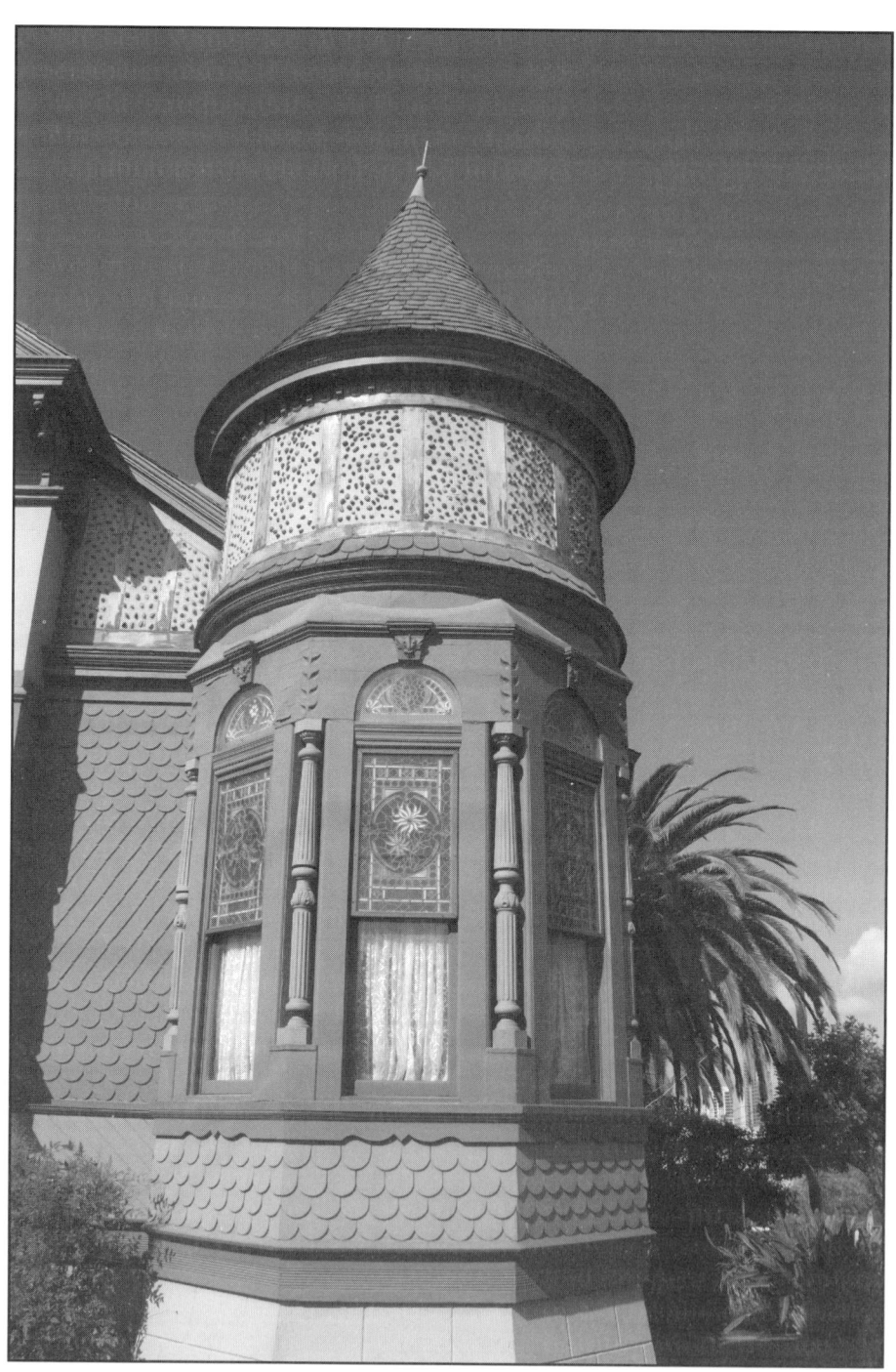

Villa Montezuma Museum, San Diego.

1968, but a judge later ruled the sale unwise, because the elderly lady—Amelia Jaeger—was unaware of the value. The home (est. at $26,000) was sold after this to the Historical Society. By the 1970s, the structure was in need of a major renovation and the city of San Diego took over ownership. The home was restored and opened to the public in 1972.

Visitors to Villa Montezuma claim to still hear Jesse Shepard playing his piano. Music is heard coming from Jesse Shepard's music room, though it is empty. Did his séances raise a few spirits who decided to stay on in Villa Montezuma? Around the room where he held his séances are hidden corridors and above the room is a crawl space. These features may have been used during séances. Besides the spirits of past musicians, there is also rumored to be the ghost of a custodian who killed himself in the tower room. Sudden drops in temperature signal this ghost's presence.

Though we have been in the home when open and several times peer as we might into the stained glass windows, no one ever looked back. But when standing in front of the home, a strong presence is felt that casts a spell over those in its shadow. {53, 54}

Location

1925 K Street
San Diego, CA
The home is currently not open for public tours as it is undergoing renovations. For information, see the Web site: www.villamontezuma. org.
Tours of the Sherman Heights District where the home is located are held on the first and third Sunday of each month from 1pm until 3 pm.

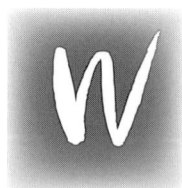

Whaley House
San Diego

"I think paranormal experiences are very personal.."
—Andrea Corr

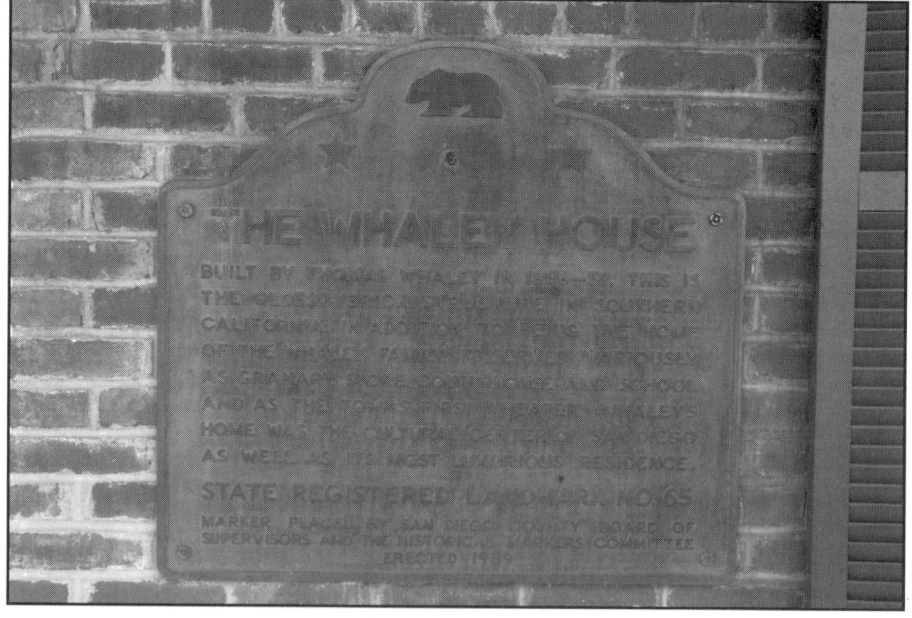

Whaley House official plaque, Old Town San Diego.

Curators at the Whaley house often hear loud footsteps coming from the upper level, but no one else is there. Visitors tell of a sensation of being strangled on the lower floor, in the exact spot "justice" was carried out. Over active imaginations or is there a disgruntled ghost coming back to haunt the good people of San Diego? The same "good people" that sent him to the gallows over a hundred years ago.

A single noose hung from the scaffold. A large crowd gathered to see the man who tried to steal Captain James Keating's schooner. The

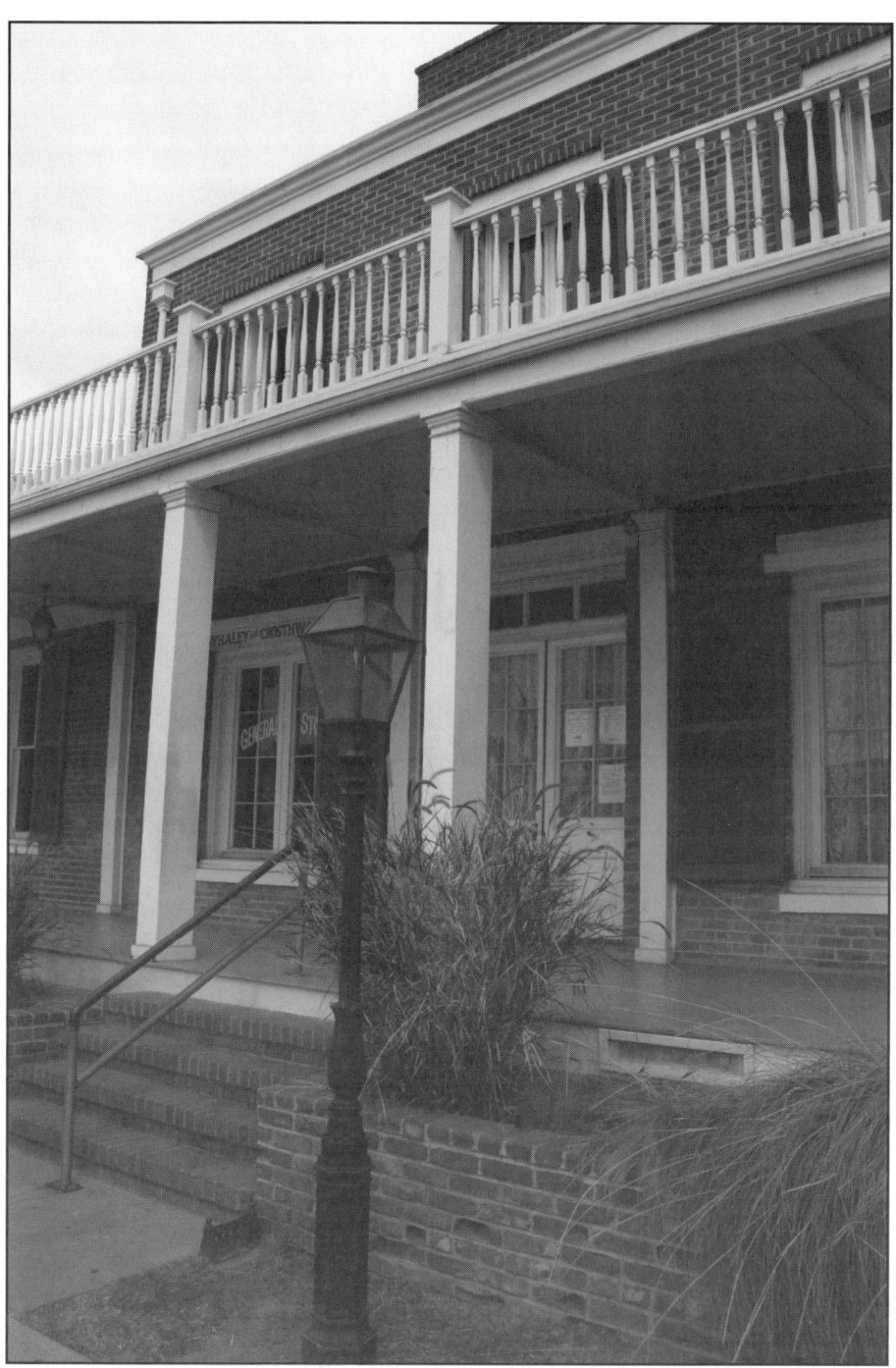

Whaley House Museum, Old Town San Diego.

culprit was first brought to public attention as the Sheriff successfully apprehended "the man in the red shirt." Of course, Yankee Jim, whose real name was Jim Robinson, denied he was trying to steal the schooner. He claimed he was simply rowing in its direction—in a stolen rowboat no less. The jury didn't take long to come back with a guilty verdict. Hanging the thief was the "right thing to do," and some thought giving the man a trial in the first place had been a waste of time.

September the eighteenth was hanging day for Yankee Jim. According to reports in the History of Placer County 1882, Yankee Jim didn't really believe he would be hung. But the people gathered on San Diego Avenue that day were not there to give him a good scare. While the other suspects involved in the case may have been reprieved, Jim was going to hang. After given an opportunity to say his last words, Sheriff Crosswaite gave the orders. The crowd cheered as the wagon was pulled from beneath Jim.

Unfortunately for Jim, no one had taken into account his height. He was a tall man even by today's standards at 6'4", and the scaffold had been built only for a person with the maximum height of six feet. Instead of a quick death, the crowd gathered in front of the scaffold watched Jim slowly suffocate. Perhaps it was this agonizing death that prevents the spirit of Yankee Jim from resting.

The Whaley House was built in 1856, on the site of those gallows. Thomas Whaley traveled from New York by way of Cape Horn to San Francisco in 1849. After a few business setbacks, he would make his way to San Diego—a climate he compared to Italy. In 1853, he married Ana Eloise De Lannay and they settled in San Diego. He wrote to his mother of the new home he was building facing San Diego Avenue. "My new house and store will soon be complete, and when furnished will be the handsomest and most convenient and comfortable place in this section of the country…"

Four years later, Thomas Whaley's sunny outlook on his home changed. He would write about the phantom of Yankee Jim in his home. Mysterious sounds of a man walking about the home he attributed to Yankee Jim.

This was just a hint of the misfortune that would befall the family in this home. A son born to the Whaleys would die. And it is this child's cries, which from time to time, echo in the home. A neighbor's daughter, Annabella Washburn, was killed after slicing her neck on Anna Whaley's low-slung clothesline. In addition, Whaley's oldest daughter, distraught over a failed marriage, killed herself at the home.

The "most haunted house in America" attracts the famous and not so famous. When Regis Philbin was a local San Diego announcer, he tried to spend the night in the home, but after possibly seeing the image of Anna Whaley, fled the property.

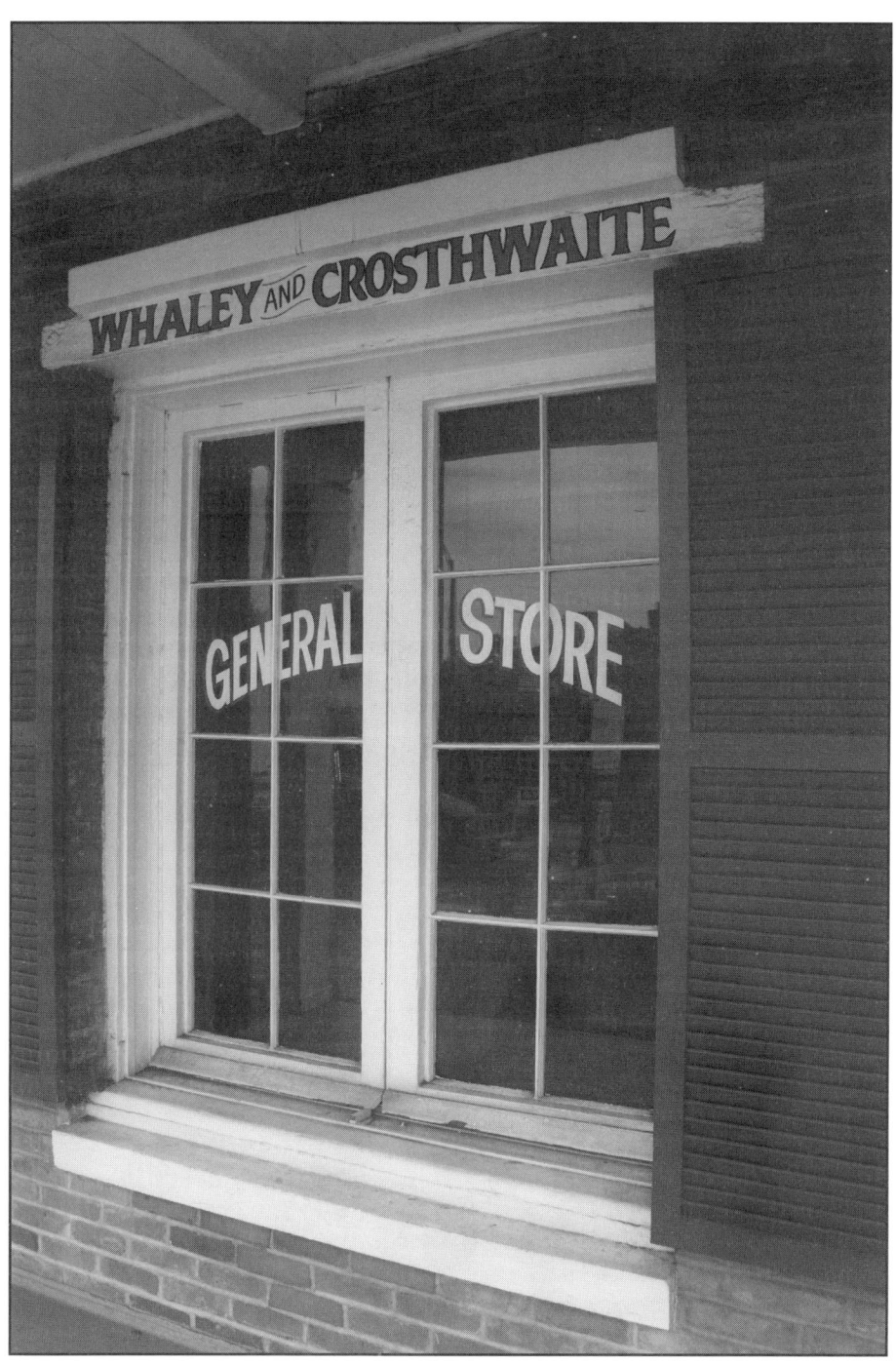

Whaley House Museum, Old Town San Diego.

From the moment you turn the worn knob on the Whaley House door, be prepared for a memorable visit. There are at least four spirits here. Cigar smoke from Mr. Whaley's pipe greets you upon entering. Don't mind him, he is still welcoming guests to his home, even though he passed on in 1890. His wife, Anna, won't be far behind. Her presence is indicated by the scent of a floral perfume. Daisy, the white terrier naturally likes the porch out front. And then there is Yankee Jim whose heavy footsteps give him away. It was designated a haunted historical site in the 1960s by the U.S. Commerce Department.

Location

The Whaley House is located in Old Town San Diego
2476 San Diego Avenue
San Diego, CA 92110
Be sure to check the Web site for hours of operation, which do change with seasons. Private tours of the home are also available.
Web site: www.whaleyhouse.org
(619) 298-2482

Wild Goose
Catalina Island

"I have never yet heard of a murderer who was not afraid of a ghost."
—John Philpot Curran

Although John Wayne's boat is now used as a charter boat, maintenance workers and others are said to have seen the Duke roaming the decks or waving from the top deck of his former yacht.

Shortly before he died of complications from stomach cancer in 1979, John Wayne sold the *Wild Goose* to a Santa Monica lawyer named Lynn Hutchins. Stories that his ghost haunts the vessel quickly began to swirl. Lynn Hutchins told the *National Enquirer* she'd seen Duke's ghost twice while onboard and felt his presence on many occasions. "...I was sleeping in The Duke's stateroom. I remember waking up with a start in the middle of the night. The room was black and the boat was uncannily silent. As my eyes got used to the dark I suddenly became aware of someone standing by the door to the port gangway. I froze because I was alone on the boat. Then I leaped out of bed and the figure vanished into

164

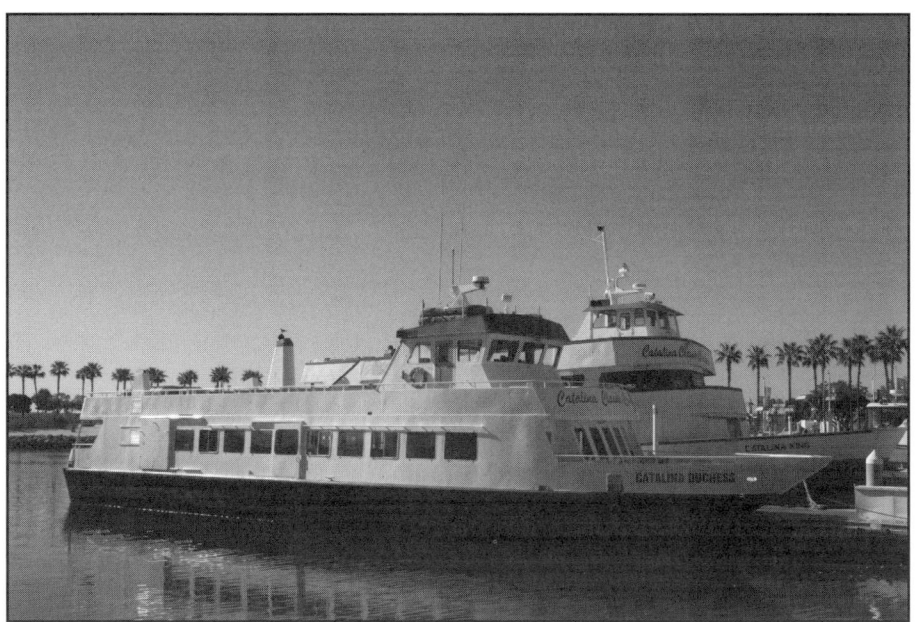

Day excursions to Catalina Island from Long Beach.

thin air! Later I talked to Bert Minshall a former captain of the boat and he said that the ghost was John Wayne."

In another report, his ghost is said to have been seen in a mirror behind the bar as beer glasses rattled. A psychic, Pat Hayes, who investigated the incidents, said Duke's spirit was returning because of his "deep emotional attachment to the vessel."

His last trip aboard *Wild Goose* came on Easter weekend 1979. It was a cruise to Catalina Island.

Location

For day cruises to Catalina Island: see Web site at www.catalinainfo. com.

William Desmond Taylor
Los Angeles

"There was always something hard to shake off about the ghost story; it is so old and so universal."

—*Robert Leffingwell*

One of the most famous murder cases in Hollywood was that of William Desmond Taylor. Three hundred people confessed to the crime, but to this day, his murder is unsolved. Taylor was a successful actor turned director who, after his death, was discovered to be involved in a love triangle with a nineteen-year-old starlet named Mary Mile Minter and screen vamp Mabel Normands. The forty-nine-year-old director had been shot in the back inside his bungalow at the Alvarado Court Apartments.

There was no shortage of witnesses who claimed to have seen a person, wearing a scarf around the head exiting Mr. Taylor's home. A key witness was a servant in the employ of Douglas MacLean—soon afterward, she gave up her job. "She declared that she had seen not only the murderer but the ghost of the murdered man as well." Several of her successors affirmed that they had seen the same phenomena. According to servants, the spectral visitor made its appearance at the hour when the shot that killed William Desmond Taylor was fired. This information comes from an *Oakland Tribune* article dated May 13, 1923.

Neither Douglas MacLean or his wife had glimpsed the ghost of William Desmond Taylor, but so many servants had quit, they had little choice but to move. The MacLeans relocated to a house in Beverly Hills where they were never bothered by the specter again.

It is not known if the current occupants ever crossed paths with the actor or if his "haunting" was simply media-induced hype over his death. There are Web sites devoted to his murder and a few books published about his death. {55}

Location

404-B South Alvarado Street
Westlake Park, CA

William S. Hart Park
Santa Clarita

"Communicating with spirits has always raised eyebrows. The following is a timeline from 1876 up until present day of some interesting thoughts on spiritualists, mediums, ghost seekers, and the paranormal. They are interesting for what they reveal about common thoughts and practices."

—Author unknown

Welcome to La Loma de Los Vientos or Hill of the Winds which William Hart (King of the Cowboys) named his ranch in Newell, California. There are a few spirits said to be at the ranch.

The ghost of Mr. Hart is said to appear wandering in the direction of his beloved horses. There are few sightings of his spirit, which made this author wonder if the ghost of Mr. Hart was more a nostalgic wish by his fans. But how did this rumor of a haunted ranch begin? The current generation may not be aware of how strongly William Hart was associated with his horse, Fritz. From *The Times Standard*, May 17, 1969, comes this quote: "William S. Hart was the cowboy movie hero. He loved his horse. No movie was complete until he kissed his horse goodbye. 'So long, Old Paint. I reckon I must mosey.'" When William Hart retired from movies, so did his horse, Fritz, thaat he kept with him at his ranch. "Fritz stayed in the backyard because Hart had to see him and talk with him everyday," wrote a reporter in *The Fresno Bee*, 1938. When the horse died, William Hart erected a monument to the horse and told reporters, "I'd give both my shoes—with my feet in them—to have him back."

In 1944, William Hart came to West Hollywood to dedicate another of his homes as a park. He told of a dream in which Will Rogers told him: "Hello there, Bill. What you hangin' back there with the drag fer, Bill? Why don't you come up here and ride point with me? Your old paint horse is here, Bill, trailin' alongside with me right now, but the saddle—your saddle—is empty." Two years later, William Hart was dead.

It is left up to you, the reader, to wonder whether horse and rider were reunited in death or do the spirits of William Hart and Fritz still roam the property in Newall? {56, 57}

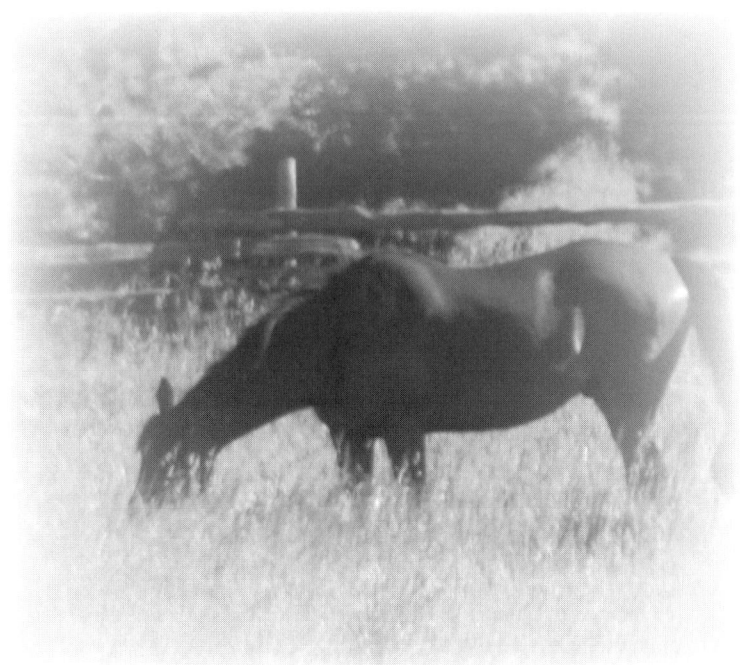

Background

Though William Hart began acting in his twenties, it wasn't until the age of forty-nine that he made his way to Hollywood. Not many people begin a career in film at forty-nine! He did Western plays, which lead to his debut as a cowboy in 1914. The ranch he purchased in 1921, he lived on until his death in 1946. The homes and surrounding land was left to the County of Los Angeles. The two-story home belonged to the family of Henri M. Newhall. It is located at Heritage Junction; enter at William S. Hart Park, then make a left.

Location

24151 Newhall Avenue
Newhall, California
(616) 254- 4584
Web site: www.hartmuseum.org
Hours: Mid September to Mid June; Wednesday to Friday 10 am to 1 pm; Saturday and Sunday 11 am to 4 pm
Consult the site to see tour times.

Conclusion

The coastline of Southern California is a patchwork of sandy beaches, rugged mountains, deserts, and urban activity. Each town has its own character. As such, it is little wonder the fascinating history of California lends a distinctive flavor to its supernatural stories. Visiting the sites in this book will not only inspire you to see more of the state, but to learn more legends surrounding some of its most famous landmarks.

And perhaps you too will have a ghost story to share with your friends.

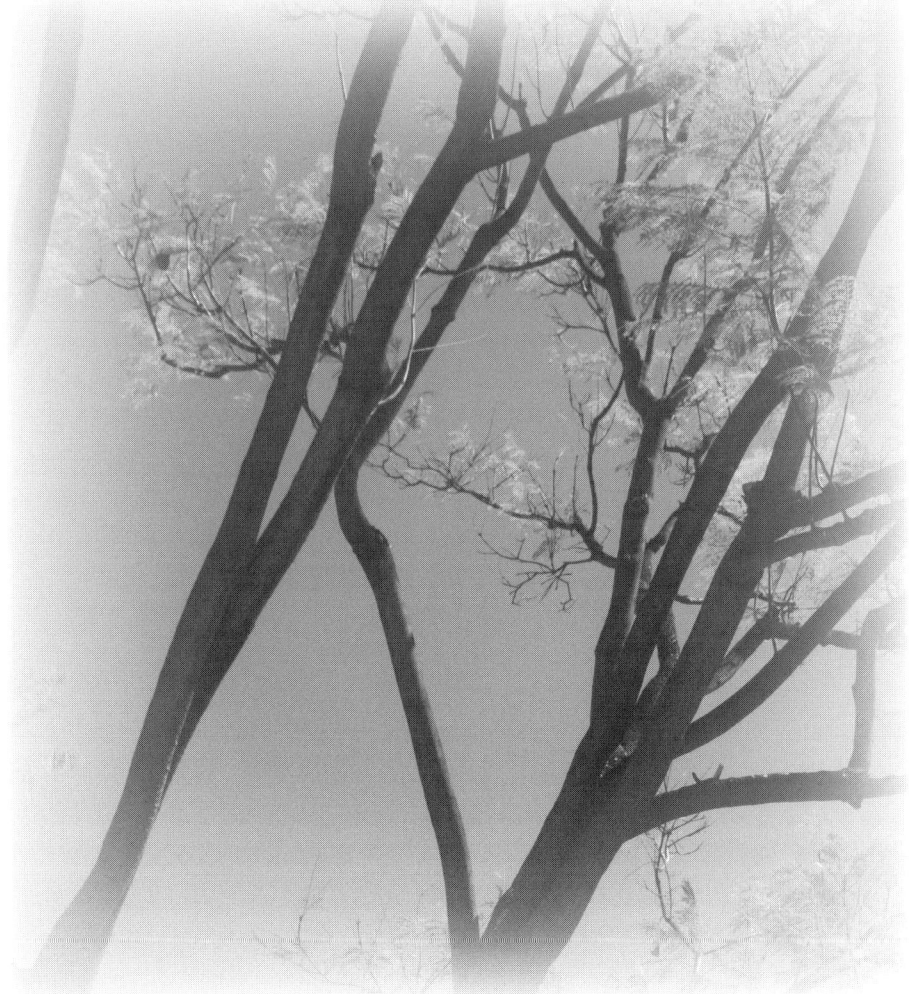

Top Ten Places To Find A Ghost

The following information is provided by author and ghost investigator, Fiona Broome and appears in her book, *Ghosts of Austin, Texas*. For more information, visit http://hollowhill.com/.

No matter where you are, certain locations are usually haunted. These sites don't always have ghosts, but they're the best places to start when you're looking for unreported visitors from beyond the grave.

Theatres

Ghosts frequent places where people have performed on stage. These include movie theatres that were once performance halls. There are three kinds of ghosts at these locations: First, at least one actor who is still seen on or near the stage. Second, a stagehand lingers backstage, usually around the lighting or the curtain controls. Finally, someone appears towards the back of the hall, especially during rehearsals. He or she almost always smokes a cigarette that people can smell, or they'll see the smoke or the burning ember.

Battlegrounds

Almost every battleground has some residual energy from the violent and tragic deaths that occurred there. Some battlegrounds are actually haunted by the spirits of the men and women who died there, too. Between Texas' battles for independence, Indian attacks, and Civil War conflicts, you'll find many locations with ghost stories… and real ghosts.

Cemeteries

It's a cliché but a true one: Ghosts haunt cemeteries. Modern graves—burials that occurred less than fifty years ago—are rarely haunted for very long.

For the most powerful hauntings, look for graves that are at least a hundred years old. Only a few are haunted, but you'll find elevated EMF levels at many of graves, especially if they're unmarked.

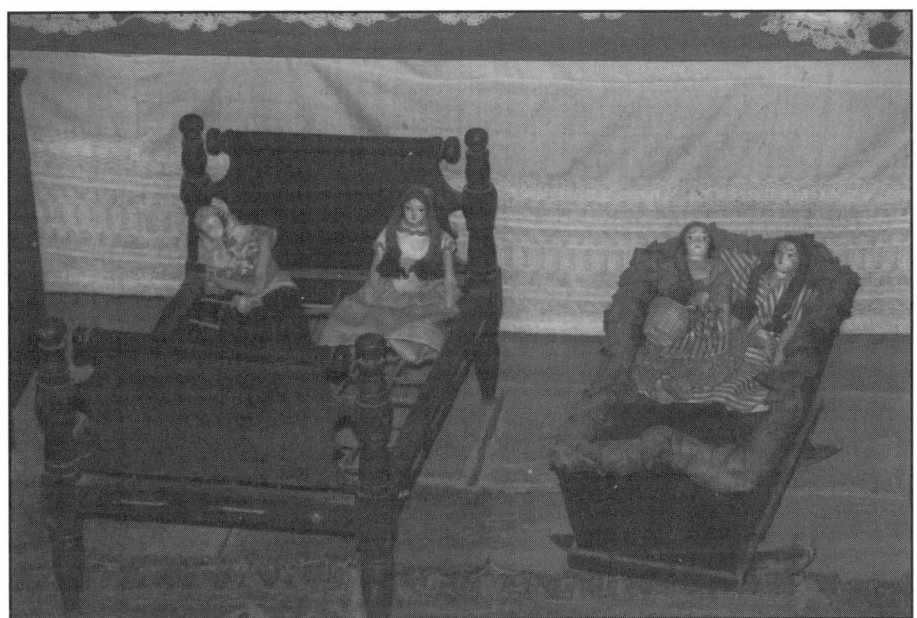

La Casa de Estudillo, Old Town San Diego.

Colleges

Almost every college or university reports at least one ghost. Most also report poltergeist phenomena. The performing arts center is often the most haunted location on campus. In Austin, the University of Texas campus is probably the most haunted college.

Summer Camps

Most camps—especially Scout camps—have a ghost or two. Usually, these are benevolent ghosts of former camp counselors or the camp manager. An aroma of perfume or pipe smoke is usually reported, related to someone who worked there.

Very Old, Large Homes and Buildings

Like most ancient castles, many very old, large buildings have ghosts. In an older home, a woman who lived there lingers to be sure that the house and its occupants remain safe. She usually wears a green dress.

Another ghost is mad and lurks in the attic, basement, or an outbuilding. A variation on this is a ghost in the nearby woods or a field next to an old homestead. These hauntings are almost predictable.

Old Hotels

Many hotels are haunted by the same people who visited them in life. They're usually happy ghosts who return to relax and enjoy themselves.

Classic haunted spots in hotels include the top floor, the elevator, and the lobby. This is true of the Driskill Hotel, Austin's most haunted and elegant hotel, and a favorite destination for visiting ghost hunters.

Around Austin, this category of haunting extends to former brothels. In the late nineteenth century, dozens of feisty, independent-minded madams owned "boarding houses" around downtown Austin. Today, these sites are often clubs, bars, and restaurants in the entertainment and warehouse districts of Austin. And, most of them have great ghost stories to share.

Hospitals, Retirement Homes, Morgues and Funeral Parlors

As you'd expect, some people aren't willing to leave the last place where they were seen and called by name. However, if these sites are still in use, they're usually off-limits to ghost hunters.

Instead, look for former locations of these kinds of buildings. They're usually haunted by perplexed and sometimes angry ghosts.

Around Austin, there are probably hundreds of unreported ghosts. If you follow these suggestions, you'll find even more ghosts than are included in these pages.

Glossary
of Common Ghost Hunting Terms

The following infotrmation is provided by author and ghost investigator, Fiona Broome and appears in her book, *Ghosts of Austin, Texas*. For more information, visit http://hollowhill.com/.

There are many words that ghost hunters use in reference to ghosts and haunted places. You're probably familiar with most of these words, but some may be new or have different meanings when they refer to haunted places.

Afterlife

One of several terms used interchangeably to refer to life after death. The word "afterlife" has been used since 1615, and is generic enough to use in almost any setting and culture. Other popular terms include "crossing over," "the Otherworld," and "the other side."

Most ghost hunters avoid specific religious terms such as "heaven" and "the Summerland" when discussing ghosts, hauntings, and an afterlife.

Aliens

Visitors from other planets. We differentiate aliens from visitors that live in parallel worlds, the Otherworld, or what's generally characterized as the afterlife. Some ghost hunters believe in UFOs and aliens; others don't. Generally, ghost hunters don't mix the two studies.

Anomaly

Something that is out of place and unexplained. In paranormal studies, this word refers to any phenomena that we cannot explain. Example: A lens flare in a photo is not an anomaly if you can see the light source that created it. A orb that cannot be explained is an anomaly.

Apparition

Since the early seventeenth century, this word has referred to a ghost that seems to have material substance. If it appears in any physical form, including a vapor-like image, it may be called an apparition.

Banshee

From the Irish, bean sidhe, meaning female spirit. Most families with Irish ancestors have at least one banshee story if you do enough research, but many people are reluctant to discuss this subject. Her wail does not always mean death. She does not cause anyone to die. She's generally not a ghost.

Clearing, or Space Clearing

This is a process of ridding an area of lingering unpleasant energy. It does not "kill" a ghost. Space clearing may encourage ghosts to cross over, or at least leave the haunted location.

Immediately after a space clearing, ghosts can be noisier or more hostile than usual. An effective space clearing may take three to five days to work. In the most haunted settings, it's usually necessary to repeat the space clearing several times.

Demons

Historically, this term has included deceased individuals. However, since the early eighteenth century, the word "demon" usually refers to an evil spirit, sometimes more powerful than man, but less than Deity. Today, we generally do not use this term to indicate a deceased human being. The female demon, very rarely mentioned, is a demoness.

Demons and possessions are treated like UFOs and aliens. That is, most ghost hunters have an opinion about them, but they rarely discuss them in connection with hauntings. The "Amityville Horror" is one noted exception where the story seemed to include both ghosts and possessions.

Ghosts generally do not attempt to take over a living body. In most cases, they believe that they're still alive and—in their minds—each has his or her own body. They're not interested in anyone else's.

Doppelganger

A concept made popular in the early nineteenth century, especially by Shelley and Byron. The doppelganger is the apparition, or double, of a living person.

This may be paranormal phenomenon, but it's not a ghost. It does not forecast anything tragic.

Dowsing rods

These are usually single rods, split rods, or L-shaped wires or twigs. Some people dowse with pendulums, too. They're popularly used to locate water and oil wells, and to measure energy levels of many kinds. For ghost research, we usually use two L-shaped rods.

In ghost hunting, the investigator loosely carries one rod in each hand, and watches the movement of the rods. When the rods cross or splay wide apart, it usually indicates a haunted location.

It's easy to make your own dowsing rods from coat hanger wire. Cut the wire near the top, and again at the opposite end of the lower section. Do this with two different coat hangers to create two dowsing rods.

You can also purchase ready-made dowsing rods. Be certain that they're long enough for ghost research; the 16-inch length is recommended. Look for dowsing tools that glow in the dark. They're especially useful for ghost hunting.

Hold each one loosely in your hands with your arms extended or your elbows bent at a right angle. The rods should be pointed straight ahead of you, and able to swing on their own.

If the rods are drifting, this could be from the normal movement of your body. However, in haunted places, the pull on the rods is strong and cannot be mistaken for a casual, unconscious movement of your hands.

When you step out of the haunted area, the rods return to their original position.

Some researchers successfully use dowsing rods to find unmarked graves. With practice, it's possible to use the rods to detect other information about the body in the grave and the spirit that may haunt the site.

Ectoplasm

Often referred to as "ecto," this is the physical residue of psychic energy. It's the basis for "slime" used in the Ghostbusters movies. Ectoplasm can be seen by the naked eye, and is best viewed in dark settings, since it is translucent and tends to glow. It is very unusual.

Researchers often describe it as a vivid, *X-Files* kind of lime green. It usually fades from sight gradually.

EMF

The initials stand for Electro Magnetic Field, or Electro Magnetic Frequency. In the broadest terms, EMF is a combination of electrical and magnetic fields. You'll find EMF around power sources, fuse boxes, electrical outlets, computer monitors, microwave ovens, etc.

It's smart to study EMF so that you'll recognize the normal sources of elevated EMF readings.

Constant, clearly defined EMF fields usually have a logical explanation.

Unexplained EMF fields may indicate something paranormal. EMF fields can be measured with various tools, including an EMF meter or a hiking compass.

Entity

An entity is any being, including people, animals, and ghosts. It can also refer to aliens, faeries, mystical beasts, and a wide range of paranormal creatures. If you use this term—and many ghost hunters do—be sure that others understand your context.

ESP

ESP is the abbreviation for Extra Sensory Perception. It means the ability to perceive things beyond the usual five senses of smell, hearing, touch, taste, and sight.

Although these perceptions may be interpreted as sounds or sights, experienced ghost hunters can usually tell the difference between normal detection with the five senses, and things detected with the "sixth sense" or psychic abilities.

EVP

Electronic Voice Phenomena, or the recording of unexplained voices, usually in haunted settings. Sometimes the voices are heard during the investigation. More often, the voices are whispers, understood only when a sound recording is processed, filtered, and amplified with a computer.

When people first recorded EVP, they insisted on total silence so normal noises and talking wouldn't be confused with EVP. More recently, people have deliberately included sounds such as normal talking, white noise, and so on. Some researchers believe that ghosts may need ambient noise to create their own sounds and speech.

Most researchers use digital recorders to save EVP. Once the researcher is at home, he or she uses a computer program to filter out everyday noises, such as airplanes and passing cars. The recording may need to be speeded up or slowed down, or a range of sounds magnified above others.

Faeries

Beings that live in the Otherworld or Underworld, parallel to our world and not far from it. Many researchers who readily accept the reality of ghosts don't believe in faeries. Similar to the subject of aliens and UFOs, it's best to keep faerie research clearly separated from your ghost hunting.

Fear

Most ghost hunters have a healthy respect for ghosts and paranormal phenomena. Many ghost hunters enjoy a "good scare." However, if you feel genuinely alarmed or frightened while ghost hunting, it's prudent to leave that location. It may have been your imagination, but there may be something (or someone) truly dangerous nearby.

Ghost hunting should always be interesting, and sometimes entertaining. If it's not, you may be at risk. Ghost hunting should never become a "dare" or an endurance test.

If you're truly frightened in any setting—haunted or not—leave immediately. If this happens regularly when you're ghost hunting, choose a different hobby.

Ghost

A sentient entity or spirit that visits or lingers in our world, after he or she lived among us as a human being. We've also seen evidence of ghostly animals and pets.

Ghost hunters generally use other terms for other beings such as aliens and faeries.

Ghoul

This word has been mistakenly used to mean a ghost. "Ghoul" comes from Middle Eastern lore, where it may refer to an evil spirit that robs graves.

Haunted

Describes a setting where ghosts, poltergeists, and/or residual energy seem to produce significant paranormal activity. The word "haunt" originally meant to frequent.

Hollow Hill

Hollow Hill is the name of Fiona Broome's ghost hunting Web site! http://www.HollowHill.com/.

It is one of the oldest and most trusted ghost-related Web sites online.

Medium

This word usually refers to something in the middle, relative to size or duration.

In ghost hunting, it means anyone who is able to convey communications from departed spirits. That is, the person is able to maintain a position between the world of the living and those who've crossed over, and talk with (or for) those on the other side.

This term was popularized in the mid nineteenth century and is often used interchangeably with the word "psychic." (Compare that definition in this glossary.)Some people call themselves psychic mediums because they can communicate with the other side, but also sense other paranormal energy and/or work with ESP.

Occult

From the Latin, meaning something that is concealed or covered. Since the sixteenth century, it has meant anything that is mysterious. Today in America, it generally refers to magical, mystical and experimental studies.

Orb

An orb is a round, whitish or pastel-colored translucent area in photos. Generally, these are perfectly circular, not oval. Many researchers believe that they represent spirits or ghosts.

If you're using a digital camera, it's important to differentiate between an area of broken pixels (called an "artifact") and the translucent, circular image that is an orb.

Also, any reflective surface or light source can create a lens flare that looks like an orb. When taking photos, note glass, shiny metal, reflective signs, polished surfaces such as tables and headstones, and lights.

In most cases, ghost hunters do not see orbs when they're at a haunted site. Usually, orbs show up only in photos. They are the most common evidence for hauntings.

Critics often dismiss orbs as lens flares and artifacts. However, unexplained orbs often appear at haunted sites. They're rarely in photos at locations that aren't haunted.

Ouija

From the French and German words for "yes," this is a spelling board used with a planchette. The device is intended to communicate with and through the spirit world, obtaining answers to questions.

Generally, we don't recommend them on serious ghost investigations. Some people are vehemently opposed to Ouija boards. The biggest problem is that researchers can't tell who is really moving the planchette. Even if it is a ghost, the spirit could be playing a prank or lying; the information from Ouija boards is unreliable for ghost research.

Paranormal

The prefix, "para" indicates something that is irregular, faulty, or operating outside the usual boundaries. So, "paranormal" refers to anything outside the realm and experiences that we consider normal.

Parapsychology

The study of mental abilities and effects outside the usual realm of psychology. Parapsychology includes the study of ESP, ghosts, luck, psychokinesis, and other paranormal phenomena.

Pendulum

A small weight at the end of a cord or chain that is usually about six to ten inches long. The movement of the weight, when uninfluenced by other factors, can be used to detect areas of paranormal energy.

Poltergeist

From the German meaning "noisy ghost," this term has been in use since the early nineteenth century to mean a spirit that makes noise, or otherwise plays pranks... usually annoying. Unlike other ghosts, poltergeists can move from one location to another, following the person they've chosen to torment.

Many psychologists believe that poltergeists are not ghosts at all, but some form of psychokinesis or remote activity.

Portal

Literally, a doorway or gate, this term suggests a specific location through which spirits enter and leave our world. When there are multiple phenomena in a confined area, such as an abundance of unexplained orbs, some people call this a "ghost portal."

Possession

When an entity attempts to take control of a body that does not belong to them, it's called a possession.

In ghost hunting, this phenomenon is rare, but some psychics and mediums allow ghosts to speak through them. Sometimes, this can enable the living to communicate directly with the ghost and help him or her to cross over.

In extreme cases, a spirit can maliciously attempt to take over an unwilling person's body. Most ghost hunters will never witness this kind of possession, though it's a popular scene in horror movies. Unwilling possession is often linked to demonic activity.

Proof

There is no "proof" of ghosts when someone is a committed skeptic. People who won't believe in ghosts find other explanations for all scientific evidence of hauntings.

A profound, personal encounter with a ghost or the unexplainable is the only way to change someone's mind about haunted places.

Protection

Some researchers use objects, rituals, routines, tactics, or specific processes to protect themselves against ghostly, demonic, or paranormal intrusions and effects. This is a personal matter and rarely discussed during a ghost hunt.

When you go on a ghost hunt, it's generally smart to carry something that you feel may protect you from evil. Most ghost hunters wear a small cross, Star of David, pentacle, or other religious jewelry. They often conceal it under clothing, or wear it as a ring, earrings, or on a bracelet where it won't be noticed.

Carrying a very big, heavy Bible, an intimidating (and very visible) athame, or a large religious icon is usually considered excessive.

Psi

"Psi" or "psy" is a popular term used to mean any psychic phenomena or psychic abilities. This term is sometimes inclusive of paranormal disturbances as well.

Psychic

From the Greek word meaning *of the soul*, or *of life* (Paul used it in the Bible, I Cor ii, 14), this word usually refers to the world outside the domain of physical law.

"Psychic" can relate to the spirit or the mind, depending upon the context. When someone is described as a psychic, it usually means that he or she is able to perceive things that are outside traditional physical laws and perceptions.

Psychical

A British term used as an adjective or adverb, for what Americans call "psychic."

Psychokinesis or Psycho Kinesis

To move something with the powers of one's mind, alone. It may be a factor in some hauntings, and particularly in poltergeist phenomena. It's usually called "PK." (Also see telekinesis.)

Residual Energy

Many ghost hunters believe that emotionally-charged events leave an imprint or residue on the physical objects nearby.

What distinguishes residual energy from an active haunting is that the energy/impressions repeat consistently, as if on a tape loop. The energy level may increase or decrease, but the content remains the same with each manifestation.

By contrast, in an active haunting, the ghost may respond to environmental stimuli and direct contact.

Sixth Sense

Since normal phenomena are detected with the five senses (smell, taste, touch, hearing, and sight), anything that you experience outside those five senses may be categorized as a sixth sense. Usually, this indicates to psychic detection or ESP.

Since M. Knight Shyamalan's movie of the same name, people usually think that the sixth sense refers primarily to seeing ghosts. In reality, few people see ghosts as full figures or living people.

In ghost hunting, the sixth sense can include everything from the ability to hear ghosts whispering, to an internal visual image from the past, or even a "creepy feeling" that can't be explained.

Sparkles

This paranormal visual effect is sometimes described as the sparkle of embers falling immediately after a fireworks display. These small, sparkling lights usually occur no closer to the camera than ten feet. They are often twenty to fifty feet away, or more. Sparkles are seen during, and especially immediately after, the flash on a camera is used.

Even the most vivid sparkles will not show up on film. They are paranormal phenomena.

"Sparkles" is a proprietary term developed in the 1990s by Fiona Broome during research for Hollow Hill. Other researchers have adopted the term to describe this unique phenomenon.

Spirit

This word comes from the Latin, meaning that which breathes. It means that which animates life, or the soul of the being.

Table Tapping, Table Tipping

A method to communicate with spirits. Usually, several people sit around a table with their hands on it, or holding hands on top of the table. Then, they ask the spirits to reply to communicate by tapping on the table, perhaps once for *yes* and twice for *no*.

Others are successful asking the ghosts to lift the table very slightly to show that they are present. Then, the ghosts may tap their replies, move a Ouija-type platen, or use some other means to communicate with movement around the table.

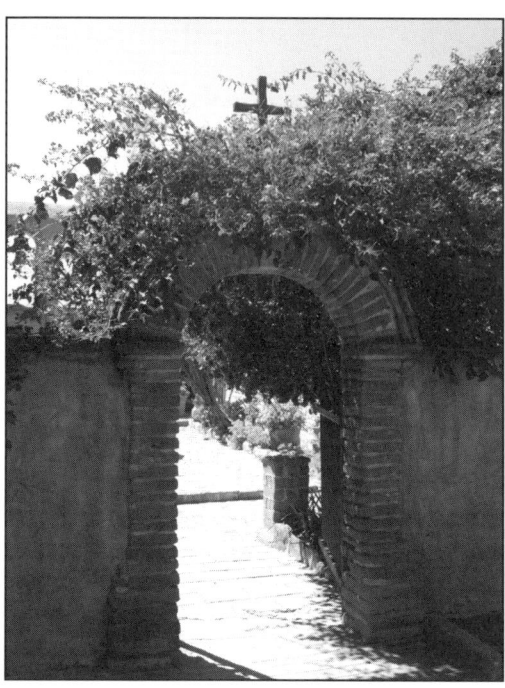

Mission San Juan Capistrano.

Tarot

The history of the Tarot deck is still unclear. However, since its use in fourteenth century Italy, "Tarot" refers to playing cards that are also used for fortune-telling or divination.

Telekinesis

From a Greek word meaning any motion that is activated from a distance. Technically, this could describe a remote-controlled toy boat, so most people use the word psychokinesis for ghost research.

Vortex

Since the time of Descartes, this has indicated the rotation of cosmic energy around a central point or axis. Beginning in the mid-nineteenth century, the word "vortex" has meant any whirling movement of energy or particles.

Some people use this term to explain lines or narrow cylinders that appear highlighted in ghost photos.

Your Own Ghost Stories

I f you would like to share your own ghost stories for possible publication send them to:

stories@anitayasuda.com

What to include:

- Where the sighting occurred.
- Number of people witnessing the event.
- Ages and or occupation of the people involved.
- Date and Year.
- History of the building or area where said event occurred.
- Describe the event as best as you can including as many details as possible. Include your feelings.

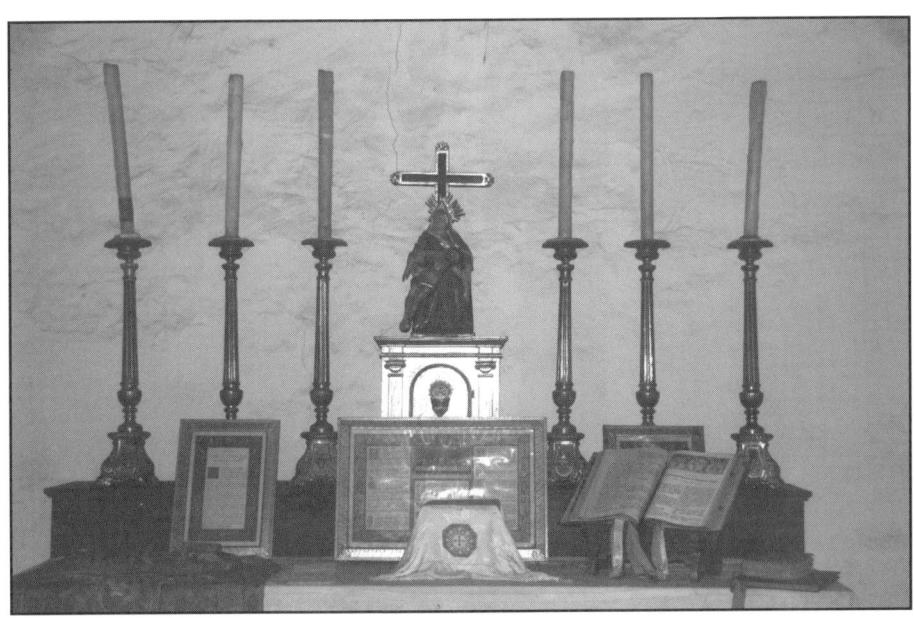

La Casa de Estudillo, Old Town San Diego.

End Notes and Selected Bibliography

The following end notes and bibliography lists publications that refer in whole or in part to paranormal occurrences in coastal California.

1. Stewart, Jay. "State's 'City of Venice'". *The Times Standard*. September 6, 1971.

2. W.E.W. "Just a Little of This & That." *The Van Nuys Newspaper*. October 10, 1930.

3. Hanrahan, Jennifer. "Experts Hunting For Signs Of Haunting." *Daily News*. October 29, 1997.

4. Drew, May. "The Santa Clarita Valley". *Van Nuys*. November 24, 1979.

5. Anon. "Camulos Rancho Sold." *Oxnard Daily Courier*. May 24, 1924.

6. Young, Gerry Prince. "Bless This House." *The Valley News*. May 7, 1970.

7. Anon. "Hunters in fog as 2-ton hippo steals away in it." *Press-Telegram*. February 24, 1978.

8. Anon. "Tiny Bubbles on stage." *Oakland Tribune*. March 13, 1978.

9. Anon. "San Miguel Island—Where Ghosts & Death Abound." *Press Courier*. May 26, 1966.

10. Anon. "It's Vacation Time." *Fresno Bee Republican*. May 23, 1957.

11. Thomey, Tedd. "Los Cerritos-Mysterious Happenings at the Ranch, Including Ghostly Footsteps, Rustling and a Spooky Tap on the Shoulder." *Long Beach Independent*, August 2, 1974.

12. Gillum, Helen L. "Rancho Los Cerritos and the legend of Uncle Mike." *Independent Press Telegram*, September 15, 1974.

13. Anon. "Spirits Braved By City Council." *Los Angeles Herald*. July 11, 1905.

14. Delling, Anna. "Love on the rocks: California's Haunted Coast." *Daily News*. June 28, 1996.

15. Anon. "Yankee Blade". *Mountain Democrat*. December 2, 1854.

16. Anon. "Total Wreck of the Yankee Blade—800 Passengers in Peril!" *Mountain Democrat*. October 14, 1854.

17. Leslie, E.J. "Curse of Rancho Feliz." *San Francisco Call*, 1903.

18. Adams, John. Rialto. *Inland Valley Daily Bulletin*. October 26, 2006.

19. Norris, Murray. "The Ghost of Foster Park." *Press-Courier*. April 16, 1967.

20. Gregory, Kim Lamb. Spirits, ghosts & demons are stars of paranormal convention next week in Santa Paula." *Ventura County Star*. July 15, 2007.

21. Crump, Spencer. "Long Beach Sands Hide Pirate Loot." *Long Beach Independent*, 1952.

22. White, Diane. "The Hotel Psychic." *The Boston Globe*, August 20, 1988.

23. Menard, Wimon. "Hoodoo Ship." *Independent Press-Telegram*. July 1, 1962.

24. Anon. "Los Angelino Yanked From Bed." *Los Angeles Herald*, 1906.

25. Leach, Eric. "Web Around Leonis Adobe Spun." *The Valley News*. October 29, 1971.

26. Bidwell, Carol. "Banditos, Bodies and Ghosts." *Daily News*. June 28, 1996.

27. Zate, Maria. "Feng Shui experts are now remedy for those looking to get rid of ghosts." *Santa Barbara News-Press*, October 21, 2004.

28. Wardwell, W.D. "The Wishing Chairs of San Miguel." *The San Francisco Call*. March 16, 1910.

29. Mariani, Teresa. "Discovering the ghost of San Miguel." *The Tribune*. September 20, 1997.

30. Frye, Matt. "Urban Legends plentiful in I.E." *The Sun*. October 27, 2006.

31. Taylor, Ron. "Tejon: Ghosts of Lebec, Beale Haunt Old Fort." *Fresno Bee*. October 15, 1967.

32. Conrad, Ralph. "Century-Old Fort Tejon Retains Charm With Military Ghosts in Quiet Oasis." *Van Nuys*. April 2, 1968.

33. Strickley, Andria. "Who's calling from room 1007? *The Tribune*. February 14, 2001.

34. Gregory, Kim Lamb. "Some say friendly apparitions are inhabiting Ventura's Pierpont Inn." *Ventura County Star*. January 11, 2008.

35. Hine, Robert V. California's Utopian Colonies. W.W. Norton & Co., NY, 1973.

36. Metzger, Ted. "Let's Look Around." *The Press-Courier*. August 4, 1966.

37. Mosqueda, Sarah. "Fullerton can be a creepy city." *The Daily Titan*. October 31, 2007.

38. Omohundro, Baxter. Young Couples Watch for Ghost of Heartbroken Girl." *Long-Beach Press Telegram*. April 30, 1950.

39. Anon. "Colorado Street Bridge." *Oakland Tribune*. 1929/1933.

40. Anon. "Freight Car." *Long Beach*,1949.

41. Alvarex, Yazmin. "Supernatural experiences leads writer to hidden passion." *The Sun*. October 26, 2006.

42. Osorio, Alma. *"San Diego State University students say ghosts haunt corridors of dorm."* University Wire. October 29, 1999.

43. Anon. "Fisherman Has To Cut Tentacle to Release Victim. *San Francisco Call*, 1910.

44. Anon. "Sea Serpent Nears Shore." *Los Angeles Herald*. September 12, 1907.

45. Anon. "The Rios Caledonia Adobe Spirit." San Luis Obispo.com. Accessed March 2008.

46. Conrad, Ralph. "New Home For Old Stage Coach Inn." *The Valley News*. December 17, 1968.

47. Thompson, Jay. "Spirit of the Bluebird." *The Tribune*. October 31, 1999.

48. Rapp, Dawn. "The Clubhouse at This Old House." *The Tribune*. June 14, 2007.

49. La Fee, Scott." *The San Diego Union Tribune*. October 31, 2001.

51. Giraud, Victoria. Haunted Retreat: House Full of Rich Film History." *Daily News Los Angeles*. July, 18, 1996.

51. Anon. Pythons Trained To Be "Sea Serpents." *Los Angeles Herald*. July 15, 1907.

52. Anon. "Valentino greeted by 30 Mediums." *Oakland Tribune*. May 7, 1948.

53. Anon. "Jesse Shepard." *Oakland Tribune*. October 14, 1875.

54. Crane, Clare. "The Villa Montezuma as a Product of its Time." *The Journal of San Diego History*. Spring-Summer 1987, Volume 33, # 2 & 3.

55. Anon. "William Desmond Taylor." *Oakland Tribune*. May 13, 1923.

56. Robb, Thomas. "William Hart Park to Open." *The Press Telegram*. September 18,1958.

57. Anon."William Hart Marks Shrine of Film Horse." *Fresno Bee*. July 2, 1938.

Index

A

Abbott Kinney 10, 11, 12
Adobe Cerritos 30, 31, 32
Adobe Leonis 70-73
Adobe Montanez 91, 92
Adobe Olivas 102, 103, 104
Adobe Rios 133, 134
Albert Pryor 12
Alice Halloran 15, 16
Aliso Canyon 21
Andres Pico Adobe 16, 17
Arguello, Concepcion 34, 35

B

Balboa Theatre 18, 19
Battlefield 128, 129
Big Yellow House 19, 20, 21
Billiwhack Dairy 21, 22
Black Lake Rising 23
Bless This Home 23
Bluebird Motel 141, 142
Brinkerhoff 73, 74, 75
Brinkerhoff Avenue 73, 74, 75
Bubbles 24, 25
Bubbles The Hippo 24, 25

C

Cabrillo's Ghost 27, 28
Cambria 141, 142
Camels 97, 98
Captain Cass 29
Casa de Rancho Los Cerritos 30, 31, 32
Cass House Historic Inn 29
Catalina Island 57, 58, 115, 144, 148, 149, 164, 165
Cayucos 29, 142
Charman 32
Cheesecloth Ghost 33, 34

Clubhouse at This Old House 142, 143
Curse of Griffith Park 36, 37
Cursed Freight Car 118

D

Del Coronado 145, 146, 147
Desmond, William 166
Drum Barracks 147, 148

E

El Adobe Restaurant 38

F

First Christian Church 40, 41
Foster Park 44,
Fullerton Theatre 44, 45

G

Garden Grove 136, 137
Gaviota 51
Gaviota State Park 51
Georgian Hotel 43, 44
Ghost of Foster Park 44
Glen Tavern Inn 46
Grand Colonial Hotel 48
Griffith Park 36
Griffith, Col. 37
Guadalupe Adobe 49, 50

H, I

Halloran, Alice 15, 16
Hart, William S. 167, 168
Haunted Gaviota Coast 51
Hippolyte Bouchard 53, 54, 111
Hollywood 154, 166, 167, 168
Horton Grand Hotel 54, 55

J

Joyita 57, 58

K

Kinney, Abbott 10, 11, 12

L

La Jolla 48, 49
La Llorona 77, 94,
La Purisma Mission 61, 62
Lady in Pink 62, 63
Laguna 87, 24, 52
Lamar Street 64, 65
Le Milagro 66,
Legend of The Swallows 68, 69
Leonis Adobe 70-73
Lompoc 61
Long Beach 90, 118, 120-123,
    130-132, 165
Los Angeles 11, 16, 17, 34, 36,
    37, 57, 64-66, 102, 120,
    130-133, 135, 154, 155

M

Malibu 132,
Mission Saint Ines Ghost 87, 88,
    89
Mission Saint Ines Legend 87,
    88, 89
Mission San Fernando Rey de
Espana 76, 77
Mission San Juan Capistrano
    78-81
Mission San Miguel 82-85
Mission Santa Barbara 85, 86, 87
Modjeska House 90, 91
Montanez Adobe 91, 92
Morey Mansion 92, 93

N

Nipomo 23

O

Ocean Park 131, 132
Old Cemetery 94,
Old Fort Tejon 96, 97, 98
Old Point Loma Lighthouse
    98-101
Olivas Adobe 102-104

P

Pasadena 116, 117
Paso Robles 105, 106
Pendalton Road 124
Pepper Tree Legend 107
Pierpont Inn 108, 109, 110
Pirate Lights 110,
Pisgah Grande 112, 113
Plummer Auditorium 113, 114
Point Vicente Lighthouse 114,
    115
Possessed Bridge 116
Pryor, Albert 12

Q

Queen Mary 120-123

R

Rancho Palos Verdes 116
Red Lady of Pendalton Road 124
Redlands 127
Rialto's First Christian Church
    40, 41
Rios-Caledonia 133, 134

S

San Antonio Valley 82
San Bernardino 98, 124-126
San Bernardino High 126, 127
San Diego 127, 128, 133,
    137-140, 145, 150, 153,
    155-157
San Diego State University 127
San Fernando 16, 17, 24, 76, 77
San Juan Capistrano 12-15, 38,
    68, 69, 78-81
San Luis Obispo 102, 126, 133,
    141-143
San Miguel 27, 82-85, 133, 134, 149
San Pasqual Battlefield 128-130
Santa Barbara 135, 149
Santa Clarita 97, 166, 167,
Santa Monica 37, 43, 44, 150,
    164,
Santa Rosa 149

Santa Susana Mountain Park 112, 113
Sparkuhl, Theodore 151
Sea Serpent 130, 131, 152, 153
Shepard, Jesse 155-159
Smugglers Beach 110- 112
Spirit of the Rios-Caledonia Adobe 133, 134
Stage Coach Inn 134
Stanley House 136
Star of India 137-140
Summerland 19, 20, 85, 108, 173

T, U

Taylor, William Desmond 166
The Bluebird Motel 141-142
The Cass House Historic Inn 29
The Clubhouse at This Old House 142, 143
The Del Coronado 145-147
The Drum Barracks 147, 148

V

Valentino 154, 155
Van Nuys 17, 23, 24
Venice Beach 10, 11

Ventura 22, 32, 44-46, 66, 70, 90, 102, 104, 108, 110-112, 134, 135
Villa Montezuma 155-159

W

Wayne, John 164, 165
Whaley House 3, 160-164
Whaley, Thomas 162-164
Wild Goose 164, 165
William S. Hart Park 167, 168
Wilmington 57, 147, 148

X, Y, Z

Yorba Linda 62-64,